Foucault: A Critical Reader

Foucault: A Critical Reader

Edited by
David Couzens Hoy

Basil Blackwell

© Basil Blackwell Ltd 1986

First published 1986
Reprinted 1986

Basil Blackwell Ltd
108 Cowley Road, Oxford OX4 1JF, UK

Basil Blackwell Inc.
432 Park Avenue South, Suite 1503,
New York, NY 10016, USA

British Library Cataloguing in Publication Data
Foucault: a critical reader.
  1. Foucault, Michel
  I. Hoy, David Couzens
  194 B2430.F724

ISBN 0–631–14042–5
ISBN 0–631–1403–3 Pbk

Library of Congress Cataloging in Publication Data
Foucault : a critical reader.
  Includes index.
  1. Foucault, Michel. I. Hoy, David Couzens.
B2430.F724F68 1986   194   86–6786
ISBN 0–631–14042–5
ISBN 0–631–14043–3 (pbk.)

Printed in the USA

Contents

Contributors

Arnold I. Davidson, Professor, Committee on the Conceptual Foundations of Science and Department of Philosophy, University of Chicago

Hubert L. Dreyfus, Professor, Department of Philosophy, University of California, Berkeley

Jürgen Habermas, Professor, Department of Philosophy, Johann Wolfgang Goethe University, Frankfurt-on-Main

Ian Hacking, Professor, Institute for the History and Philosophy of Science and Technology, Victoria College, University of Toronto

David Couzens Hoy, Professor, Board of Studies in Philosophy, University of California, Santa Cruz

Martin Jay, Professor, Department of History, University of California, Irvine

Mark Poster, Professor, Department of History, University of California, Berkeley

Paul Rabinow, Professor, Department of Anthropology, University of California, Berkeley

Richard Rorty, University Professor of Humanities, University of Virginia

Edward W. Said, Parr professor of English and Comparative Literature, Columbia University

Barry Smart, Department of Sociological Studies, University of Sheffield

Charles Taylor, Professor, Departments of Philosophy and Political Science, McGill University

Michael Walzer, Professor, School of Social Science, Institute for Advanced Study, Princeton, New Jersey

Introduction

DAVID COUZENS HOY

The life of the mind requires controversy, and the essays in this book confront the issues provoked by the work of Michel Foucault. Early plans for this collection called for critical essays ranging from quarrels over particular claims to attacks on his entire position. Many books on Foucault were appearing, but they were often interpretative in character. Combating misunderstandings of Foucault's sometimes difficult texts and accounting for his apparent changes are, of course, necessary first steps in interpreting him fairly. Beyond questions in interpretation, however, are questions about the validity of his ideas and the coherence of his position. The idea for this reader was to gather essays representing careful counterarguments to Foucault's own theses, or assessments of his thought by other contemporary thinkers with their own visions. The essays by Michael Walzer and Charles Taylor are paradigms that gave shape to the initial project.

When Foucault was still alive such an anthology could have included a response by Foucault to his critics. Excellent examples of how productive this kind of exchange can be are the rejoinders by Jürgen Habermas to his critics in *Habermas: Critical Essays* and *Habermas and Modernity*.[1] With Foucault's death, however, plans for this book had to be changed. Since he could no longer respond for himself, the collection was broadened to include some more sympathetic readings of his works as well. For the sake of fairness the book now includes essays that are useful in rebutting some common criticisms by showing that his ideas are not what the standard objections assume them to be. In soliciting new pieces for this reader, I asked for critical discussions of Foucault, but left decisions about the tone, content, and stance of the essays to the discretion of the contributors. In this introduction I shall review some of the main criticisms of Foucault's method and sketch a potential line of rebuttal.

My remarks do not substitute for a close reading of these rich essays, but they may convey the problems confronting critical readers of Foucault now that he is unable to provide his own rejoinders.

Self-criticisms

The task of giving critical assessments of Foucault is particularly difficult in that his career as an author shows him covering an astonishing range of topics. As he moves from one topic to another, however, his methods and purposes seem to change. So there may not be a single 'Foucault'. Critics must first be interpreters, and criticisms of a particular aspect of his thought may not count against, or may even be obviated by, other aspects.

Some commentators deal with these changes of direction by identifying various periods in Foucault's development. Foucault himself continually reflects on his own development and offers his own interpretations of it, often with honest self-criticisms. Not all these self-interpretations seem readily compatible, however. For instance, in 1961 Foucault described his project in *Madness and Civilization* as an analysis of experience: 'We must try to return, in history, to that zero point in the course of madness at which madness is an undifferentiated experience, a not yet divided experience of division itelf.'[2] By the end of the 1960s Foucault was decrying any such attempt to recapture a 'zero point' of human experience.[3] A search for origins smacks of anthropologism, the empirical belief in a conceptual abstraction called 'man'. He sees linguistics as one human science that detaches itself from the assumption that it is uncovering the essence of 'man' by studying language. Structuralist linguistics manages instead to perceive that 'things attain to existence only in so far as they are able to form the elements of a signifying system'.[4] Foucault then seems to build this linguistic nominalism into his own conception of archaeological method, creating difficulties I shall describe shortly.

By the middle of the 1970s, however, Foucault no longer understands himself as theorizing about discourse exclusively. He focuses instead on practices, both discursive and nondiscursive. His central topic becomes what he calls power/knowlege. Reflecting on his earlier works in an interview from 1977, he remarks, 'When I think back now, I ask myself what else it was that I was talking about, in *Madness and Civilization* or *The Birth of the Clinic* but power?'[5]

In 1981, however, the notion of power is displaced. 'The goal of my work during the last twenty years,' he says, 'has not been to analyse the phenomena of power, nor to elaborate the foundations of such an analysis.'[6] What replaces it? In the preface to one of his last publications, the second volume of his *History of Sexuality*, Foucault maintains that what he has always been interested in after all is experience. Admitting that his earlier conception of experience in *Madness* was 'floating', he now defines it by specifying three levels that he thinks any historian could study, although the levels correspond to what others might consider three distinct periods of his own development.[7] The three levels making up historically concrete human experience are first, a field of knowledge with concepts, theories, and diverse disciplines; second, a normative collection of rules (for instance, those operant in distinguishing the permitted and the forbidden, the normal and the pathological, or the decent and the indecent); and third, a mode of relation to oneself (for instance, by which one recognizes oneself as a sexual subject among others). These three levels can be found together in any of his works, but the study of the asylum focuses on the first, the study of the prison on the second, and the later volumes of the history of sexuality on the third.

The Limitations of Archaeological Epistemology

Arnold Davidson provides us here with a reading of how Foucault's three levels of analysis, archaeology, genealogy, and ethics, fit together in a complementary way. Davidson argues for the compatibility of the two methods of archaeology and genealogy, citing Ian Hacking's description of Foucault's method in the first essay of this collection. Hacking was instrumental in bringing Foucault to the attention of other North American philosophers. Foucault according to Hacking is not defending some irrationalist theory of truth, but is more usefully studying the empirical conditions under which scientific statements come to be counted as potentially true or false.[8]

While Richard Rorty agrees with Hacking that Foucault can avoid standard epistemological pitfalls, Rorty prefers to see Foucault as avoiding epistemology altogether.[9] Rorty thinks that Foucault's *Archaeology of Knowledge* is a mistaken attempt to make archaeology the successor subject to epistemology. Describing without commending the Nietzschean turn of the later Foucault away from the search for a theory of knowledge, Rorty suggests that the maxims of genealogy are negative rather than positive. The maxims are simply injunctions to the critical historian not to believe that history as a whole is inherently characterized by progress, or rationality, or teleology, or freedom, or necessity. Rorty undercuts standard worries about the epistemological implications of Foucault's theory and method by suggesting that since these maxims are purely negative, they do not constitute either a theory or a method.

Davidson's reading contrasts to that of Hubert Dreyfus and Paul Rabinow in their comprehensive and indispensable book on Foucault.[10] Like Rorty, Dreyfus and Rabinow see *The Archaeology of Knowledge* as an aberration and they stress its philosophical difficulties. Their confrontation with these problems leads their reading to bring out the discontinuities between Foucault's various turns, although in the end they think that he is successful in formulating a coherent method for cultural analysis that they call interpretive analytics.

Whereas those who are more critical of Foucault might take the shifts in Foucault's self-understanding as vacillations, the book by Dreyfus and Rabinow shows Foucault learning from his mistakes as he follows a central theme. Throughout his career he continually investigates both how human beings constitute themselves as subjects and how they treat one another as objects. Citing Foucault's own description of his project as a slalom, Dreyfus and Rabinow emphasize in particular the difference between his quasi-structuralist insistence during the late 1960s on the autonomy of discourse in *The Order of Things* or *The Archaeology of Knowledge* and his poststructuralist focus in the 1970s in *Discipline and Punish* on how social practices condition cognitive discourse. They see the mistake of the *Archaeology*, on Foucault's own admission, to be the tendency to treat language as autonomous and as constitutive of reality.

Vestiges of idealism lurk in the structuralist suggestion that discourse organizes not only itself but also social practices and historical epochs. While critics of Foucault were attacking his alleged linguistic idealism, Foucault continued to work on his real concern, which was not to prove the autonomy of language. Since he never thought of language as a subjective or mental phenomenon, both structuralism and philosophical idealism, with their postulation of universally constitutive categories, were foreign to his central purpose. For Dreyfus and Rabinow, Foucault's intention was to show instead that the human subject is not given with permanent structures that constitute or condition reality, but is produced historically from its social world.

Discipline and Punish surprised many because it seemed to be admitting that discourse did not constitute social reality. Instead, discursive knowledge is shown to be produced in the service of an expanding social power that increasingly penetrates modern institutions like prisons, armies, schools, and factories. Discourse is now recognized to be a social practice itself, and Dreyfus and Rabinow believe that Foucault correctly comes to see that the background of social practices can never be completely articulated. Foucault thus rejects the holism essential to idealism, and opposes the traditional philosophical goal of constructing a total theory that can explain the entire social reality.

Dreyfus and Rabinow argue that Foucault's later studies of social power represent the development of a method that avoids idealism and holism more successfully. On their account, genealogy or 'interpretive analytics' meets the difficulties that plague Foucault's archaeological suspension of disbelief while investigating the history of the human sciences. The weakness of Foucault's structuralist period is that his insistence on the radical discontinuities between autonomous, self-referential discourses makes it impossible for him to say how social change, including social improvement, could come about, or why anyone should care. Archaeology seems to some critics to relativize knowledge to whatever discourse happens to be spoken at a particular time, and to deny that there is anything like serious truth.

The problem persists. Whereas Hacking and Rorty offer accounts of how Foucault can avoid the charge of epistemological relativism, Charles Taylor argues that Foucault never succeeds in thinking through his paradoxical stance on truth. The difficulty is, as presented by Dreyfus and Rabinow in their book, that the archaeologist seems to be trying to believe that those who entertain serious beliefs or engage in serious argument never do so except under illusion.[11] Foucault's archaeological method gives the impression of nihilistic non-seriousness insofar as it makes truth relative to an *archive* or *episteme*, that is, to what in the Anglo-American philosophical vocabulary could be called a scientific paradigm or conceptual framework. Since these are subject to abrupt, unexplainable changes, discourses and truth seem historically relative, and perhaps even arbitrary.

As supposedly true descriptions of past discourses, the archaeologist's own utterances have to except themselves from this

relativity, producing Foucault's contradictory attitude as he shifts
from the stance of the disinterested, objective historian to that of the
partisan, engaged social critic. The archaeologist cannot criticize either
past or present discourses by appealing to truth and falsity. Archaeology is designed to avoid the Whiggish assumption of the necessary
superiority of later theories (for instance, our own) over earlier ones.
A historian's method, archaeology shuns the scientific-realist view
that this superiority results from the deliberate replacement of the
earlier, false theory by a later, true one in a cumulative progression
toward a clearer picture of things as they really are.

Foucault also wishes to use archaeology to show that humanistic
sciences of 'man' are warped and twisted forms of reflection.
Commentators have been struck by the extent to which his method is
equivalent to the procedure whereby certain historians of science
identify a research programme as reaching a point of stagnation or
even degeneration when the programme declines into repetitive
reassertion of its own earlier discoveries or mere redescription of
competitors' discoveries. This approach invites objection, however,
when used as a tool not only for historiographical research but also
for contemporary social criticism. The social critic who treats the
present as already past must pretend either to transcend any given
historical standpoint or to speak from a fictitious future. The
historian can show a research programme to be degenerative when no
one, or only a few, still pursue it earnestly. Yet if almost everyone is
still talking in the vocabulary of modern enlightenment humanism,
and arguably ought to continue to do so, then the identification of
that discourse as degenerating can result only by projecting backward
from an as yet fictitious future standpoint. The archaeologist may be
correct in believing that people will not always talk as we now do, but
in the absence of any analysis of how they will talk (and of how we
could understand them), the critique of current humanistic discourse
is empty.

Power Struggles

As an antidote to these epistemological problems Foucault develops
and applies his method of genealogy by writing what Nietzsche calls
critical history and Foucault labels 'history of the present'. Genealogical historiography generates its own problems, however, when the
polemic turns political. Unlike the neutral, disinterested, archae-

ological historian, the Nietzschean genealogist admits the polemical interests motivating the investigation and critique of the emergence of modern social power. No longer claiming to be archaeologically outside the social practices being analysed, genealogy takes the practices seriously and does not deny the need to rectify the malignancies it diagnoses. Physician rather than philosopher, Foucault as genealogist lets his histories tell their own story.

More problematically, however, he also lets the patients themselves decide both the veracity of his diagnosis and the cure. Foucault's continued refusal to specify either a prescription or a prognosis for the social illness he diagnoses suggests to some readers that genealogy is as unserious and irresponsible as archaeology. Genealogy may be a better model of social analysis, since it permits social change to be at least contemplated. Nevertheless, whether genealogy can go beyond mere contemplation to active advocacy of social change is not clear. Unlike archaeology, which avoids causal explanation of social change by restricting itself instead to the identification of self-contained discourses demarcated by abrupt discontinuities, genealogy can pay attention to gradual, continuous processes of social change. Genealogy charts the emergence and growth of social institutions as well as the social-scientific techniques and disciplines that reinforce specific social practices. Although his genealogical histories thus have the advantage of being less static by focusing more on continuous emergence than on discontinuous ruptures, Foucault still wishes to avoid the use of certain causal explanations in historiography. His history of the prison is thus a reworking of an earlier one by two members of the Frankfurt School, Rusche and Kirchheimer, whom Foucault criticizes for relying on quasi-materialist explanations of the emergence of the prison as a causal result of underlying economic forces. For Foucault such explanations are inadequate because they do not explain in a sufficiently detailed way the techniques and changes that occur without being directly correlative to other social and economic changes. He therefore thinks his model is a better analytic tool, but can he wield it critically?

The use of functional rather than causal explanation standardly leads to consequences Foucault himself would not accept. Foucault's model for analysing 'systems' of thought seems to borrow from sociological functionalism, which sees social life as systematically interconnected, such that change in any part affects every other part and reconfigures the whole. Since each part of the social system thus appears   indispensable,   functionalism   can   lead   to   political conservatism. Functionalist explanations may imply either that the whole is so powerful that attempts to bring about social improvements by particular reforms will inevitably fail, or that the existent social institutions must be preserved since they are at least better than the social chaos that might result from efforts at social transformation.

Among the prominent critics who think Foucault gets trapped in his methodological strategy are Jürgen Habermas, Michael Walzer, Steven Lukes, Charles Taylor, Fredric Jameson, and Clifford Geertz. Habermas's philosophy is the most serious challenge to Foucault's enterprise in Europe today. The short article published here is an encapsulated statement of Habermas's interpretation and critique of Foucault, which is argued more extensively in chapters 9 and 10 of *Der philosophische Diskurs der Moderne*. Habermas contends that Foucault's critique of modernity fails because Foucault loses his sense of direction. This loss occurs because Foucault is both a 'crypto-normativist' and an 'irrationalist'. The former label applies because Foucault cannot explain the standards Habermas thinks must be presupposed in any condemnation of the present. Habermas cites Nancy Fraser's pointed questions, 'Why is struggle preferable to submission? Why ought domination to be resisted? Only with the introduction of normative notions of some kind could Foucault begin to answer this question. Only with the introduction of normative notions could he begin to tell us what is wrong with the modern power/knowledge regime and why we ought to oppose it.'[12] Foucault inherits the appellation of 'irrationalist' because of Nietzsche's influence. Whereas the early Foucault echoes Nietzsche's critique of the will-to-knowledge, Habermas thinks the later Foucault is forced by the resultant epistemological paradox to avow the will-to-knowledge after all.

The dispute between Habermas and Foucault turns on whether Foucault is understood to be criticizing modernity from a postmodern or a premodern perspective.[13] Habermas is willing to defend his own reconstruction of the progressive presuppositions of the modern enlightenment tradition against those critics of modernity whom he considers to be anti-modern because of the reactionary implications of their views, however radical they may seem. In an earlier essay he associates Foucault with such a group:

> The *Young Conservatives* recapitulate the basic experience of aesthetic modernity. They claim as their own the revelations of a decentered

subjectivity, emancipated from the imperatives of work and usefulness, and with this experience they step outside the modern world. On the basis of modernistic attitudes, they justify an irreconcilable anti-modernism. They remove into the sphere of the far away and the archaic the spontaneous powers of imagination, of self-experience and of emotionality. To instrumental reason, they juxtapose in manichean fashion a principle only accessible through evocation, be it the will to power or sovereignty, Being or the dionysiac force of the poetical. In France this line leads from Bataille via Foucault to Derrida.[14]

From Habermas's perspective Foucault's belittling of the progressive character of modern enlightenment and rationality is mistaken. He thinks Foucault's generalization of panoptical or conformist forces to the entire process of the modernization of society is false.[15] Also, by ignoring the progress achieved through the modern guarantees of liberty and legality, Habermas thinks that Foucault fails to see clearly that the real problem is that the legal means for securing freedom also endanger it.[16] Finally, Foucault's attacks on the human sciences for being unconsciously manipulative and thus uncritically co-opted are out-of-date since for Habermas these fields are genuinely hermeneutical and critical by the 1970s.[17]

In their response to Habermas here, Dreyfus and Rabinow, whose interpretation Habermas cites in presenting his account of Foucault's development, argue that Habermas nevertheless misrepresents Foucault. They object to classifying Foucault with those whom they call anti-thinkers, and thus to representing Foucault as someone who is necessarily opposed to all features of the enlightenment tradition. Richard Rorty's piece also takes issue with Habermas's critique of Foucault. He sees Foucault's critical histories as correctly subverting the quasi-metaphysical comfort implied by Habermas's argument for the necessity of presupposing convergence in the long run on the rational standards of an 'ideal speech community'.

In contrast to Rorty, Dreyfus, and Rabinow, Martin Jay's subtle analysis of Foucault suggests a different way of pursuing lines of criticism motivated by Habermas's philosophy. Our foremost historian of the Frankfurt School, Jay offers a detailed critique of Foucault in the epilogue to his impressive recent book, *Marxism and Totality: The Adventures of a Concept from Lukács to Habermas* (Berkeley: University of California Press, 1984). The present article is a genealogy of Foucault's own genealogy, studying how Foucault's corpus fits into and continues twentieth-century French philosophy's troubled and sometimes unconscious denigration of the privilege given by the philosophical tradition to vision. The essay represents independent evidence for Habermas's suspicion that such an investigation would show how Foucault fails, in Jay's words, 'to see' beyond the horizon of his own *episteme* and question the premises and implications of the 'anti-ocular counter-enlightenment'.[18]

Michael Walzer's article is a good place to start for the reader who wants a clear and incisive representation of the social and political issues more from an Anglo-American perspective. Walzer begins by accusing Foucault's account of being inadequate on empirical grounds. Foucault is said to underestimate the difference between being in prison and being out of it in a carceral society, or between being in a carceral yet social democratic society and being in a Gulag.

But finally Walzer maintains that the problem is more serious, and that Foucault's political epistemology is simply incoherent. Foucault calls for resistance but offers no account of what would constitute good reasons both for criticizing that which is to be resisted and for explaining how it should be resisted: 'Foucault believes that truth is relative to its sanctions and knowledge to the constraints that produce.it. There would appear to be no independent standpoint, no possibility for the development of critical principles.'[19]

This last sentence illustrates the belief of many of Foucault's critics that critical principles can be developed only from a standpoint independent of the social one being criticized. By denying the possibility of an independent standpoint, Foucault appears to such critics to be not simply a functionalist, but a nihilistic, fatalistic one. Thus Walzer interprets Foucault as a functionalist who presupposes that society is a whole governed by an invisible hand rather than by an accountable, legitimate state power and a rational rule of law. As an anarchist, Foucault is said to disavow any political structure but also any human nature that could persist without social systems. So Foucault seems to believe that social improvement is impossible short of abolishing modern society altogether. But Walzer thinks that this radical abolitionism is nihilistic because 'either there will be nothing left at all, nothing visibly human; or new codes and disciplines will be produced, and Foucault gives us no reason to expect that these will be any better than the ones we now live with. Nor, for that matter, does he give us any way of knowing what "better" might mean.'[20]

Other critics stress particular aspects of this line of criticism. Steven Lukes thinks that Foucault treats power exclusively as an impersonal, deterministic structure and thereby fails to explain how power is exercised by individuals who bear the responsibility for their actions.[21] Although Charles Taylor does not share Lukes's conception of power as 'power-over', he too objects to Foucault's conception of power. For Foucault social power is intentionality without a subject, a phrase that sounds as if he were talking about purposefulness without purpose, or action without agency. Taylor agrees that the patterns of human action do not have to be explained as the direct, intended results of conscious willing, but he argues that the patterns nevertheless have to be intelligibly related to conscious action, even if only indirectly. He maintains that Foucault's explanations fail to satisfy the latter condition.[22]

Foucault's deliberate attempt to avoid writing teleological histories of human purpose may backfire in rhetorical as well as conceptual ways. Genealogy is supposed to be an antidote to the historiographical method of writing about history as if it were a Kantian or Hegelian story about the progress of freedom in the world. Yet Clifford Geertz believes that in reading *Discipline and Punish* 'we seemed to be faced with a kind of Whig history in reverse – a history, in spite of itelf, of the Rise of Unfreedom'.[23] If Foucault's project is to do social criticism without appealing to a utopian, teleological philosophy of history, his use of the rhetoric of negative or dystopian functionalism is paradoxical. While dystopian stories can be told to counter the belief in utopias, they are equally as mistaken as the utopian stories if the goal is to avoid all stories about where history as a whole is going. Furthermore, the reverse Whiggish narrative has a decided moral or practical disadvantage when contrasted to the progressive narrative. The story of the inevitable slide into catastrophe evokes attitudes of fatalism and quietism, which make social criticism pointless since individual agents are helpless to rectify the resented social practices and institutions.

Other critics have noted that Foucault's rhetoric often conflicts with his more considered articulation of his method. Fredric Jameson argues that Foucault is trapped in a rhetorical strategy that Jameson identifies as a '"winner loses" logic':

> What happens is that the more powerful the vision of some increasingly total system or logic – the Foucault of the prisons book is the obvious example – the more powerless the reader comes to feel. Insofar as the theorist wins, therefore, by constructing an increasingly closed and terrifying machine, to that very degree he loses, since the critical capacity of his work is thereby paralyzed, and the impulses of negation and revolt, not to speak of those of social transformation, are increasingly perceived as vain and trivial in the face of the model itself.[24]

Foucault's texts often call for resistance to the exercise of power, and genealogy as a method should be used to disrupt the complacent tendency to assume that the generally progressive character of present society justified its shortcomings, or at least makes its dangers less urgent. Yet his rhetoric suggests to some that he is only displacing one form of invisible hand explanation with another, when his intention is to avoid any explanations that are incompatible with the form of resistance represented by the critical use of genealogy in writing histories of the present.

Political Differences

As archaeology gives up the contrast between true and false, genealogy remains peculiarly silent about the distinctions between liberty and power or the just and the unjust. Political theorists like Walzer and Taylor think that Foucault's social criticism tacitly presupposes the ideals of freedom, truth, justice, and progress that he discounts. Foucault's line of response has been the indirect one of denying that he either is or needs to be a political theorist. Not a political theorist but instead a critical historian, his interests are different, and require no political self-justification.

As a historian he has been trying to locate cases where these traditional ideals have served only as empty notions blinding humanitarian theorists to the historical reality of the spread of oppressive and conformist tendencies in modern societies. He discounts these values because he is looking at another level than that usually addressed by political theorists, who are concerned more with principles that individual and collective agents can explicitly espouse and deliberately pursue. Broad, impersonal social and historical developments may have little direct connection with what agents choose to do or what they think they are doing. As a historian of movements of longer duration, Foucault's scope of analysis may not seem to include factors that individuals could normally take into account in formulating their own plans of action.

Thus his history of the birth of modern prisons and the extension of the 'carceral' system to other institutions suggests that the spread of this system throughout the social fabric is accompanied by a corresponding moulding of people into 'normal' as opposed to 'abnormal', 'delinquent', or 'deviant' individuals. He calls this process 'normalization', and means by it the imposition of a model of well-ordered human activity on all aspects of social life. Foucault plays on two different but related senses of 'discipline' to suggest that the social process of inculcating discipline into individuals through the homogenizing techniques used in prisons, armies, and schools develops hand in hand with the scientific disciplines required to acquire knowledge about human social life.

He is clearly critical of the progress of this social cancer, and calls his book a 'history of the present' to admit frankly that the account is not a neutral, objective description, but is intended to subvert and disrupt the growth of this malignancy. Yet his critics believe that he fails insofar as he has no social alternatives to offer, and no moral or political standards on which to base his angry charge that modern society is becoming more and more like a prison, however progressive and benevolent it appears to those who have let themselves be successfully normalized. Given his injunction that genealogy can work only within a given social context, how can he regret the increasing normalization of society? Does his genealogical method prevent him from arguing either that the past was any better, or that the future should be different?

Respondents for Foucault think that such charges may be off-target. Barry Smart gives a broad, social scientific context for understanding Foucault on power in his lucid book, *Foucault, Marxism and Critique* (London: Routledge & Kegan Paul, 1983). In his article written for the present volume Smart extends his project to consider similar points of comparison between Foucault and Gramsci. Gramsci also figures in Edward Said's article, which adds a crucial supplement to Said's influential earlier analysis of the divergent implications for literary theory of the approaches of Foucault and Derrida.[25] Both Said and Smart wrestle with the difficulty that Foucault describes power as so pervasive and irresistible as to make resistance seem futile.

Foucault's critics have grounds for their readings and are right to attack his often incautious statements in interviews. Even his more considered methodological self-justifications may not be the best interpretation of his enterprise. So interpreters who think that criticisms, however justified by Foucault's own remarks, do not capture what is most interesting about Foucault's approach to social criticism have to propose their own readings of his method and results.

One line of defence I can suggest is to argue for genealogy as a plausible method of immanent social criticism, one that can work without presupposing an independent, utopian standpoint. As a genealogist Foucault is able to diagnose the organizing trends of our culture only because he, too, is subjected to them. If he is, then so are others. Borrowing from Nietzsche, his method is not to construct an alternative model, but to get us to recognize his frustration and resentment, and thereby the motivation for criticism of the present, in ourselves as well. Foucault paints the picture of a totally normalized society, not because he believes our present society is one, but because he hopes we will find the picture threatening. He could hope for this effect on us only if we have *not* been completely normalized.

As someone who rejects holism and the ideal of totalization, Foucault probably also believes that it does not even make sense to speak of society as entirely normalized, since there is no theoretical standpoint from which this claim could be defensibly asserted. He knows full well that his dissenting voice is a counterexample to his own suggestion that the entire social body has become subjected to carceral techniques and normalizing tendencies. He believes that the resistance to social developments can come only from within the society and from those places that have not been fully co-opted. His point is therefore that if, counterfactually, it could be said that the social normalization were total, then there would be no grounds for social criticism. There would be no way that the members of such a society could see themselves any differently from the way they were. Their perspective might seem disturbingly indistinguishable from that of real historical groups who show no understanding for and toleration of social differences. The ideal of the normalized society thus seems inhuman to us now. This recognition would justify Foucault's genealogical method of searching for normalization's insidious workings, however one might feel about the plausibility of his empirical analysis of them.

From Power to Ethics

Even if the interpretations more sympathetic to Foucault clarify his analysis of social power, his later work on the history of sexuality and the formation of the self adds further complexity, but also a further line of self-defence. Should we think that as a result of criticism Foucault learned that his approach to studying power was a blind alley, as Habermas thinks? Is his interest in human subjectivity and selfhood, traditional concerns of French philosophy before the linguistic turn of structuralism and poststructuralism, inconsistent with the methods of archaeology and genealogy? Is his return to the theme of the self a welcome advance or a defensive retreat?

However one interprets the last turn in Foucault's career, independent assessments can be given of his unfinished studies of a level of ethics below that usually studied by moral philosophers. Professors Hacking and Davidson argue for the value of this move beyond the study of power to the history of ethical self-understandings, and they do not see it as inconsistent with the best aspects of his earlier work. A dissenting voice providing a different assessment of the studies in volumes 2 and 3 comes from the historian Mark Poster, whose book *Foucault, Marxism and History* interprets Foucault as Marx without metaphysics.[26] With Foucault's shift from modern power to ancient and medieval ethics, he moves away from the preoccupations of social theorists to what may seem like arcane philological studies. Without the volumes that would tie the studies to the present, the effort might be said to fall short of being another genealogical 'history of the present' that effectively disrupts current beliefs and practices.

The posthumous publication of remaining materials in another volume of the *History of Sexuality* could still affect these assessments. The available writings can serve, however, as a sketch of an argument that Foucault's genealogical method is not inherently functionalistic, nihilistic, fatalistic, or relativistic. The topics of some of his applications of the method may suggest these labels, but his later work deflects them by studying a different level of human activity.

Genealogy studies how we constitute ourselves as human subjects. For the most part this self-constitution is not the result of active, conscious decisions, but of subliminal socialization. Like Nietzsche who attacks the idea of a fixed human nature or essence, Foucault is studying features of human beings that individuals generally take to be fixed but that historical study shows to be malleable. Even the human body (as experienced), which seems to be the lowest common denominator throughout history, is transformed over time by technologies such as the prison system or confession or sexual mores. Incarceration is more impersonal than confession or sexuality, since we do not do it to ourselves voluntarily. But there is also much in our sexual self-understanding that is not voluntary, even though to call it involuntary would miss the extent to which we form our identities by conforming ourselves over time to tacitly understood norms and generally accepted practices.

By applying genealogy to the study of how sexual ethics has been understood in different historical periods, then, Foucault no longer sounds as if he is offering impersonal, functionalist explanations for why people act as they do. He pays attention to the practices by which individuals train themselves to become a certain sort of person. Confession is one such practice that emerged from Christianity, for instance, but Foucault also notes the less institutionalized practices such as a husband might exercise on himself to keep himself faithful to his wife. Unlike the prison book, then, which studies how people constrain others, the history of sexuality studies how people constrain themselves.

If Foucault is writing a history of ethics, however, he is not writing a history of moral codes. Although the phenomena he is investigating are more conscious than those studied in his prison book, they are not fully self-conscious events such as reflections on principles for conduct. Unlike traditional moral philosophy, Foucault's study of ethics is not of sets of principles that people explicitly espouse however much they may live up to them. Unlike Kant he does not try to ground the moral code containing explicit prescriptions or commandments, since he thinks these do not have an interesting history and are generally stable throughout the different historical periods. His project owes an acknowledgement to Hegel, who criticizes Kant for looking only at the explicit moral rules instead of at the underlying 'ethical substance' that allows the moral code to function. For Hegel and Foucault the ethical substance includes .the background of shared understanding of what it is to belong to a particular community and to aspire in practice to being a good person there.

So Foucault investigates how the conception of the self changes from the Graeco-Roman idea of taking care of the self to the Christian goal of self-renunciation. He traces how sexual subjectivity alters as the Greek interest in *aphrodisia* changes into the Christian desire of the flesh. Both the Greeks and the Christians valued the ascetic restraint of sexual desires, but they interpreted this asceticism differently. For the Greeks asceticism does not mean a renunciation of the self but instead involves '*le souci de soi*', the care for the self described in volume 3. Foucault argues that Greek asceticism entails making the self aesthetically pleasing, and his central theme in volume 3 is asceticism in the larger sense of techniques that agents practise on themselves to make themselves into the persons they want to be. In *L'Usage des plaisirs* he offers evidence that sexuality is a specific historical concept, and in particular a product of the nineteenth century. He insists that the Greeks found sexual conduct as problematic as moderns do, but in different ways. For them it was not how or with whom one had sex that was crucial, as it supposedly is now, but whether one was master or slave of one's passions. So the Greeks could not have been opposed to what came to be called perversion or deviancy, but only to the aesthetic ugliness of any degree of physical excess.

As I understand Foucault's volumes on the history of sexuality, he is presenting evidence for the plausible belief that physical events such as bodily couplings are always understood under a particular mode of description, however tacitly. Furthermore, this mode of description or self-understanding will condition those physical events, such that human action properly understood must involve the former as well as the latter. Thus, in *The History of Sexuality* volume 1, Foucault suggests that sex is not a biological given onto which types of sexuality are somehow grafted as the result either of how the individual personality is formed or of what is permitted culturally. Foucault wants to get us to start thinking differently about sexuality by suggesting that only recently has it seemed necessary to think of human beings as if their possession of certain organs determined their gender and behaviour, or as if sexuality and personality were totally conditioned by particular orientations toward how these organs are used.

In volumes 2 and 3 of the *History of Sexuality*, Foucault goes beyond this critique of the modern idea of sexuality to study how sexual self-understanding has been different in the past. As a historian he wants to point to a level below the explicit moral precepts or other factors that are for the most part reflectively available to individual agents. His investigation of the underlying background of self-understanding is an exercise in the history of thought, but 'thought' for Foucault means more than what the agents might have said explicitly about themselves.

What I am calling self-understanding for Foucault is thus not the same as self-consciousness. Genealogy is not a vestige of the Cartesian philosophy of consciousness, but a historian's tool for studying observable manifestations of historically variable experiences of the self. A possible source of influence on Foucault here is Heidegger, for whom self-understanding is not revealed introspectively through access to a private, internal domain. Instead, self-understanding is shown in actions, and especially through patterns of action. I take Foucault to believe that although these patterns of action may appear to the practitioners to be coherent, intelligible, and tolerable, a critical history shows the practices to be not as rational, inevitable, or invariable as they are thought to be. Self-understanding is not a matter either of biological programming or of explicit, autonomous decision procedures. But self-understanding can be studied objectively through a matrix of social and discursive practices. To the extent that these practices turn out to vary historically, self-understanding will vary as well.

Someone with more Cartesian assumptions may object that the way individuals experience sexuality may be historically invariable, or at least different from the way historically variable public statements and institutions interpret it. This view presupposes, however, that there is no connection between the true experience of the individual self and the historian's investigation of public, cognitive discourse about sex as well as of social ways of recognizing its practice. The objection ignores the argument that if experience is not a given that is then interpreted, but is itself already interpreted, observable changes in patterns of interpretation and action will be the same as changes in subjective experience.

Since Foucault is focusing on processes that can be objectively discerned even though they may never be articulated self-consciously, he is studying a larger background that could be called the 'system of thought' since it is never fully explicit. But if 'system' connotes a static set of interconnected, articulatable elements and rules, this word fails to do justice to Foucault's historicist sense that there is change going on all the time, and at different rates at different levels. So while the moral precepts change slowly, the background understanding of these rules can alter at a different pace. From the historian's perspective agents will understand only incompletely why they act as they do. How individuals in one historical period understand themselves and therefore, given Foucault's premises, what they are doing will not be generalizable for other times. Over time these modes of self-understanding, and thus the experience people have, will change.

Since Foucault is now dealing with ethical issues about the formation of values, he cannot be accused of ignoring values and being nihilistic. Nevertheless, he still avoids constructing an independent standpoint from which to assess the present as well as the earlier value configurations. Since the historian is investigating different self-understandings to which individuals have adapted themselves with reasonable success, there is no standpoint from which to say that one self-understanding is better or worse than another. Foucault is of course critical of the present, and the contrast between the present and the past serves in part to underline this criticism. Yet Foucault insists that we cannot go back to these earlier modes of understanding. Hence, he avoids asserting that they are better or worse than our own, since such an assertion is not really intelligible.

His implicit reasoning is, I believe, that we can genuinely evaluate only those alternatives or options that are real or live for us. On his analysis the ancient Greek configuration is now recognizably foreign and remote. Contemplating its differences may help us to think differently about elements of our own self-understanding, but we cannot simply choose to understand ourselves and act now as the Greeks once did. As for Christianity Foucault pointedly does not imitate Nietzsche's tirades, probably because Christian worries about the flesh are no longer live options and thus do not warrant shrill polemics. Of course, part of Foucault's point is that the modern understanding of sexuality (as manifested, for instance, in psychiatry or sexual liberation movements) is suspect insofar as it derives from Christian views about the soul and the practice of self-confession. But Foucault also believes that the Christian and the modern formulations for sexual comportment are incommensurable. The Christian formula, for example, would eradicate desire, whereas according to the modern formula desire should be liberated.

Does Foucault's refusal to explain how to improve on the present suggest again the fatalistic conclusion that we cannot do anything at all to change ourselves now? To give a history of sexuality is for him to describe how different ages have always found sexual relations problematic although in intriguingly different ways. So he is not saying that we must simply reconcile ourselves to our present conceptualization of sexuality. Resignation to the sexual status quo would be inconsistent with his depiction of modern sexuality as being deeply problematic for us.

Of course, seeing that sexuality was problematic for the Greeks as well does not make our own problems go away. Since the radical differences in the backgrounds of beliefs and practices prevent us from adopting previous sexual self-understandings, Foucault's analysis of the different sexual problematics does not supply a corrective for our own. But from that it does not follow that his analysis has no practical, critical value for us. Although he does not construct a totally different ideal to which we could aspire, his history does make us more aware of the shortcomings in our own self-understanding and practices. The imperative to change must come from within ourselves if it comes at all. Foucault can only hope that his historiography will help to subvert what he thinks are our self-deceptive tendencies to deny any such imperative.

If we deceive ourselves, there must be a truth about ourselves that we falsify. Is Foucault covertly bringing back appeals to truth values? Whatever one thinks about Foucault's archaeological method for studying knowledge, the epistemological questions raised there do not obviously trouble his analyses of ethics. That he rejects epistemological relativism is especially apparent from his attack on Derrida's reading of Plato.[27] Foucault believes that the method of textual deconstruction tries incorrectly and unsuccessfully to bracket all questions about the truth claims of texts. He does not hesitate to claim that there are truths about how people do understand themselves and what sort of life they esteem. He does not address the further question whether there are lives to which everyone everywhere ought to aspire. As a historian he is not required to do so. As a philosopher he could give arguments that the question is misguided because it presupposes both an inflated conception of what a philosophical theory of morality can establish and an inadequate moral psychology that ignores the social and historical background supporting the moral code.

Foucault's efforts in working on the genealogy of ethics are thus intended to correct what some might consider his own earlier mistakes or what others will think to be mistaken understandings of what he was up to all along. If his study of the emergence of conditions for taking different factors as potentially true or false about how human beings understand themselves is not paradoxically relativistic, his serious interest in the cultural basis of morality deflects as well the accusation of nihilism. Also, instead of being a functionalist who believes that all aspects of society and culture are tied together so tightly that no part can change or be improved independently of all the other parts, he insists that some aspects of the ethical substance change while others persist. Foucault gives up the tool of hypothesizing total historical discontinuities when it no longer has any heuristic value. As a result his account of sexual ethics does not seem fatalistic, since individuals at this level do have some practical capacity to influence their own self-formation. They can try to correct and improve factors they discover to be problematic since they can change some features of themselves without simultaneously changing all other social and political practices.

Beyond Enlightenment?

However Foucault's trajectory is described, and whether his genealogical method is practicable, he arrives finally at a clear philosophical assessment of his own efforts. Oddly enough, his last formulation of his relation to the philosophical tradition is worked out through an interpretation of the philosopher who all along appeared to be his antithesis. Any comparison with the unhistorical, transcendental philosopher Kant, the defender of enlightenment belief in the necessary progress of rationality, presumably would serve only to highlight Foucault as an extreme representative of the anti-rationalist counter-enlightenment.

Hilary Putnam, for instance, identifies Foucault as a relativist, and then uses an argument from Kant to show that relativism is logically unintelligible.[28] Putnam says, for instance, that 'Foucault is not arguing that past practices were *more* rational than they look to be, but that all practices are *less* rational, are, in fact, mainly determined by unreason and selfish power.'[29] So described, Foucault's position is self-refuting, for if every cultural standpoint, including Foucault's, is irrational, then there is no standpoint from which Foucault could assert that every cultural standpoint is irrational. On such a view asserting or denying anything becomes nothing more than 'crazy behaviour'.[30]

If Foucault treads dangerously close to this paradox during his archaeological phase, he does not claim that genealogy establishes any conclusions about the irrationality of *all* our beliefs and practices. He settles for the more modest, less totalizing claim that successful genealogies would show the irrationality only of some specific beliefs and practices.

This clarification suggests that he does not consider himself an enemy of enlightenment. He might not even take exception to Putnam's thesis, advocated also by Kant and Habermas, that we must (for logical reasons) believe in the regulative ideal of reason or of 'a just, attentive, balanced intellect'.[31] There may be affinities between Kant and Foucault that are distorted by Foucault's attack on Kantian humanism in *The Order of Things*. In the last essay of this collection Ian Hacking points out that Foucault was a 'remarkably able Kantian', and that *The Order of Things* itself grew out of Foucault's plans for an introduction to his translation into French of Kant's *Anthropologie*. Hacking argues that Foucault's notion of freedom resembles Kant's to such an extent that 'those who criticize Foucault for not giving us a place to stand might start their critique with Kant'.[32]

In his last years Foucault was fascinated by Kant's little essay, 'What is Enlightenment?' Instead of attacking Kant's efforts there, Foucault identifies that essay as giving birth to the critical tradition that forms his own heritage. This tradition asks about the specific features of the present that make us distinctively who we are. Admittedly this is a different critical tradition from the principal one of analysing the transcendental conditions for all possible experience, as undertaken in the *Critique of Pure Reason*. Foucault concludes a lecture on Kant's enlightenment essay by remarking:

> It seems to me that the philosophical choice with which we find ourselves confronted at present is this one: we can opt either for a critical philosophy presenting itself as an analytic philosophy of truth in general, or for a critical thinking that takes the form of an ontology of ourselves or an ontology of the present. The latter form of philosophy, from Hegel to the Frankfurt School passing through Nietzsche and Max Weber, has founded a form of reflection in which I have tried to work.[33]

After having criticized Kant in *The Order of Things* for starting the tradition of philosophical anthropology and thereby sanctioning the sciences of man, Foucault returns to Kant as the originator of a different role for philosophy. Foucault was working toward the end of his life on an essay also called 'What is Enlightenment?'[34] Here he insists that he is not a 'counter-enlightenment' thinker, if by that is meant someone who denies that 'we still depend in large part' on the enlightenment.[35] Foucault recognizes that his efforts to show the extent to which the present is historically conditioned by the enlightenment are guided by the enlightenment's own 'principle of a critique and a permanent creation of ourselves in our autonomy'.[36] So while he still wishes to criticize humanism for borrowing a specific theological and metaphysical conception of human nature, he admits that he cannot claim to stand outside the enlightenment tradition itself.

If he prefers to be agnostic about the possibility of the success of the drive for enlightenment, that is because faith in enlightenment is paradoxical for reasons he surely learned from the *Dialectic of Enlightenment* by Adorno and Horkheimer. The pious belief in the unqualified value of enlightenment contradicts the enlightenment's own aspiration for rational autonomy. Rational autonomy is itself an empty ideal, however, unless it is exercised critically through the genealogical study of specific, limited historical features of ourselves. Remaining within the enlightenment tradition does not mean that the purpose of these specific historical inquiries should be exclusively to preserve the '"essential kernel of rationality"' especially since, Foucault now insists, this kernel 'would have to be preserved in any event'.[37]

He is thus implying that a strictly retrospective use of critical history to justify the enlightenment would show the enlightenment to be stagnant or even degenerating. So Foucault is not claiming that the enlightenment tradition is dead, but only that it would die if we stopped doing genealogical investigations that explore the '"contemporary limits of the necessary"'.[38] To ensure the vigour of enlightenment we should continue to question our limits, experimentally pushing ourselves to think about 'what is not or is no longer indispensable for the constitution of ourselves as autonomous subjects'.[39]

Some of his critics may think that this minimal concession to reason does not salvage his enterprise so much as vindicate their objections. Others may find the call for 'permanent critique' either too subversive or too empty. Foucault may be right, however, in his assessment of the predicament confronting any philosopher and social critic today. By exemplifying that predicament and confronting it with honest and difficult work, Foucault deserves our attention. Given his own insistence on the continuous need for criticism, he would not object if that attention were critical. All he would ask is that it represent productive 'work on our limits, that is, a patient labor giving form to our impatience for liberty'.[40]

Notes

1 *Habermas: Critical Essays*, ed. John B. Thompson and David Held (Cambridge, Mass.: MIT Press, 1982). *Habermas and Modernity*, ed. Richard J. Bernstein (Cambridge, Mass.: MIT Press, 1985).
2 Michel Foucault, 'Preface', *Madness and Civilization: A History of Insanity in the Age of Reason*, trans. Richard Howard (New York: Random House, 1965), p. ix.
3 See Foucault, *The Order of Things: An Archaeology of the Human Sciences* (New York: Random House, 1970), p. 332.
4 Ibid., p. 382.

5 Michel Foucault, 'Truth and Power', in *Power/Knowledge: Selected Interviews and Other Writings 1972–1977*, ed. Colin Gordon (New York: Pantheon, 1980), p. 115.

6 Michel Foucault, 'Why Study Power: The Question of the Subject', an afterword to *Michel Foucault: Beyond Structuralism and Hermeneutics* by Hubert L. Dreyfus and Paul Rabinow (University of Chicago Press, first edition, 1982; second edition, 1983), p. 208.

7 See Paul Rabinow (ed.), *The Foucault Reader* (New York: Pantheon, 1984), p. 336; this version of the preface to volume 2 is a different one than was finally published in the book itself.

8 See Ian Hacking, *The Emergence of Probability: A Philosophical Study of Early Ideas About Probability, Induction and Statistical Inference* (Cambridge University Press, 1975), and in 1983 from the same publisher, *Representing and Intervening: Introductory Topics in the Philosophy of Natural Science*, for examples of his own approach to the history of science.

9 For Rorty's own critique of epistemology see in particular Part 3 of *Philosophy and the Mirror of Nature* (Princeton University Press, 1979) and the introduction to his *Consequences of Pragmatism (Essays: 1972–1980)* (Minneapolis: University of Minnesota Press, 1982).

10 Hubert L. Dreyfus and Paul Rabinow, *Michel Foucault: Beyond Structuralism and Hermeneutics* (University of Chicago Press, 1982, 1983). I review both the first edition of this book in 'Foucault's slalom', *London Review of Books*, vol. 4, 4–17 November 1982, pp. 18–20, and the supplemented second edition in a survey entitled 'After Foucault', *London Review of Books*, vol. 6, 1–14 November 1984, pp. 7–9. Some of the following remarks are anticipated in those reviews.

11 See Dreyfus and Rabinow, *Michel Foucault* (second edition), pp. 85–103.

12 Nancy Fraser, 'Foucault on modern power: empirical insights and normative confusions', *Praxis International*, vol. 1 (1981), p. 238; cited by Habermas, *Der philosophische Diskurs der Moderne: Zwolf Vorlesungen* (Frankfurt: Suhrkamp, 1985), p. 333. See her critique of my own and other defences of Foucault in 'Michel Foucault: a "Young Conservative"?' in *Ethics*, vol. 96 (October 1985), pp. 165–184.

13 See my discussion of this issue in 'Foucault: Modern or Postmodern?' (forthcoming in Jonathan Arac (ed.), *After Foucault: Humanistic Knowledges, Postmodern Challenges*). I treat Habermas's critique of Foucault at greater length in my forthcoming book from Basil Blackwell, *Critical Theory, For and Against*, co-authored with Thomas McCarthy.

14 Habermas, 'Modernity versus Postmodernity,' *New German Critique*, no. 22 (Winter 1981), p. 13.

15 Habermas, *Der philosophische Diskurs der Moderne*, p. 338.

16 Ibid., p. 340.

17 Ibid., p. 321.

18 See below, p. 196.

19 See below, p. 64.

20 See below, p. 61.
21 See my discussion of Lukes and Foucault in 'Power, Repression, Progress' (below, pp. 123 ff.) Professor Lukes plans to include this account and a further response to Foucault's work in his forthcoming anthology from Polity Press entitled *The Dimensions of Power*.
22 See William E. Connolly's rebuttal to Taylor's critique of Foucault, and Taylor's rejoinder, in their exchange in *Political Theory*, vol. 13 (August 1985), pp. 265–85.
23 Clifford Geertz, 'Stir crazy', *The New York Review of Books*, 26 January 1978, p. 6, where Geertz concludes that Foucault 'has not escaped so completely from the vulnerable *épistéme* of historicism as he might like or imagine . . . But perhaps like half-revolutions, half-escapes are enough, and will suffice. It is just such a half-escape, whatever he intended, that makes *Discipline and Punish* so fascinating . . . As with so many prisoners, of so many kinds, it is not getting out but wanting out that generates in Foucault a strange and special vision.'
24 Fredric Jameson, 'Postmodernism, or, the cultural logic of late capitalism', *New Left Review*, vol. 147 (September 1984), p. 57.
25 In addition to *Beginnings* (New York: Basic Books, 1975), see Edward Said, 'Criticism between Culture and System' in *The World, the Text and the Critic* (Cambridge, Mass.: Harvard University Press, 1983).
26 Mark Poster, *Foucault, Marxism and History: Mode of Production versus Mode of Information* (Cambridge: Polity Press, 1984), p. 159.
27 In addition to volume 2 of the *History of Sexuality*, see the interview 'On the Genealogy of Ethics', appended to the second edition of the book by Dreyfus and Rabinow (pp. 245f.) and published as well in Rabinow's *Foucault Reader* (pp. 363f.).
28 Hilary Putnam, *Reason, Truth and History* (Cambridge University Press, 1981); see pp. 121, 155–62.
29 Ibid., p. 162.
30 Ibid., p. 162.
31 Ibid., p. 163.
32 See below, p. 239.
33 Translated from 'Un cours inédit de Michel Foucault', a reworked transcription from 1983 published in *Magazine littéraire*, no. 207 (May 1984), p. 39.
34 Published posthumously in Paul Rabinow (ed.), *Foucault Reader*, pp. 32–50.
35 Foucault, 'What is Enlightenment?', p. 42.
36 Ibid., p. 44.
37 Ibid., p. 43.
38 Ibid., p. 43.
39 Ibid., p. 43.
40 Ibid., p. 50.

The Archaeology of Foucault

IAN HACKING

Power/Knowledge is a collection of nine interviews, an essay, and a pair of lectures in which Michel Foucault tries to work out new ways to talk about power.[1] This is one more stage in a remarkable adventure of ideas that began in the late fifties. 'Key words' in Foucault's work would be, for example: Labour, Language, Life, Madness, Masturbation, Medicine, Military, Nietzsche, Prison, Psychiatry, Quixote, Sade, and Sex. Be neither attracted nor repelled by this adolescent list of topics. Foucault has an original analytical mind with a fascination for facts. He is adept at reorganizing past events in order to rethink the present. He engagingly turns familiar truisms into doubt or chaos. Even though his present thoughts about power and knowledge have not yet matured, they are plainly part of a fermentation worth learning about.

What are the relationships between power and knowlege? There are two bad short answers: (1) knowledge provides an instrument that those in power can wield for their own ends; (2) a new body of knowledge brings into being a new class of people or institutions that can exercise a new kind of power. These two assertions parallel two opposed theses about ideology: (1) a ruling class generates an ideology that suits its own interests; and (2) a new ideology, with new values, creates a niche for a new ruling class. Virtually nobody likes either side of these simple dichotomies. Foucault is one of many who want a new conception of how power and knowledge interact. But he is not looking for a relation between two givens, 'power' and 'knowledge'. As always he is trying to rethink the entire subject matter, and his 'knowledge' and 'power' are to be something else.

Nobody knows this knowledge; no one wields this power. Yes, there are people who know this and that. Yes, there are individuals and organizations that rule other people. Yes, there are suppressions and repressions that come from authority. Yes, the forms of knowledge and of power since the nineteenth century have served the bourgeoisie above all others, and now also serve a comparable class in Eastern Europe. But those ruling classes don't know how they do it, nor could they do it without the other terms in the power relation – the functionaries, the governed, the repressed, the exiled – each willingly or unwillingly doing their bit. One ought to begin an analysis of power from the ground up, at the level of tiny local events where battles are unwittingly enacted by players who don't know what they are doing.

Now this sort of project is not novel. Foucault's genius is to go down to the little dramas, dress them in facts hardly anyone else had noticed, and turn these stage settings into clues to a hitherto unthought series of confrontations out of which, he contends, the orderly structure of society is composed. For all the abstract schemes for which Foucault has become famous, he is also the most concrete of writers. He is a fact-lover. One of the interviews ends on a typical note. He's asked when bottle-feeding of infants was invented or at least introduced into France. He does not know and is delighted when his interlocutors can tell him, and at the same time curses himself for being so dumb not to have asked the question himself.

Foucault is, then, no spinner of verbal fantasies. I enjoy his long books rather than these short interviews just because the books are denser with facts. The editor of *Power/Knowledge* is right, however, when he says that the interviews can help us to understand the books. The interview is a French art form used to present work in progress which is destined, at first, for limited circulation, and which is couched in terms suitable for discussion among one specific audience. Hence there is a directness here that is often missing from the long and elaborately constructed books. But Foucault's notions of power and knowledge are so divorced from common speech that I need to recall how he arrived at them. His sequence of books is, despite its ups and downs, an intellectual progress, and I shall try to describe it by way of explaining the interviews.

Madness and Civilization was a somewhat romantic work.[2] It seems to have started with the hesitant belief, never stated, that there is a pure thing, madness, perhaps a good in itself, which is not something that we can capture in concepts. It is certainly not what the sciences of the insane call madness. We classify and treat and put away the mad by systems of our own creation. Our institutions create the phenomena in terms of which we see insanity. This first major book by Foucault hints at an almost Kantian story in which our experience of the mad is a mere phenomenon conditioned by our thought and our history, but there is also a thing-in-itself which can be called madness and which is uncorruptible. Moreover reason is also only a phenomenon whose very existence requires its opposite to define itself against. In English the book is ironically subtitled, 'A History of Madness in the Age of Reason'.

By the time that the book had been written it was clear that this romantic conception of a pure and prior madness was a mistake. There could be no such thing as this preconceptual way of being. The book had become a book about something else. What? That was not so clear, at first. 'When I think back now,' Foucault said in a 1977 interview, 'I ask myself what else it was that I was talking about, in *Madness and Civilization* or *The Birth of the Clinic*, but power?'[3]

The plot of the madness book, which is repeated in several of its successors, is plain enough. There are two notable events. First comes 'the great exclusion' in mid-seventeenth century: a frantic locking up of deviants and a building of lunatic asylums. Much later, at the time of the French Revolution, there was a spurious liberation, when a new body of psychiatric knowledge invented new ways to deal with the insane. At least in the old asylums, Foucault suggests, the mad were left to themselves in all the horror that implied. Yet the horror was not worse than the solemn destruction of the mad by committees of experts with their constantly changing manuals of nostrums.

Foucault's stories are dramatic. He presents a reordering of events that we had not perceived before. The effect is heightened by brilliant before-and-after snapshots taken on either side of the great divide during which one tradition is transformed into another. We are given one snippet of description of a brain around 1780 and another twenty-five years later. The very 'same' organ on the marble slab plays a role in the later physiology that corresponds to nothing in 1780.

Scholars remind us that the facts are vastly more complex than what Foucault describes. His predilection for French examples projected onto European history leads to mistakes.[4] There are two extremes of French historiography. The *Annales* school goes in for long-term continuities or slow transitions – 'the great silent motionless bases that traditional history has covered with a thick layer of events' (to quote from the first page of Foucault's *Archaeology of Knowledge*).[5] Foucault takes the opposite tack, inherited from Gaston Bachelard, Georges Canguilhem, and Louis Althusser. He posits sharp discontinuities in the history of knowledge. In one interview he grants that this obsession with breaks creates an account of knowledge that fits some facts, but is not a general model. Now not only do we find that the facts are sometimes not quite right, that they are overgeneralized, and that they are squeezed into a model of brusque transformations; we also find that many of Foucault's dramas have already been told in calmer terms, by other people.

No matter. His histories stick in the mind. We can add our own corrective footnotes at leisure. These histories matter because they are in part political statements. They are also what I call philosophy: a way of analysing and coming to understand the conditions of possibility for ideas – not only ideas of disease or insanity or imprisonment but also the traditional concept of epistemology, namely knowledge, and of ethics, namely power.

An exclusion is an exercise of power. It is a putting away. Despite all the fireworks, *Madness and Civilization* follows the romantic convention that sees the exercise of power as repression, which is wicked. The dramatic and fundamental feature of Foucault's recent work is the rejection of this idea. But do not turn at once to his writings on power, for it is in his reflections on knowledge that this conversion occurs.

The psychiatrists, hygienists, forensic scientists, theorists of the prison, of education or population that emerge in the nineteenth century form a new band of experts. They had lots of hypotheses and prejudices and tidy theories that were constantly being revised, but which were embedded in an underlying conception of disease or crime or whatnot. Foucault used the French word *connaissance* to stand for such items of surface knowledge, while *savoir* meant more than science; it was a frame, postulated by Foucault, within which surface hypotheses got their sense. *Savoir* is not knowledge in the sense of a bunch of solid propositions. This 'depth' knowledge is more like a postulated set of rules that determine what kinds of sentences are going to count as true or false in some domain. The kinds of things to be said about the brain in 1780 are not the kinds of things to be said a quarter-century later. That is not because we have different beliefs about brains, but because 'brain' denotes a new kind of object in the later discourse, and occurs in different sorts of sentences.

The knowledge of *Power/Knowledge* is the *savoir* I'm calling 'depth' knowledge. Maybe no one is conscious of this knowledge. We should expect that Foucault's 'power' will turn out to be some sort of 'depth' power that no one wittingly exercises. Foucault's worries about knowledge and power will not, then, be the important but trite questions about how geneticists or nuclear physicists are to use their new-won surface knowledge for the good or ill of our species.

A new knowledge is involved in the liberation of the insane as they are brought under the care of the medical man. New things are to be said and thought about the mad. Foucault's book on medicine has a connected story. *La clinique* denotes both an institution, the teaching hospital, and the clinical lecture, a way of talking. *The Birth of the Clinic* (1963) is another book about exclusion and about new candidates for truth-or-falsehood. It is also about the creation of a self-constituting class of experts located within a new knowledge. What makes this development possible? A familiar history of science would tell us a tale of heroes. We would learn of their problems, their goals, their luck, their experiments, their mistakes, their visible and invisible colleges, and their funding. Foucault does not aim at such a history of who said what and why, but a story about the web of specific sentences that were uttered, and a theory, called archaeology, of what made it possible for those sentences to be uttered (largely regardless of who uttered them). This impossible task will produce a bizarre account of what we might call pure knowledge. The first and probably last masterpiece in this genre is *The Order of Things*.[6]

The Order of Things tells of four epochs. The periodization is already familiar. There is the age of reason, from Descartes to the Revolution. There is a historicist nineteenth century that leads on to the present. There is the predecessor era that we call the renaissance. Finally there is a future, starting now.

'Life, labour and language' are concepts formed in the nineteenth century as the material of biology, economics, and linguistics. These sciences have objects that don't correspond with or 'map onto' their pre-Revolutionary predecessors of natural history, the theory of wealth, or general grammar. Those fields of inquiry have, in turn, no parallel in the Renaissance, says Foucault. Such non-mappings result not so much from new discoveries as from the coming into being of new objects of thought for which new truth and falsehoods are to be uttered. *The Order of Things* is about how one 'depth' knowledge can mutate into another, and with what consequences.

The book is not only a new sort of historical performance. It is also a tract against the human sciences. The American reader should not identify these with the social sciences, for the French classification will include some admixture of psychoanalysis and ethnography, certain kinds of literary analysis and various reflections of a Marxist origin. Foucault's book is about *Man*, a figure of less interest for our anglophone culture. 'Man' is two-faced, knower and object of knowledge. He was formally announced when Kant one year put a new question into his annual Logic lectures: 'What is Man?'

The ensuing philosophical anthropology – it was Foucault, who edited a French edition of Kant's *Anthropologie* (1964) – generates an illicit way to talk that pretends to look like biology or linguistics. This is not the familiar criticism that says the method of the social sciences is inept. The method is all too well modelled on legitimate science. Foucault is denying that the human sciences have a genuine object to talk about. Luckily, he informs us, Man is on the way out. Discourse is coming in, pure discourse without the knowing subject who utters the words.

Some of this antagonism to the knowing subject is merely typical of Parisian discussions of the day. Phenomenology was detested and despised by figures such as Lévi-Strauss. Foucault's own literary criticism – some of which can be read in a collection of his essays translated as *Language, Counter-Memory, Practice*[7] – argues that the concepts of 'author' and '*oeuvre*' must be exchanged for less personal ways of grouping sentences. He also urges that literature is extinct. My very phrase 'literary criticism' is a solecism in describing Foucault. So much was the high fashion of the day. But in addition Foucault had, if not a theory, at least a body of speculations that give sense to it. He held that the class of sentences that can be uttered in a specified time and place is not determined by the conscious wishes of the speakers. The possibility of being true-or-false does not reside in a person's desire to communicate. Hence the author himself is irrelevant to the analysis of such 'conditions of possibility'.

Discourse is, then, to be analysed not in terms of who says what but in terms of the conditions under which those sentences will have a definite truth value, and hence are capable of being uttered. Such conditions will lie in the 'depth' knowledge of the time. This vision leads us far from material conditions of the production of sentences. Inevitably *The Order of Things* looks like an idealist book, reminiscent once again of Kant. Perhaps in self-mockery Foucault briefly accepted the label of 'the historical *a priori*'. Where Kant had found the conditions of possible experience in the structure of the human mind, Foucault does it with historical, and hence transient, conditions for possible discourse,

This obsession with words was too fragile to stand. Foucault had to return to the material conditions under which the words were spoken. Not wanting to go back to individual speakers or authors, he at least had to consider the interests which spoken and written words would serve. The illegitimate sciences of Man were not just a lot of talk. They included the legal medicine which in the nineteenth century was busy reclassifying deviants (inventing even the concepts of norm and of pathology), and then allotting them to treatment. This legal reformism devised new architectures of prisons, schools, and hospitals, which are described in *Discipline and Punish: The Birth of the Prison*.[8] There are overt forms of power such as the judicial machinery with its new crowd of experts to testify on the mental health of the prisoner. Everywhere discipline is to the fore. It is revealed in the factory as well as in buildings avowedly erected for disciplining. Even the working man's cottage shall have its rooms divided and allotted to ensure the strictest morality.

Knowledge became power, all right. A new conception of human beings as disciplinary objects means one is to do something new with people. Not that anyone 'knew' much that we would now call sound belief. If you read through the volumes of the *Annales d'hygiène publique et de médecine légale*, which commence in 1829, you will give credence to very little except the statistics, but you will be able to dine out for a year on horror stories, especially if you Xerox some of the engravings.

Foucault lifted from these *Annales* an event of 1835 now published as *I, Pierre Rivière, having slaughtered my mother, my sister and my brother . . .* (1973).[9] For almost the first time a horde of experts stood about in court theorizing about the supposedly crazed killer. The categories into which they slot him will determine what is to be done with him. That is one small way in which knowledge is power. It is less the facts about Pierre than the possibility of thinking of him in these ways that fixes his fate.

In his interviews Foucault subscribes to the common wisdom that the failed Parisian revolts of May 1968 jolted him out of a one-sided fascination with discourse and also created a new audience that could discuss knowledge and power. There are also good internal reasons for at the very least expanding the project undertaken in *The Order of Things*. If you hold that a discourse consists in the totality of what is said in some domain, then you go beyond reading the intellectual highs of the heroes of science and you sample what is being said everywhere – including not only the annals of public hygiene but also the broadsheets of the day. You inevitably have to consider who is doing what to whom.

At that point Foucault makes his fundamental break with tradition. Out with the who and the whom. He is primed by the denial of the knowing subject that I have just described. The old model of repression says there is a who: some identifiable party is organizing the lives of other people; or, as a result, we are not allowed to do certain things. Volume 1 of *The History of Sexuality* (1976) is a polemic against that model.[10]

This book is, as Foucault remarks in one interview, not about sex. 'Sexuality' denotes (in one dictionary definition) recognition of, or preoccupation with, sex. The book is partly about this preoccupation. The French title of volume 1 is *La Volonté de savoir*, the will to knowledge, 'depth' knowledge. The will in question is nobody in particular's will; indeed the title is also an allusion to Schopenhauer. There is a will to create the possibility of saying truths and falsehoods about sex. Unlike the other figures of Foucault's histories, this will to knowledge turns out to have been around for a long time.

Like the prison, sexuality has its own immediate interest, but Foucault's abiding concerns also call his attention to a certain positive knowledge of populations and what he calls biopolitics. Great webs of bureaucracy evolve endless ways to count and classify people. Birth, death, sickness, suicide, fertility: these inaugurate the modern era, the era of statistical data. There is an avalanche of numbers early in the nineteenth century. It occurs not because people can count better but because new kinds of facts about populations are taken to be the things to find out.

Sexuality for Foucault is not only a preoccupation with sex. It intersects with a larger circle of ideas, of consciousness of the body, of bodies. It has to do with 'political technologies of life'. Two axes of sexuality are offered: 'disciplines of the body, of harnessing, intensification and distribution of force, the adjustment and economy of energies. On the other hand ["sexuality"] was applied to the regulation of populations.' Both 'an entire micro-power concerned with the body', and 'comprehensive measures, statistical assessments and interventions' aimed at the entire social body: 'Sex was a means of access both to the life of the body and the life of the species.'

We once had a sovereign who exercised power upon subjects. Around the beginning of the nineteenth century there arises what Foucault describes in an interview as 'a new type of power, which can no longer be formulated in terms of sovereignty'. It is one of the great inventions of bourgeois society. In one dimension this power is to be called 'disciplinary', but discipline is only one aspect of it. New kinds of truth and falsehood are another. '"Truth"', Foucault tell us, 'is to be understood as a system of ordered procedures for the production, regulation, distribution and operation of statements. "Truth" is linked in a circular relation with systems of power which produce and sustain it.' This 'truth' is at one step removed from what we normally understand. It is an abstract underlying element that takes its place with the 'depth' knowledge and power. We are specifically enjoined not to think of all this in terms of ideology and Marxian super- structure, i.e., self-conceptions used after the fact to legitimate an economic arrangement. The truth, knowledge, and power are on the contrary the conditions of possibility for the bourgeois mode.

Most readers have already had a hard time making sense of Foucault's anonymous knowledge, discourse with a life of its own. Unowned power is even more mysterious. 'All the same', one interviewer begins with a touch of exasperation, 'does someone initiate the whole business or not?' Prisons were under discussion. Foucault's answer goes like this. The new technology of power does not originate with any identifiable person or group. We do indeed get individual tactics invented for particular needs. Prison architecture is modified to make it harder for prisoners to hang themselves – but always with a certain model of how a prison is to be built. The tactics take shape in piecemeal fashion without anyone's wittingly knowing what they add up to. If we turn to the practice of collecting information about populations, each new classification, and each new counting within that classification, is devised by a person or a committee with a straightforward, limited goal in mind. Then the population itself is increasingly classified, rearranged, and administered by principles each one of which is innocently put forward by this or that technocrat. We obtain 'a complex play of supports in mutual engagement, different mechanisms of power'.

Let us not, therefore, ask why certain people want to dominate, what they seek, what is their overall strategy. Let us ask, instead, how things work at the level of on-going subjugation, at the level of those continuous and uninterrupted processes which subject our bodies, govern our gestures, dictate our behaviours etc. In other words, rather than ask ourselves how the sovereign appears to us in his lofty isolation, we should try to discover how it is that subjects are gradually, progressively, really and materially constituted through a multiplicity of organisms, forces, energies, materials, desires, thoughts etc. We should try to grasp subjection in its material instance as a constitution of subjects. This would be an exact opposite of Hobbes' project in *Leviathan* ...[11]

The *exact* opposite: Foucault is not concerned with how the subjects shall form a constitution determining who or what is sovereign. He wants to know how the subjects themselves are constituted. Just as there was no pure madness, no thing-in-itself, so there is no pure subject, no 'I' or 'me' prior to the forms of description and action appropriate to a person. Literary historians have long noted that a person did not conceive of himself as a poet – as *that* kind of person – before the Romantic era. One just wrote poems. Liberationists urge that the category of 'homosexual' (and hence 'heterosexual') did not exist until the doctors of deviancy invented it. There were acts, but not a homosexual *kind* of person. It is a Foucaultian thesis that every way in which I can think of myself as a person and an agent is something that has been constituted within a web of historical events. Here is one more step in the destruction of Kant: the noumenal self is nothing.

I have just quoted Foucault saying, 'Let us not, therefore, ask why certain people want to dominate ...' Out of context you might wonder if he is telling us never to ask why Roosevelt, Stalin, or de Gaulle wanted to dominate. Are we not to ask why these very persons had vices and virtues, and how they left their marks upon hundreds of millions of subjects? Foucault implies no such thing. Compare his earlier work. At the height of his enthusiasm for abrupt changes in knowledge, he never denied the importance of the *Annales* methodology with its search for underlying stability. When he lashed out at the concept of 'author' as critical tool, he never lost his affection for his favourite authors and their best books. In short, his own investigations do not preclude others. In context his quotation says, for *my* purposes, don't ask why certain people want to dominate.

There are two distinct points here. One is that he is embarking on new inquiries about the constitution of the subject. The other is that the old inquiries, about the power of a particular despot, say, are distorted by the blind conception of the power always stemming from above. We may indeed, in a particular story, have a complete causal chain from a directive signed 'Stalin' down to a particular victim in a Gulag. But that there should have been a Gulag-type institution is not, according to Foucault, personal or historical caprice. It looks as if this type of evil is inextricably connected with Eastern European socialist states, and its explanation will require an archaeology of communism. I have no idea how Foucault would write one, but there are hints in these interviews. Moreover, to give an archaeological account is in no way to excuse or to fail to make distinctions. Don't, he urges, fall prey to the rhetoric that says we all have our own Gulags here at our own door, in our cities. That is false, but it is not power exercised from the top that has made it false.

Foucault propounds an extreme nominalism: nothing, not even the ways I can describe myself, is either this or that but history made it so. We may have been led along this route by reflections on knowledge and language, but we should drop the metaphors that they suggest. Instead turn to power, 'war and battle. The history which bears and determines us has the form of a war rather than that of a language: relations of power, not relations of meaning.' Every new way in which to think of a person – and hence a way in which people can think of themselves, find their roles, and choose their actions – 'is the pursuit of war by other means'.

The Order of Things ends by prophesying a new era in which self-conscious discourse is not about Man or the thinking subject but about discourse alone. A good deal of this project remains in what Foucault now calls genealogy: 'a form of history which can account for the constitution of knowledges, discourses, domains of objects, etc., without having to make reference to a subject which is either transcendental in relation to the field of events or runs in its empty sameness throughout the course of history'. But *The Order of Things* spoke as if there would be no reflective talk except talk about talk. Perhaps we should not see this book as bringing in a new era of such pure talk, but rather as the final instalment in a century or so of philosophical writing obsessed with language. Foucault's new concern with relations of power, rather than relations of meaning, should lead us away from the escapist metaphors about conversation that flow from a fixation on language.

It is not that language shall be deemed unimportant. Foucault's forthcoming history of the confessional must among other things be the history of a certain kind of talk. He is likewise still concerned with the project of understanding how certain classes of sentences come up for grabs as true or false, at definite locations in history. Such investigations are now, however, to be embedded in an account of the possibilities of action and the springs of power. The murmuring at the confessional is an 'irrigation' (his word) of power. The word 'irrigation' bears not only the familiar agricultural sense but also refers to medical hygiene. Perhaps both senses are intended here. Confessions keep the power relation hygienic, and also run channels of water from one area to another so the whole can flourish. Without the performance of the individual acts of irrigation, the power would rot or dry up.

Even such events of pure philosophical inquiry as the introduction of the Cartesian *ego* into discourse may be seen in this light. The *ego* collects together a lot of fairly unrelated activities: hoping and hurting and proving theorems and seeing trees. Why should there be one thing – a substance, as Descartes had it – that is the subject of all these predicates? Suppose we guess that the confessional for novitiate monks is the place where people were first made to talk not only about what they have done, but also about what they have felt and thought and seen and above all dreamed. The *Rules* of Descartes for the direction of the mind, seemingly so purely concerned with the search for, and foundations of knowledge, may then appear to be one more item in a sequence of monastic *regulae*, rules in which a very specific type of talking integrates a system of bodily discipline.

Let power and knowledge be something like what Foucault has glimpsed. What then shall we do? We seem led to an immensely pessimistic body of doctrine. The politics of the left is usually founded upon a Romantic conception of getting back to the origin, as in Rousseau, or on to the end, as with Marx. Foucault makes plain that he has been discussing (and detesting) not only the discipline of bourgeois society. There will be an archaeology of Gulags too. In any particular context we can go some way without the Romantic illusions of the left, for there remains *praxis*, Marxist and somewhat Spinozan. We can distinguish the Gulag institution, which like the prison is to be studied and understood by a Foucault-like history, from the Gulag question, i.e., what is to be done about these monsters, at this very moment? The Gulag, as well as being a historical object, is also 'a positive present'.

So are French prisons. One may well understand that prison reform is almost coeval with the penitentiary, as if it were an auxiliary to the institution, and still try to make prisons less intolerable, right now. But although prison reform might be a popular front on which many of us can agree, Foucault clearly finds more radical transformations attractive. But if the Romantic revolutionary illusion of liberation is in principle abandoned, how is it to be replaced? 'It's not a matter of emancipating truth from every system of power . . . but of detaching the power of truth from the forms of hegemony, social, economic and cultural, within which it operates at the present time.' Liberation is the wrong concept for Foucault, but 'detachment' might be possible. Now what is to 'detach' truth from present hegemony?

There is published elsewhere a joint interview with Foucault and Noam Chomsky.[12] The linguist comes across as a marvellously sane reformist liberal: let's get justice working right. Foucault sounds more like an anarchist: destroy the judicial system. Is that a way to 'detach' a power of truth from forms of hegemony? Maybe. *Power/ Knowledge* begins with a 1972 interview with French Maoists. At the start of a revolution don't create people's courts, he urges. Don't reinstitute precisely the institutions of hegemony used to separate and control the masses. In 1980 the courtroom ironically reopens for the Gang of Four, television rights for $40,000. Foucault is no anarchist, partly because anarchy is impossible. To have a regime for saying true and false things about ourselves is to enter a regime of power and it is unclear that any detaching from that power can succeed.

We might have been content with the thought of replacing our 'forms of hegemony' by others so long as we had the Romantic illusion of a true humankind, a true me, or even a true madness. But whatever Foucault means by detaching truth from forms of hegemony, he does not want the comfort of the romantic illusions. Minute radical acts of protest and reform are not to make sense against a backdrop of progress toward the hopes of the traditional left. That way leads to desolation. Foucault, let's say, has been completing a dialogue with Kant. Each question of Kant's is deliberately inverted or destroyed. 'What is man?' asked Kant. Nothing, says Foucault. 'For what then may we hope?' asked Kant. Does Foucault give the same *nothing* in reply?

To think so is to misunderstand Foucault's reply to the question about Man. Foucault said that the concept Man is a fraud, not that you and I are as nothing. Likewise the concept Hope is all wrong. The hopes attributed to Marx or Rousseau are perhaps part of that very concept Man, and they are a sorry basis for optimism. Optimism, pessimism, nihilism, and the like are all concepts that make sense only within the idea of a transcendental or enduring subject. Foucault is not in the least incoherent about all this. If we're not satisfied, it should not be because he is pessimistic. It is because he has given no surrogate for whatever it is that springs eternal in the human breast.

Notes

1 M. Foucault, *Power/Knowledge: Selected Interviews and Other Writings 1972–1977*, ed. Colin Gordon, trans. Colin Gordon *et al.* (New York: Pantheon, 1980).

2 *Folie et déraison. Histoire de la folie à l'âge classique* (Paris: Libraire Plon, 1961). An abridged version is translated as *Madness and Civilization* (New York: Random House, 1965). During the rest of this review, dates of publication of other works refer to the French originals. The translations of these are not abridgements.

3 M. Foucault, *The Birth of the Clinic: An Archaeology of Medical Perception* (London, Tavistock, 1973). Translated from *Naissance de la Clinique* (Paris: Presses Universitaire de France, 1963).

4 See for example H. C. Erik Midelfort, 'Madness and Civilization in Early Modern Europe: A Reappraisal of Michel Foucault' in Barbara C. Malament (ed.), *After the Reformation, Essays in Honor of J. H. Hexter* (Philadelphia: University of Pennsylvania Press, 1980).

5 M. Foucault, *The Archaeology of Knowledge* (New York: Pantheon, 1972). Translated from *L'Archéologie du savoir* (Paris: Gallimard, 1969).

6 M. Foucault, *The Order of Things: An Archaeology of the Human Sciences* (New York: Random House, 1970). Translated from *Les Mots et les choses* (Paris: Gallimard, 1966).

7 M. Foucault, *Language, Counter-Memory, Practice* (Ithaca, N.Y.: Cornell University Press, 1977).

8 M. Foucault, *Discipline and Punish: The Birth of the Prison* (New York: Vintage, 1979). Translated by Alan Sheridan from *Surveiller et punir* (Paris: Gallimard, 1975).

9 M. Foucault, in collaboration with Blandine Barret-Kriegel *et al.*, *I, Pierre Rivière, having slaughtered my mother, my sister and my brother . . .: A Case of Parricide in the 19th Century* (New York: Pantheon, 1975). Translated by F. Jellinek from *Moi, Pierre Rivière, ayant égorgé ma mère, ma soeur et mon frère . . . Un cas de parricide au XIXe siècle* (Paris: Gallimard, 1973).

10 M. Foucault, *The History of Sexuality*, Volume 1: An Introduction, trans. Robert Hurley (New York: Pantheon, 1978).

11 M. Foucault, *Power/Knowledge*, p. 97.

12 N. Chomsky and M. Foucault, 'Human Nature: Justice versus Power' in Fons Elders (ed.), *Reflexive Water* (London: Souvenir Press, 1974), pp. 133–99.

Foucault and Epistemology

RICHARD RORTY

Does Foucault give us a sketch of, or a basis for, something like a new theory of knowledge? Or should we perhaps conceive of his 'archaeology' as a sort of successor discipline to the theory of knowledge, or perhaps a supplement to it? It seems to me that Foucault says a lot of things which suggest that he wants such a theory, and a lot of other things which suggest that he doesn't. My own hunch is that, whatever he may want, he has set things up so that he cannot *have* such a theory.

Ian Hacking says in his 'Michel Foucault: Immature Science' that *The Order of Things exemplifies* a theory of knowledge.[1] However, the six hypotheses that he goes on to list are hard to hook up either with *Erkenntnistheorie* or with *Wissenschaftslehre*. Rather, they look like warnings to the young historian who might be tempted to imitate Macaulay or Hegel or Engels or Acton. To put it another way, they are suggestions to the historian who would like to take Foucault himself as a paradigm. But if one wants to work these concrete suggestions up into a theory of knowledge, or ground them upon a theory of knowledge, it is hard to know where to start. One might try, however, by looking for a theory of 'how objects constitute themselves in discourse'. When Foucault uses such phrases as this, I think he is offering the following account of his relation to the epistemological tradition:

'Whereas Descartes and Locke and Kant and the positivists and the phenomenologists have assumed that the job of signs was to represent

This essay is a slightly revised version of a response to Ian Hacking, read at the Western Division meetings of the American Philosophical Association in 1979. I have not attempted to update it by taking account either of Foucault's later work or of the changes in my own view of him which that later work induced. (Footnote added in 1985.)

pre-existent reality (even if only phenomenal reality, constituted by consciousness), I will show you a new way to look at what people say. From this new perspective, you will not see words as linked to things by relations like "impression" or "symbolization" or "synthesis" or "reference" or "truth". Instead you will see them as nodes in a network of texts, and this network as making up "practices that systematically form the objects of which they speak".[2] As a new sort of theory of knowledge I shall give you a theory of such practices, one which has nothing to do with the traditional epistemological question of the accuracy of representation.'

Some such prospectus as this is common to Foucault, Derrida, Barthes, Hayden White, and many others who, as Hacking says, think that ideological purity requires us to speak of texts rather than facts. But it is not clear that they have a constructive theory to offer, as opposed to simple polemic against traditional notions. Further, it is tempting to give a deflationary interpretation of this insistence on texts. One might simply take Foucault to be saying, in the manner of Wittgenstein, that we should remind ourselves of something we already know quite well: namely, that the way people talk can 'create objects', in the sense that there are lots of things which wouldn't exist unless people had come to talk in certain ways. Examples of such things are universities, contracts, governments, international monetary exchange mechanisms, traditions of historiography, revolutions in philosophy, and so on. When we want to know how we know about such objects as these, we do and should turn not to the epistemologist but to the intellectual historian. Our curiosity about such matters is not about how to answer the epistemological sceptic, but about how practices of talking in certain ways came into being. On this deflationary interpretation, however, 'attempting to understand how objects constitute themselves in discourse' is *not, pace* Hacking, a 'central topic of the theory of knowledge'. For we *already* know quite well, without benefit of theory, how this trick is turned. We have examples of such constitution around us all the time, ranging from the way in which faculty gossip constitutes a new pecking order among the deans, to the way in which the discourse of Hacking himself, his critics and his admirers, has constituted an event called 'the emergence of probability', to the way in which the talk of our students in the sixties constituted objects called 'the environment' and 'life-styles'. We not only know how the trick is turned, we are engaged in performing it ourselves a good deal of the time. It seems doubtful that anything remotely like a theory of knowledge could help us understand better how we manage it.

make identities

make races

Foucault would not accept this deflationary interpretation of the notion of 'constitution'. He appears to think there *is* something philosophical and theoretical to be done with the notion of 'discursive practices' which will be more useful than what Hegel or Husserl did with the notion of 'consciousness'. *The Archaeology of Knowledge*, which strikes me as his least successful book, does seem to be trying to sketch a 'successor subject' to epistemology. As far as I can see, however, Foucault never quite decides what that subject is. Thus he says he wants a 'general theory of discontinuity',[3] yet that very phrasing is prima facie self-contradictory. He sounds much like Husserl when he talks about a 'project of a *pure description* of discursive events as the horizon for the search for the unities that form within it'.[4] Yet he mocks Husserl's enterprise of 'pure description' in terms which would apply equally to his own. He seems to be unconsciously imitating Descartes, another of his *bêtes noires*, when he describes his own methodological scrupulousness and rigour as follows: 'I have undertaken, then, to describe the relations between statements. I have been careful to accept as valid none of the unities that would normally present themselves to anyone embarking on such a task. I have decided to ignore no form of discontinuity, break, threshold, or limit'.[5]

In such passages, Foucault writes like a contented inhabitant of the 'system of possibilities' offered by French academic philosophy, a system which forbids you just to settle for being clever enough to have found interesting new descriptions to replace boring old ones. Instead, it commands you to exhibit your discovery of such unities as the application of a rigorous method, an illustration of a general theory, the result of having adopted the right starting-point. Nevertheless, notions of 'method', 'starting-point' and 'theory' are, officially, anathema to Foucault. He insists that he wants to 'question our will to truth, to restore to discourse its character as an event, and to abolish the sovereignty of the signifier'.[6] So he seems caught in the following dilemma. On the one hand, he wants to give up all the traditional notions which made up the 'system of possibilities' of a theory of knowledge. On the other hand, he is not content simply to give a genealogy of epistemology, to show us how this genre came into being (something he does very well). Rather, he wants to *do* something like epistemology. In what follows, I want to spell out this dilemma more fully.

Let me begin by dividing the possible attitudes towards the idea of a 'theory of knowledge' into three clumps: the Cartesian, the

Hegelian and the Nietzschean. The Cartesian attitude is the source of the traditional academic preoccupation with epistemology. It says that we can divide up culture into the areas in which we have 'objectivity' and 'rationality' – the hard or mature sciences – and softer areas such as religion and morals and art in which we have discourse which may not count as 'knowledge'. We then study the general sorts of relations between statements and objects found in the hard sciences, isolate thereby the secret of the success of such sciences in corresponding to reality and thereby isolate 'the nature of knowledge'. With this in hand, we divide up soft areas into immature sciences which *want* objectivity but haven't yet got it, and non-cognitive, non-scientific areas which will *never* have it. Whenever anyone suggests that rationality is not the same thing in all ages, the Cartesian replies that this historicist suggestion throws doubt on the independence of thought from its object, and thus is 'idealistic' and 'relativistic'. Rational inquiry, the Cartesian says, is the process of insuring that representations correspond to reality – so a fixed reality means a fixed method.

The Hegelian attitude, on the other hand, takes for granted that rationality is to be viewed sociologically and historically. From this angle, the phrase 'objective reality' is no more than an automatic and empty compliment that any discipline will pay the objects it has just finished constituting. For the Hegelian, the satisfaction the Cartesian takes in correspondence and accurate representation is replaced by the thrill of being up-to-date, of being in touch with the latest developments of the Spirit in its march towards larger syntheses and more inclusive discourses. The Hegelian praises our culture for its superiority over the past, rather than for its tighter fit to an ahistorical reality. He does not see the hard sciences as more objective than the soft, or as having a methodological secret of success which *Wissenschaftslehre* may reveal. He pooh-poohs the idea that knowledge has a 'nature' to be studied by a philosophical discipline called *Erkenntnistheorie*. When the Cartesian charges him with relativism, he replies that the progress of thought, its convergence to the end of inquiry, should take the place of the dubious Cartesian notion of 'correspondence' in underwriting our struggle for 'objectivity' and our intuition that Truth is One. He sees scientific progress as of a piece with social and moral progress – all of these exhibiting the same dialectical character and the same achievement of even larger, more fruitful syntheses. He sees history as doing what the Cartesian thought epistemology should do – exhibiting the superiority of the present to the past, and giving helpful hints to backward areas of culture as to how they might catch up with the more progressive areas.

Given this rough distinction, we can put Carnap, Hempel, Chisholm and the like on the Cartesian side, and Dewey, Wittgenstein, Kuhn, Sellars, Harré, Hesse and the like on the Hegelian side. Foucault too might seem to be on the Hegelian side. He spends a great deal of his time making anti-Cartesian historicist points. His attack on the 'sovereignty of the signifier' can easily look like a Wittgensteinian attack on the notion of language-as-picture. His attention to discontinuities between discourses looks Kuhnian, allowing for the difference Hacking notes between concentrating on paradigmatic achievements and concentrating on anonymous banalities. His refusal to see any neat distinctions between the hard sciences, the soft sciences and the arts sounds Deweyan. A lot of what he says can be read as an extension of Sellars in the direction of Goodman and Cassirer. So one is tempted to think of him as a somewhat twitchy and overwrought member of the Hegelian team.

Doing so, however, is a mistake – one produced by an illusion of distance and a narrow education. It is a mistake I made when I first read Foucault. Most of us are products of postwar Anglo-Saxon training in philosophy, and so Hegelian historicism looks to us about as far out as one can go. It takes us a while to grasp a point that Hacking has patiently tried to teach us – that historicism is as old hat on the Continent as positivism is over here. For philosophers brought up (as most of us were) to smile condescendingly at the mention of Collingwood and Croce, the suggestion that there is no such thing as an ahistorical nature of knowledge or of rationality to be discovered by philosophical analysis is so titillating that we assume that Foucault must be getting the same kick out of it that we are. But in fact Foucault thinks of historicism as just a variation of Cartesianism. He sees the mighty opposites in contemporary *Wissenschaftslehre* as *both* so completely subservient to the 'will-to-truth' that their differences count for nothing. Whereas we think it daring to suggest that Hegelian history of ideas might replace Cartesian epistemology, Foucault thinks that Hegelian 'progressive' histories are just a self-deceptive continuation of the original Cartesian project. What binds the Cartesians and the Hegelians together – Chisholm with Dewey, Hempel with Kuhn – is the conviction that there is a way of rising above the present and viewing it in relation to inquiry in general. The Cartesian does this by discovering the ahistorical nature of rational inquiry. The Hegelian does it historically by contrasting the present state of inquiry with the Peircian convergence towards the true and the real which we would expect given both the 'ideal speech situation' and unlimited grant money. The Cartesian purports to have views about representation or reference or correspondence. The Hegelian purports to have views about progress and synthesis and the self-correcting character of the scientific enterprise. Both, however, say something general and optimistic about the way things have been going for the last few centuries. Foucault's *Nietzschean* attitude towards the idea of epistemology is that there is *nothing* optimistic to say. To question, with Nietzsche, the 'will-to-truth' is to reject the common motive of Cartesian epistemology and Hegelian eschatological historiography. The Nietzschean wants to *abandon* the striving for objectivity and the intuition that Truth is One, not to redescribe it or to ground it.

To see Foucault as a Nietzschean enemy of historicism rather than as one more historicist enemy of Cartesianism, we need to see him as trying to write history in a way which will destroy the notion of historical progress. His aim, he says, is to 'introduce into the very roots of thought' the notions of 'chance, discontinuity and materiality',[7] and thereby to help us drop the notion that later and more inclusive thought is automatically closer to the real. This aim comes out most clearly, perhaps, in an essay called 'Nietzsche, Genealogy, History'.[8] There he describes genealogy (Nietzsche's term for non-eschatological, non-edifying historiography) as follows:

> Genealogy must record the singularity of events outside of any monotonous finality; it must seek them in the most unpromising places, in what we tend to feel is without history – in sentiments, love, conscience, instincts; it must be sensitive to their recurrence, not in order to isolate the gradual curve of their evolution, but to isolate the different scenes where they engaged in different roles.[9]

Foucault says he is interested in 'the historical sense' only insofar as it

> can evade metaphysics and become a privileged instrument of genealogy . . . Given this, it corresponds to the acuity of a glance that distinguishes, separates and disperses – the kind of disassociating view that is capable of decomposing itself, capable of shattering the unity of men's being through which it was thought that he could extend his sovereignty to the events of the past.[10]

For Foucault, as for Heidegger and Derrida, Cartesianism and Hegelianism are simply varieties of 'metaphysics', of the desire to rise above human activities and to see them as instances of a type, or as approximations to an ideal. Or, equivalently, they are varieties of 'humanism', a term that Foucault defines as 'everything in Western civilization that restricts *the desire for power*'.[11] He sees the desire for power as contrasting with the will-to-truth. He sees the whole Western project of philosophical reflection on the nature and prospects of human activity as part of a vast organization of repression and injustice.[12] He sees his own historical work as of a piece with his anarchist politics – as exposing the subtlety of the repressive mechanisms which the ruling classes have installed.[13]

In presenting Foucault's Nietzschean attitude I am not commending it. I have no wish to do so, especially since much of Foucault's so-called 'anarchism' seems to me self-indulgent radical chic. Rather, I am contrasting his Nietzschean attitude with the Cartesian and Hegelian attitudes towards 'theory of knowledge' in order to emphasize the difficulty Foucault must face in attempting to offer a 'theory of discursive practices' or, indeed, a *theory of anything*. Whereas the Hegelian wants history to substitute for theory of knowledge and for philosophical theories generally, a Nietzschean must not want *any* substitute for theories. He views the very idea of 'theory' as tainted with the notion that there is something there to be contemplated, to be accurately represented in thought. So, once again, I would question Hacking's suggestion that Foucault has something analogous to a theory of knowledge to offer. As far as I can see, all he has to offer are brilliant redescriptions of the past, supplemented by helpful hints on how to avoid being trapped by old historiographical assumptions. These hints consist largely in saying: do *not* look for progress or meaning in history; do *not* see the history of a given activity, of any segment of culture, as the development of rationality or of freedom; do *not* use any philosophical vocabulary to characterize the essence of such activity or the goal it serves; do not assume that the way this activity is presently conducted gives any clue to the goals it served in the past. Such purely negative maxims neither spring from a theory nor constitute a method.

Setting aside all the anarchist claptrap about repression and all the Nietzschean bravura about the will-to-power, isn't there something worth preserving in Foucault's claim that the Hegelian reaction against the Cartesian idea of epistemology still doesn't go far enough?

theory – stories accounts

It seems to me there is, and that it lies in his claim that we ought to write history, and do philosophy, in the light of the possibility that the Peircian idea of convergence or the Habermasian idea of an 'ideal speech community' may be a fake. It may be a fake because the vocabulary *any* community – even an ideal one – uses is just one more vocabulary, and may be as incommensurable with its predecessors as ours with Paracelsus's. Hegelian, Peircian and Habermasian eschatology may be a fake because the movement of thought may be just *too* jerky, the distance between successive human self-descriptions *too* wide. Maybe we *cannot* put together a history of thought which is both honest and continuous. Foucault might just possibly be right in saying that the stories we tell about how our ancestors gradually matured into ourselves are *so* 'Whiggish', *so* anachronistic, as to be worthless.

One can develop this unpleasant possibility in another way. The urge to tell stories of progress, maturation and synthesis might be overcome if we once took seriously the notion that we only know the world and ourselves *under a description*. For doing so would mean taking seriously the possibility that we just *happened* on that description – that it was not the description which nature evolved us to apply, or that which best unified the manifold of previous descriptions, but just the one which we have now *chanced* to latch onto. If we once could feel the full force of the claim that our present discursive practices were given neither by God, nor by intuition of essence nor by the cunning of reason, but *only* by chance, then we would have a culture which lacked not only a theory of knowledge, not only a sense of progress, but *any* source of what Nietzsche called 'metaphysical comfort'. I do not know what such a culture would be like, and I am uncertain about both its possibility and its desirability. But I sometimes think that Foucault has caught a glimpse of it. A culture that had genealogies but no eschatology, that actually *did* 'accept the introduction of chance as a category in the production of events',[14] would be so utterly unlike ours that the very notions of 'the constitution of objects' or of 'discursive practice' would hardly make sense. So we should not expect Foucault to give us a philosophical *theory* that deploys these notions. Still, philosophy is more than theories. We can be grateful to Foucault for doing another of the things that philosophers are supposed to do – reaching for speculative possibilities that exceed our present grasp, but may nevertheless be our future.

Notes

1 Published in *Nous*, vol. 13, 1979.
2 Cf. Michel Foucault, *The Archaeology of Knowledge* (New York: Pantheon, 1972), p. 49.
3 Ibid., p. 12.
4 Ibid., p. 27.
5 Ibid., p. 31.
6 Ibid., p. 229.
7 Ibid., p. 231.
8 Published in Michel Foucault, *Language, Counter-Memory, Practice: Selected Essays and Interviews*, ed. Donald F. Bouchard (Ithaca, N.Y.: Cornell University Press, 1977).
9 Ibid., pp. 139–40.
10 Ibid., p. 153.
11 Ibid., p. 221.
12 Cf. ibid., p. 164.
13 Cf. ibid., pp. 205–34.
14 Foucault, *Archaeology of Knowledge*, p. 231.

The Politics of Michel Foucault

MICHAEL WALZER

I

My concern here is not primarily with Michel Foucault's political positions, the statements he has made, the articles he has written, his response to 'events' – May '68, the prison revolts of the early seventies, the Iranian revolution, and so on. Though he insists that he doesn't have a political position and doesn't want to be situated on the chessboard of available positions (he doesn't play chess, or any other game whose rules the rest of us might know), he does indeed respond to events, and his statements and articles have a fairly consistent character. They are of the sort I was taught to call, in the political world where I grew up and learned to talk, 'infantile leftism', that is, less an endorsement than an outrunning of the most radical argument in any political struggle. But Foucault's infantile leftism is not my main concern.

I want to deal instead with his political theory – though he also insists that he doesn't have a political theory. His purpose, he says, is 'not to formulate the global systematic theory which holds everything in place, but to analyse the specificity of mechanisms of power . . . to build little by little a strategic knowledge'.[1] But stategic knowledge implies to my mind a coherent view of reality and a sense of purpose, and it is on these two things that I will focus: first, on Foucault's account of contemporary power relationships and their history or 'genealogy', and second, on his attitude toward these relationships and his purpose in writing about them.

I make a number of assumptions. I take Foucault to be an author in the conventional sense of that term, responsible for the books he

This discussion of the political views of Michel Foucault was first presented as a lecture at Princeton University in February 1982. Reprinted from *Dissent*, vol. 30 (Fall 1983), pp. 481–90.

writes, the interviews he gives, the lectures published under his name. I believe that he makes arguments (even, in some large sense, *an argument*) and that he has a purpose. This is to make Foucault into a subject, an academic subject, perhaps to impose upon him structures of knowledge that he wants to shatter. He is an anti-disciplinarian (his own word), at war with the established intellectual disciplines. That might be a just war; at any rate, it is an exciting one, and I don't mean to quarrel with it so long as Foucault takes on the disciplines one by one, medicine, psychiatry, criminology, political science, and so on. But each of these campaigns must still take place within the overall discipline of language and the rules of plausibility (if not of Truth).

Foucault's books are fictions, he says, but only because the power relations and the disciplinary establishments within which they could be validated don't yet exist.[2] At the same time, he has many readers who seem to inhabit such establishments, for they take his genealogies to be accurate and even indisputable; and he has students and followers who pursue the research lines he has laid out. His books are full of statements that lay claim to plausibility here and now. He writes in declarative sentences, at least sometimes, though he is fonder of conditional and interrogative forms, so that his arguments often have the character of insinuations. They are bolstered in any case by extensive footnotes and a rather erratic but (he assures us) painstaking documentation. So I take him to be saying something we are invited to believe – and then to disbelieve its opposite, that is, 'to detach the power of truth from the forms of hegemony ... within which it operates at the present time'.[3] I take him to be making an argument that is right or wrong or partly right and partly wrong.

Toward this argument, I shall adopt a 'constructionist' position. Since Foucault never presents it in anything like a systematic fashion, I shall put it together out of his more recent (and more political) books and interviews, ignoring passages that I don't understand, ignoring too his denials and evasions, and refusing to live at the heights of his flamboyance. I will do what I always do with any book I read: try to puzzle out what the author is saying. So great minds are subdued ... Reading Borges's Chinese encyclopedia I would sit struggling to design a proper index.

One last assumption, which I had best make explicit since Parisian reputations are not hard currency in the United States today: I assume that my effort is worthwhile, not only because Foucault is influential but also because his account of our everyday politics, though often annoyingly presented and never wholly accurate or sufficiently nuanced, is right enough to be disturbing – and also because it is importantly wrong. I might sum up the argument to come by comparing Foucault to his great antagonist in the world of political theory, Thomas Hobbes. ('We must eschew the model of Leviathan,' Foucault says, 'in the study of power.')[4] The comparison won't stand up with regard to insight or lucidity, only with regard to the general views of the two writers. Hobbes gives us an importantly wrong account of political sovereignty; rhetorically inflated and drained of moral distinctions, it nevertheless captures something of the reality of the modern state. Foucault gives us an importantly wrong account of local discipline; rhetorically inflated and drained of moral distinctions, it nevertheless captures something of the reality of contemporary society.

II

Foucault's political argument starts with the following two-part proposition, the second part largely unstated because it is so entirely accepted on the French intellectual left: (1) the king is the actual ruler, the visible, effective, necessary agent, the concrete embodiment of political power in the monarchic state; but (2) the people are not the rulers and not the embodiments of power in the democratic state; nor are their representatives. Elections, parties, and assemblies are entirely absent in Foucault's 'discourse of power', and the absence is eloquent. It requires only the briefest of explanations. 'Power is not built up out of "wills" (individual or collective), nor is it derivable from interests.'[5] There is no general will and no effective coalition of interest groups; sovereignty works only when there is a physical sovereign. In contemporary Western societies, power is dispersed, but not as democrats hoped to disperse it, not to citizens who argue and vote, and so determine the politics of the central government. Citizenship and government alike have been superseded. And yet the whole point of modern political theory, since the absolutist state provided the ground on which it was constructed, has been to account for these two things.

Theorists still try to answer the Hobbist questions, which Foucault puts this way: 'What is the sovereign? How is he constituted as sovereign? What bond of obedience ties individuals to the sovereign?'[6] So they reveal the genealogical constraints of their enterprise, first worked out to account for a set of power relations that have now collapsed. This is another reason, perhaps, why Foucault does not want to call himself a political theorist. When the king's head was cut off, the theory of the state died too; it was replaced by sociology, psychology, criminology, and so on.

The king is headless, the political world has no practical centre. Foucault nicely finesses the 'legitimation crisis' so hotly debated on the other side of the Rhine: the state has not been legitimate for a long time. The exercise of power, and the acceptance or endurance of power, now occurs somewhere else. The argument of Hobbes and his theoretical heirs was that subjects created and legitimized their own subjection by ceding (some of) their rights to the state; hence the state was rightful and a defender of rights. This state still exists, more or less, but it merely 'conceals' the 'actual procedures of power', 'the mechanisms of disciplinary coercion', which operate beyond the effective reach of the law. Now there is a new subjection, which creates and legitimizes new subjects – not the carriers of rights but of norms, the agents and also the products of moral, medical, sexual, psychological (rather than legal) regulation. Our interest shifts, because the action shifts, from the singular state to a pluralist society.

Many years ago, in a graduate seminar with Barrington Moore, I studied a group of American political scientists and sociologists, called 'pluralists', who argued that power was radically dispersed in American society. There was no sovereign, no political elite, no ruling class, but a pluralism of groups and even of individuals. Everybody or almost everybody had a little power; nobody had so much as to be sure of getting his own way all the time. I was taught that this was a conservative doctrine. By denying the existence of a directing centre, it robbed radical politics of its object. And yet, of course, there was such a centre, if not always visible or self-conscious or highly organized: law and policy had a shape, corresponded to a set of interests; and the interests imposed the shape, dominating if they did not absolutely control the making of law and policy.

Foucault can be read, and not inaccurately, as a pluralist; he too denies the existence of a centre. 'Power comes from below . . . there is no binary and all-encompassing opposition between rulers and ruled at the root of power relations . . . Power is not something that is acquired, seized, or shared . . . power is exercised from innumerable points . . .'[7] Again: 'At every moment, power is in play in small individual parts.'[8] And again: 'Power is employed and exercised through a netlike organization . . . individuals circulate between its threads; they are always in a position of simultaneously undergoing and exercising power. They are not only its inert or consenting targets; they are always also the elements of its articulation.'[9]

This is not, of course, the same argument that the American pluralists made. Foucault is concerned not with the dispersion of power to the extremities of the political system, but with its exercise at the extremities. For the Americans, power was dispersed to individuals and groups and then recentralized, that is, brought to bear again at the focal point of sovereignty. For Foucault there is no focal point, but rather an endless network of power relations. Still, his account does appear to have conservative implications; at least (and this is not the same thing), it has anti-Leninist implications. There can't be a seizure of power if there is nothing at the centre to seize. If power is exercised at innumerable points, then it has to be challenged point by point. 'The overthrow of these micro-powers does not obey the law of all or nothing.'[10] 'There is a plurality of resistances, each of them a special case.'[11] This begins to sound like a reformist politics, and Foucault indeed has been accused of reformism. Challenged from the left, he occasionally stands firm, if uneasy: 'It is necessary,' he told the editorial collective of a radical magazine, 'to make a distinction between [the] critique of reformism as a political practice and the critique of a political practice on the grounds that it might give rise to a reform. This latter . . . critique is frequent in left-wing groups and its employment is part of the mechanism of micro-terrorism by which they have often operated.'[12]

This is certainly right and conceivably, in a certain context, brave, but it avoids conceding the truth for which the collective was reaching: that Foucault is not a good revolutionary. He isn't a good revolutionary because he doesn't believe in the sovereign state or the ruling class, and therefore he doesn't believe in the take-over of the state or the replacement of the class. He doesn't believe in a democratic revolution, for the *demos* doesn't exist in his political world. And he certainly doesn't believe in a vanguard revolution: the vanguard is nothing more than the monarch *manqué*, one more pretender to royal power.

III

Foucault's political theory is a 'tool kit' not for revolution but for local resistance. In order to understand what that might mean and whether it is possible, we must consider more carefully the forms of social discipline that replace royal power. Every human society has its own discipline, and in every society above a certain size this discipline is exercised at micro- as well as macro-levels.

On Foucault's understanding, as I understand it, the old regime required only a rather loose discipline at the micro-level; or perhaps, and this is after all a traditional view of traditional societies, habitual routines and customary rules worked with little more than intermittent coercion. Political interventions were dramatic but occasional – like those horrifying punishments Foucault describes in the opening section of *Discipline and Punish*, which made royal power visible and were entirely consistent with a generally ineffective system of law enforcement. But we live in a different age, where economy and society alike require (and get) a far more detailed control of individual behaviour. This is a control that no single person or political elite or ruling party or class can establish and sustain from a single point: hence Foucault's 'innumerable points' and his endless networks in which, he says, we are all enmeshed.

Many writers before Foucault have suggested that we live in a more disciplined society than has ever existed before. This doesn't mean that behaviour is more routinized or predictable (it isn't), but that it is more intimately subjected to rules, standards, schedules, and authoritative inspections. Some fifteen years ago in an article on the welfare state, I argued that

> the most impressive feature of modern welfare administration is the sheer variety of its coercive and deterrent instruments. Every newly recognized need, every service received, creates a new dependency and a new social bond ... even [the] recognition of individuals – our hardwon visibility – becomes a source of intensified control. Never have ordinary citizens been so well-known to the public authorities as in the welfare state. We are all counted, numbered, classified, catalogued, polled, interviewed, watched, and filed away ...

And so on: lots of people wrote that way. But Foucault has succeeded in extending and dramatizing this view with a series of books that are rather like the king's punishments: rhetorical statements of great power, though often ineffective in what we might think of as scholarly law enforcement – the presentation of evidence, detailed argument, the consideration of alternative views. The books focus on three or four institutional networks of social discipline, asylums, hospitals, prisons, with side glances at armies, schools, and factories, and it is impossible to read them, whatever disagreements one has, without a sense of recognition.

I will come back to this sense of recognition, and so to the actual experience of living within the network of disciplines. But first I need to say a word about the general character of the network. For it does have a general character, even if it isn't governed by a single will. Foucault is not the Kafka of the prison or the asylum; his account is neither surreal nor mysterious. The disciplinary society is a *society*, a social whole, and in his account of the parts of this whole, Foucault is a functionalist. No one designed the whole, and no one controls it; but as if by an invisible hand, all its parts are somehow fitted together. Sometimes Foucault marvels at the fit: 'This is an extremely complex system of relations, which leads one finally to wonder how, given that no one person can have conceived it in its entirety, it can be so subtle in its distribution, its mechanisms, reciprocal controls and adjustments.'[13] Sometimes he is quite matter of fact: 'If the prison institution has survived for so long, with such immobility, if the principle of penal detention has never seriously been questioned, it is no doubt because this carceral system . . . carried out certain very precise functions.'[14]

The complex system within which these functions are carried out is presumably modern industrial society, but Foucault sometimes prefers a more precise name. In his account of how sexuality was 'constituted' in the nineteenth century, he writes: 'this bio-power was without question an indispensable element in the development of capitalism; the latter would not have been possible without the controlled insertion of bodies into the machinery of production and the adjustment of the phenomenon of population to economic processes. But this was not all capitalism required; it also needed . . .' etc.[15] Capitalism gets what it needs, though how the process works Foucault doesn't reveal, and his account of the local uses of power would appear to make the revelation less likely than it might be within a more conventional Marxist theory.

Some kind of functionalist Marxism, nonetheless, provides the distant underpinning of Foucault's account of power. In one of those dancelike interviews in which he both takes and doesn't take political positions, Foucault is led to say that the class struggle stands to the local power struggles as their 'guarantee of intelligibility'.[16] What this intelligibility might mean in his thought is a question that I am not going to reach here. But I do want to notice that the guarantee exists, like Bishop Berkeley's God, and that Foucault's stress on the particularist character of power relations is not an argument for disconnection or radical autonomy. He is, after all, in search of strategic, not merely tactical, knowledge. He argues from the bottom up, but this is a mode of analysis that suggests, at least by its direction, that the world is not all bottom. If he cannot find a state to seize, he still hopes to locate somehow, somewhere, in the complex system of modern society or of the capitalist economy, a comprehensible antagonist.

Foucault begins, however, with tactics, with local power relations, with the men and women at the lowest levels of the social hierarchy or, as he would say, caught in the fine meshes of the power networks, with you and me. We can't understand contemporary society or our own lives, he argues, unless we look hard and close at this kind of power and at these people: not state or class or corporate power, not the proletariat or the people or the toiling masses, but hospitals, asylums, prisons, armies, schools, factories; and patients, madmen, criminals, conscripts, children, factory hands. We must study the sites where power is physically administered and physically endured or resisted.

In fact, this is not quite what Foucault does: he is more a theorist than a historian, and the materials out of which he constructs his books consist mostly of the written projects and proposals for these sites, the architectural plans, the handbooks of rules and regulations, rarely of actual accounts of practices and experiences. Still, it is exciting to see how the projects proliferate, how similar designs are repeated for different institutions, how the rules and regulations, though they often have the perfectionist character of an anti-utopia, as if in anticipation of *1984* or *Brave New World*, begin nevertheless to suggest the outlines of our everyday lives. This is the area of Foucault's strongest work, and it is strong even though, or perhaps because, it offers us no 'guarantee of intelligibility'. It does point, though, to a certain sort of coherence.

For it is Foucault's claim, and I think he is partly right, that the discipline of a prison, say, represents a continuation and intensification of what goes on in more ordinary places – and wouldn't be possible if it didn't. So we all live to a time schedule, get up to an alarm, work to a rigid routine, live in the eye of authority, are periodically subject to examination and inspection. No one is entirely free from these new forms of social control. It has to be added, however, that subjection to these new forms is not the *same thing* as being in prison: Foucault tends systematically to underestimate the difference, and this criticism, which I shall want to develop, goes to the heart of his politics.

IV

I have suggested that all micro-forms of discipline are functional to a larger system. Foucault sometimes calls this system capitalism, but he also gives it a number of more dramatic names: the disciplinary society, the carceral city, the panoptic regime and, most frightening (and misleading) of all, the carceral archipelago. But whatever this larger system is, it isn't the political system, the regime or constitution. It isn't determined by a Hobbist sovereign shaped by a legislator or a founding convention, controlled through a judicial process.

The crucial point of Foucault's political theory is that discipline escapes the world of law and right – and then begins to 'colonize' that world, replacing legal principles with principles of physical, psychological, and moral normality. Thus in his book on prisons: 'Although the universal juridicism of modern society seems to fix limits on the exercise of power, its universally widespread panopticism enables it to operate, on the underside of the law, a machinery both immense and minute . . .'[17] And the code by which this machinery operates is a scientific, not a legal code. The function of discipline is to create useful subjects, men and women who conform to a standard, who are certifiably sane or healthy or docile or competent, not free agents who invent their own standards, who, in the language of rights, 'give the law to themselves'.

The triumph of professional or scientific norms over legal rights and of local discipline over constitutional law is a fairly common theme of contemporary social criticism. It has given rise to a series of campaigns in defence of the rights of the mentally ill, of prisoners, hospital patients, children (in schools and also in families). Foucault himself has been deeply involved in prison reform or – I had better be careful – in a political practice with regard to prisons that might give rise to reforms. And indeed there have been reforms (in the USA at least, but I suspect in Europe too): new laws about consent, confidentiality, access to records; judicial interventions in the administration of prisons and schools. Foucault has little to say about this sort of thing and is obviously sceptical about its effectiveness. Despite his emphasis on local struggles, he is largely uninterested in local victories.

But what other victories can he think possible, given his strategic knowledge? Consider:

(1)   that discipline-in-detail, the precise control of behaviour, is necessary to the (unspecified) large-scale features of contemporary social and economic life;

(2)   that this kind of control requires the micro-setting, the finely meshed network, the local power relation, represented in ideal-typical fashion by the cellular structure of the prison, the daily timetable of prison events, the extra-legal penalties inflicted by prison authorities, the face-to-face encounters of guard and prisoner;

(3)   that the prison is only one small part of a highly articulated, mutually reinforcing carceral continuum extending across society, in which all of us are implicated, and not only as captives or victims;

(4)   and finally, that the complex of disciplinary mechanisms and institutions constitutes and is constituted by the contemporary human sciences – an argument that runs through all of Foucault's work, to which I will return. Physical disciplines and intellectual disciplines are radically entangled; the carceral continuum is validated by the knowledge of human subjects that it makes possible.

Given all this – leave aside for the moment whether it adds up to a fully satisfactory account of our social life – how can Foucault expect anything more than a small reform here or there, an easing of disciplinary rigour, the introduction of more humane, if no less effective, methods? What else is possible? And yet sometimes, not in his books but in the interviews – and especially in a series of interviews of the early 1970s, which still reflect the impact of May '68 – Foucault seems to see a grand alternative: the dismantling of the whole thing, the fall of the carceral city, not revolution but abolition. It's for this reason that Foucault's politics are commonly called anarchist, and anarchism certainly has its moments in his thought. Not that he imagines a social system different from our own, beyond discipline and sovereignty alike: 'I think that to imagine another system is to extend our participation in the present system.'[18]

It is precisely the idea of society as a system, a set of institutions, that must give way to something else – what else, we can't imagine. Perhaps human freedom requires a nonfunctionalist society whose arrangements, whatever they are, serve no larger purpose and have no redeeming social value. The nearest thing to an account of such arrangements comes in an interview first published in November 1971. 'It is possible,' says Foucault, 'that the rough outline of a future society is supplied by the recent experiences with drugs, sex, communes, other forms of consciousness, and other forms of individuality.'[19] In that same interview, with some such vision in mind, he repudiates the likely reformist results of his own prison work: 'The ultimate goal of [our] interventions was not to extend the visiting rights of prisoners to 30 minutes or to procure flush toilets for the cells, but to question the social and moral distinction between the innocent and the guilty.'[20]

As this last passage suggests, when Foucault is an anarchist, he is a moral as well as a political anarchist. For him morality and politics go together. Guilt and innocence are the products of law just as normality and abnormality are the products of discipline. To abolish power systems is to abolish both moral and scientific categories: away with them all! But what will be left? Foucault does not believe, as earlier anarchists did, that the free human subject is a subject of a certain sort, naturally good, warmly sociable, kind and loving. Rather, there is for him no such thing as a free human subject, no natural man or woman. Men and women are always social creations, the products of codes and disciplines. And so Foucault's radical abolitionism, if it is serious, is not anarchist so much as nihilist. For on his own arguments, either there will be nothing left at all, nothing visibly human; or new codes and disciplines will be produced, and Foucault gives us no reason to expect that these will be any better than the ones we now live with. Nor, for that matter, does he give us any way of knowing what 'better' might mean.

V

Is Foucault then committed to his anarchism/nihilism? He has a way of turning on anyone who imitates it or tries to act it out politically, and I am inclined to think it is intended to have descriptive, not normative, force. In a 1977 interview he is savagely critical of some of his comrades in 'the struggle around the penal system' who have fallen for 'a whole naive, archaic ideology which makes the criminal . . . into an innocent victim and a pure rebel . . . The result has been a deep split between this campaign with its monotonous, lyrical little chant, heard only among a few small groups, and the masses who have good reason not to accept it as valid political currency.'[21]

For Foucault, obviously, the prisoner cannot be an innocent victim, for he has denied the distinction between guilt and innocence. But his argument does seem to suggest that every act of resistance at every micro-setting of the carceral continuum, whatever its motives, is a 'pure rebellion' against the continuum as a whole – and one with which he is always ready to sympathize. What 'good reasons' do ordinary men and women have for discriminating among these acts?

The same problem of discrimination arises when Foucault confronts young leftists who confuse the carceral archipelago with the Gulag archipelago, a confusion to which Foucault's terminology in this instance and, more generally, the language of all his books, are a perpetual incitement. He himself resists the incitement and is severely critical of those who succumb. 'I am indeed worried,' he says, 'by a certain use that is made of the Gulag–Internment parallel . . . which consists in saying, "Everyone has their own Gulag, the Gulag is here at our door, in our cities, our hospitals, our prisons, it's here in our heads." ' And he goes on, forcefully, to reject the 'universalizing dissolution of the [Gulag] problem into the denunciation of every possible form of internment'.[22] But he provides no principled distinction, so far as I can see, between the Gulag and the carceral archipelagos. I don't believe that he can do that, not so long as he is also committed to rejecting any sort of liberalism that 'sanctifies basic rights' and to blurring the line between guilt and innocence. Nor does he provide a genealogy of the Gulag and, what is probably more important, his account of the carceral archipelago contains no hint of how or why our own society stops short of the Gulag. For such an account would require what Foucault always resists: some positive evaluation of the liberal state.

Here again a comparison with Hobbes is illuminating. Hobbes thought that political sovereignty was a literal necessity – else life was nasty, brutish, and short. He supported every sort of sovereignty, and so for him tyranny was nothing more than 'monarchy misliked'. Foucault believes that discipline is necessary for this particular society – capitalist, modern, or whatever; he abhors all its forms, every sort of confinement and control, and so for him liberalism is nothing more than discipline concealed. For neither Hobbes nor

Foucault does the constitution or the law or even the actual workings of the political system make any difference.

In fact, I think, these things make all the difference. One of Foucault's followers, the author of a very intelligent essay on *Discipline and Punish*, draws from that book and the related interviews the extraordinary conclusion that the Russian Revolution failed because it 'left intact the social hierarchies and in no way inhibited the functioning of the disciplinary techniques'.[23] Exactly wrong: the Bolsheviks created a new regime that overwhelmed the old hierarchies and enormously expanded and intensified the use of disciplinary techniques. And they did this from the heart of the social system and not from what Foucault likes to call the capillaries, from the centre and not the extremities. Foucault desensitizes his readers to the importance of politics; but politics matters.

Power relations, he says 'are both intentional and nonsubjective'.[24] I don't know what that sentence means, but I think that the contradictory words are intended (nonsubjectively?) to apply to different levels of power. Every disciplinary act is planned and calculated; power is intentional at the tactical level where guard confronts prisoner; doctor, patient; lecturer, audience. But the set of power relations, the strategic connections, the deep functionalism of power has no subject and is the product of no one's plan. Foucault seems to disbelieve in principle in the existence of a dictator or a party or a state that shapes the character of disciplinary institutions. He is focused instead on what he thinks of as the 'micro-fascism' of everyday life and has little to say about authoritarian or totalitarian politics – that is, about the forms of discipline that are most specific to his own lifetime.

VI

But these are not the forms most specific to his own country, and Foucault does believe in sticking close to the local exercise of power. Nor does he often use terms like 'micro-fascism'. He is not a 'general intellectual' of the old sort – so he tells us – who provides an account and critique of society as a whole.[25] The general intellectual belongs to the age of the state and the party, when it still seemed possible to seize power and reconstruct society. He is, in the world of political knowledge, what the king is in the world of political power. Once we have cut off the king's head, power and knowledge alike take different forms. Foucault's more recent work is an effort to explain these forms, to work out what can be called a political epistemology. I now want to examine this epistemology, for it is the ultimate source of his anarchism/nihilism.

Sometimes Foucault seems to be committed to nothing more than an elaborate pun on the word 'discipline' – which means, on the one hand, a branch of knowledge and on the other, a system of correction and control. This is his argument: social life is discipline squared. *Discipline makes discipline possible* (the order of the two nouns can be reversed). Knowledge derives from and provides the grounds for social control: every particular form of social control rests on and makes possible a particular form of knowledge. It follows that power isn't merely repressive but also creative (even if all it creates is, say, the science of penology); and similarly, knowledge isn't merely ideological but also true. But this doesn't make either power or knowledge terribly attractive. Penology is 'constituted' by the prison system in the obvious sense that there could not be a study of prisoners or of the effects of imprisonment if there were no prisons. One form of discipline generates the data that makes the other possible. At the same time, penology provides both the rationale and the intellectual structure of the prison system. There could be no exercise of discipline, at least no sustained and organized exercise, without disciplinary knowledge.

It is a nice model, though perhaps a little too easy. In any case, Foucault proceeds to generalize it. 'Truth is a thing of this world: it is produced only by virtue of multiple forms of constraint. And it induces regular effects of power.'[26] So for every society, for every historical age, there is a regime of truth, unplanned but functional, generated somehow out of the network of power relations, out of the multiple forms of constraint, and enforced along with them. There are certain types of discourse that the society accepts 'and makes . . . true', and there are mechanisms that enable us to distinguish true and false statements – and sanctions, so that we won't make mistakes. Foucault believes that truth is relative to its sanctions and knowledge to the constraints that produce it.

There would appear to be no independent standpoint, no possibility for the development of critical principles. Of course, one can ask the obvious questions: what is Foucault's standpoint? To what set of power relations is the genealogical antidiscipline connected? Foucault is far too intelligent not to have worried about these questions. They are standard for any relativism. He responds in two ways: first he says, as I have already noted, that his genealogies are fictions waiting for the 'political realities' that will make them true. Each present invents its own past, but Foucault has invented a past for some future present. At other times, Foucault says more simply that his work is made possible by the events of '68 and by subsequent local revolts here and there along the disciplinary continuum.

As the conventional disciplines are generated and validated by the conventional uses of power, so Foucault's antidiscipline is generated by the resistance to those uses. But I don't see, on Foucault's terms, how it can be validated by resistance until the resistance is successful (and it's not clear what success would mean). But perhaps, after all, the demand that Foucault show us the ground on which he stands, display his philosophical warrants, is beside the point. For he makes no demands on us that we adopt this or that critical principle or replace these disciplinary norms with some other set of norms. He is not an advocate. We are to withdraw our belief in, say, the truth of penology and then support . . . what? Not every prison revolt, for there may be some that we have 'good reason' not to support. At this point, it seems to me, Foucault's position is simply incoherent. The powerful evocation of the disciplinary system gives way to an antidisciplinarian politics that is mostly rhetoric and posturing.

But there is more that has to be said. In those prison revolts with which we might rightly sympathize, the prisoners don't in fact call into question the line between guilt and innocence or the truth value of jurisprudence or penology. Their 'discourse' takes a very different form: they describe the brutality of the prison authorities or the inhumanity of prison conditions, and they complain of punishments that go far beyond those to which they were legally condemned. They denounce official arbitrariness, harassment, favouritism, and so on. They demand the introduction and enforcement of what we might best call the rule of law. And these descriptions, complaints, denunciations, and demands make an important point.

Foucault is certainly right to say that the conventional truths of morality, law, medicine and psychiatry are implicated in the exercise of power; that is a fact too easily forgotten by conventionally detached scientists, social scientists, and even philosophers. But those same truths also regulate the exercise of power. They set limits on what can rightly be done, and they give shape and conviction to the arguments the prisoners make. The limits are important even if they are in some sense arbitrary. They aren't entirely arbitrary, however, insofar as they are intrinsic to the particular disciplines (in both senses of the word). The truths of jurisprudence and penology, for example, distinguish punishment from preventive detention. And the truths of psychiatry distinguish the internment of madmen from the internment of political dissidents.

A liberal state is one that maintains the limits of its constituent disciplines and disciplinary institutions and that enforces their intrinsic principles. Authoritarian and totalitarian states, by contrast, override those limits, turning education into indoctrination, punishment into repression, asylums into prisons, and prisons into concentration camps. These are crude definitions; I won't insist upon them; amend them as you will. I only want to suggest the enormous importance of the political regime, the sovereign state. For it is the state that establishes the general framework within which all other disciplinary institutions operate. It is the state that holds open or radically shuts down the possibility of local resistance. The agents of every disciplinary institution strive, of course, to extend their reach and augment their discretionary power. Ultimately, it is only state power that can stop them. Every act of local resistance is an appeal for political or legal intervention from the centre.

Consider, for example, the factory revolts of the 1930s that led (in the USA) to the establishment of collective bargaining and grievance procedures, critical restraints on scientific management, which is one of Foucault's disciplines, though one that he alludes to only occasionally. Success required not only the solidarity of the workers but also at least some support from the liberal and democratic state. And success was functional not to any state but to a state of that sort; we can easily imagine other 'social wholes' that would require other kinds of factory discipline. A genealogical account of this discipline would be fascinating and valuable, and it would undoubtedly overlap with Foucault's accounts of prisons and hospitals. But if it were complete, it would have to include a genealogy of grievance procedures too, and this would overlap with an account, which Foucault doesn't provide, of the liberal state and the rule of law. Here is a kind of knowledge – political philosophy and philosophical jurisprudence – that regulates disciplinary arrangements across our society. It arises within one set of power relations and extends towards the others; it offers a critical perspective on all the networks of constraint.

This suggests that whatever the value of detailed analyses and critiques of local discipline we still require – I don't mean that society requires, or capitalism or even socialism requires, but you and I require – what Foucault calls 'general intellectuals'. We need men and women who tell us when state power is corrupted or systematically misused, who cry out that something is rotten, and who reiterate the regulative principles with which we might set things right.

But I don't want to end on this last note. I don't want to ask Foucault to be uplifting. That is not the task he has set himself. The point is rather that one can't even be downcast, angry, grim, indignant, sullen, or embittered *with reason* unless one inhabits some social setting and adopts, however tentatively and critically, its codes and categories. Or unless, and this is much harder, one constructs a new setting and proposes new codes and categories. Foucault refuses to do either of these things, and that refusal, which makes his genealogies so powerful and so relentless, is also the catastrophic weakness of his political theory.

Notes

All the books cited are by Michel Foucault.

1 *Power/Knowledge: Selected Interviews and Other Writings, 1972–1977*, ed. Colin Gordon (New York: Pantheon, 1980), p. 145.
2 Ibid., p. 193.
3 Ibid., p. 133.
4 Ibid., p. 102.
5 Ibid., p. 188.
6 Ibid., p. 187.
7 *The History of Sexuality*, Vol. 1: *An Introduction*, trans. Robert Hurley (New York: Vintage, 1980), p. 94.
8 *Power, Truth, Strategy*, ed. Meaghan Morris and Paul Patton (Sydney: Feral, 1979), p. 60.
9 *Power/Knowledge*, p. 98.
10 *Power, Truth, Strategy*, p. 126.
11 *Sexuality*, p. 96.
12 *Power/Knowledge*, p. 143.
13 Ibid., p. 62.
14 *Discipline and Punish: the Birth of the Prison*, trans. Alan Sheridan (New York: Vintage, 1979), p. 271.
15 *Sexuality*, pp. 140–1.
16 *Power/Knowledge*, p. 142.
17 *Discipline and Punish*, p. 223.
18 *Language, Counter-Memory, Practice: Selected Essays and Interviews*, ed. Donald F. Bouchard (Ithaca, N.Y.: Cornell University Press, 1977), p. 230.
19 Ibid., p. 231.

20   Ibid., p. 227.
21   *Power/Knowledge*, p. 130.
22   Ibid., pp. 134, 136–7.
23   Paul Patton, in *Power, Truth, Strategy*, p. 126.
24   *Sexuality*, p. 94.
25   *Power/Knowledge*, pp. 126ff.
26   Ibid., p. 131.

Foucault on Freedom and Truth

CHARLES TAYLOR

Foucault disconcerts. In a number of ways, perhaps. But the way I want to examine is this: certain of Foucault's most interesting historical analyses, while they are highly original, seem to lie along already familiar lines of critical thought. That is, they seem to offer an insight into what has happened, and into what we have become, which at the same time offers a critique, and hence some notion of a good unrealized or repressed in history, which we therefore understand better how to rescue.

But Foucault himself repudiates this suggestion. He dashes the hope, if we had one, that there is some good we can *affirm*, as a result of the understanding these analyses give us. And by the same token, he seems to raise a question whether there is such a thing as a way out. This is rather paradoxical, because Foucault's analyses seem to bring *evils* to light; and yet he wants to distance himself from the suggestion which would seem inescapably to follow, that the negation or overcoming of these evils promotes a good.

More specifically, Foucault's analyses, as we shall see in greater detail, turn a great deal on power/domination, and on disguise/illusion. He lays bare a modern system of power, which is both more all-penetrating and much more insidious than previous forms. Its strength lies partly in the fact that it is not seen as power, but as science, or fulfilment, even 'liberation'. Foucault's work is thus partly an unmasking.

You would think that implicit in all this was the notion of two goods which need rescuing, and which the analyses help to rescue:

freedom and truth; two goods which would be deeply linked granted
the fact that the negation of one (domination) makes essential use of
the negation of the other (disguise). We would be back on familiar
terrain, with an old enlightenment-inspired combination. But
Foucault seems to repudiate both. The idea of liberating truth is a
profound illusion. There is no truth which can be espoused, defended,
rescued *against* systems of power. On the contrary, each such system
defines its own variant of truth. And there is no escape from power
into freedom, for such systems of power are co-extensive with human
society. We can only step from one to another.

Or at least this is what Foucault *seems* to be saying in passages like
the following:

> contrary to a myth whose history and functions would repay further
> study, truth isn't the reward of free spirits . . . nor the privilege of those
> who have succeeded in liberating themselves. Truth is a thing of this
> world: it is produced only by virtue of multiple forms of constraint.
> And it induces regular effects of power. Each society has its own
> régime of truth, its 'general politics' of truth: that is, the type of
> discourse which it accepts and makes function as true . . .[1]

Is there confusion/contradiction here, or a genuinely original position? The answer I want to offer cannot be put in a single phrase, but
roughly, I think that there is some of both. However, the nature of the
combination is not easy to understand.

I

I would like to examine this issue in connection with some of the
analyses of Foucault's recent historical works, *Surveiller et punir* and
Histoire de la sexualité.[2] For the sake of my discussion, I want to
isolate three lines of analysis, each of which suggests, or is historically
connected with, a certain line of critique, but where in each case
Foucault repudiates the latter. But I have ordered these analyses so
that the argument arising from them moves towards more radical
repudiations. That is, at first sight, the second analysis will seem to
offer a reason for repudiating the good suggested by the first; and the
third analysis will seem to offer a reason for rejecting the good
implicit in the second; only to be in turn rejected. Or so it would
seem.

1

The first that I want to take up is the contrast drawn in *Surveiller et punir* between modes of punishment in the classical age and today. The book opens with a riveting description of the execution of a parricide in seventeenth-century France. The modern is appalled, horrified. We seem to be more in the world of our contemporary fanatical perpetrators of massacre, the Pol Pots, the Idi Amins, rather than in that of the orderly process of law in a civilized, well-established regime. Obviously something very big has changed in our whole understanding of ourselves, of crime and punishment.

Bringing us up against this evidence of radical historical discontinuity is what Foucault does superlatively well. For our eyes, the details of the execution of Damiens bespeak gratuitous cruelty, sadism. Foucault shows that they had another reason then. The punishment can be seen as a kind of 'liturgy' ('la liturgie des supplices').[3] Human beings are seen as set in a cosmic order, constituted by a hierarchy of beings which is also a hierarchy of goods. They stand also in a political order, which is related to and in a sense endorsed by the cosmic one. This kind of order is hard to explain in modern terms, because it is not simply an order of things, but an order of meanings. Or to put it in other terms, the order of things which we see around us is thought to reflect or embody an order of Ideas. You can explain the coherence things have in terms of a certain kind of making sense.

Certain kinds of crime – parricide is a good example – are offences against this order, as well as against the political order. They do not just represent damage done to the interests of certain other individuals, or even of the ensemble of individuals making up the society. They represent a violation of the order, tearing things out of their place, as it were. And so punishment is not just a matter of making reparation for damage inflicted, or of removing a dangerous criminal, or of deterring others. The order must be set right. In the language of the time, the criminal must make *amende honorable*.

So the punishments have a meaning. I find Foucault convincing on this. The violence done to the order is restored by being visited on the wrong-doer. Moreover this restoral is made the more effective by his participation in the (to us) grisly scenario, in particular his avowal. As Foucault puts it, one of the goals was to 'instaurer le supplice comme moment de vérité'.[4] Moreover, since the order violated includes the political order – royal power in this case – and this order is public, not in the modern Benthamian sense of touching the general interest, but in the older sense of a power which essentially manifests itself in public space, the restoral has to be enacted in public space. What to us is the additional barbarity of making a spectacle of all these gruesome goings-on was an essential part of what was being *effected* in the punishments of that age. 'L'atrocité qui hante le supplice joue donc un double rôle: principe de la communication du crime avec la peine, elle est d'autre part l'exaspération du châtiment par rapport au crime. Elle assure d'un même coup l'éclat de la vérité et celui du pouvoir; elle est le rituel de l'enquête qui s'achève en la cérémonie où triomphe le souverain.'[5]

It is clear that one of the things which makes us so different from the people of that epoch is that the whole background notion of order has disappeared for us. This has been connected to, is in a sense the obverse side of, the development of the modern identity, the sense we have of ourselves as free, self-defining subjects, whose understanding of our own essence or of our paradigm purposes is drawn from 'within', and no longer from a supposed cosmic order in which we are set. But this is not the whole story; it is not just that we have lost their background rationale. It is also that a new notion of the good has arisen. This is defined by what has often been called modern 'humanitarianism'. We have acquired, since the eighteenth century, a concern for the preservation of life, for the fulfilling of human need, and above all for the relief of suffering, which gives us an utterly different set of priorities from our forebears'. It is this, and not just our loss of their background, which makes them seem to us to barbaric.

What lies behind this modern humanitarianism? This is a big and deep story. No one can claim to understand it fully. But I have to go into it a little, because his interpretation of it is central to Foucault's position. I think one of the important factors which underlies it is the modern sense of the significance of what I want to call 'ordinary life'. I use this as a term of art for that ensemble of activities which are concerned with the sustaining of life, with its continuation and reproduction: the activities of producing and consuming, or marriage, love and the family. While in the traditional ethics which came to us from the ancients, this had merely infrastructural significance (it was the first term in Aristotle's duo of ends: 'life and the good life', *zên kai euzên*; a career, *bios*, concerned with it alone puts us on a level with animals and slaves) in modern times, it becomes the prime locus of significance.

In traditional ethics, ordinary life is overshadowed by what are identified as higher activities – contemplation, for some, the citizen life, for others. And in medieval Catholicism something like this overshadowing of ordinary lay life occurs relative to the dedicated life of priestly or monastic celibacy. It was particularly the Protestant Reformation, with its demand for personal commitment, its refusal of the notion of first- and second-class Christians (unless it be the distinction between saved and damned), its refusal of any location of the sacred in human space, time or rite, and its insistence on the Biblical notion that life was hallowed, which brought about the reversal. This reversal continues through the various secularized philosophies. It underlies the Baconian insistence on utility, and partly in this way feeds into the mainstream humanism of the enlightenment. It has obviously levelling, anti-aristocratic potential.

But more than this, it has come, I would claim, to inform the entirety of modern culture. Think for instance of the growth of the new understanding of the companionate marriage in the seventeenth and eighteenth centuries, the growing sense of the importance of *emotional* fulfilment in marriage – indeed, the whole modern sense that one's *feelings* are a key to the good life. This is now defined as involving certain emotional experiences. If I can use the term 'the good life' as an absolutely general, ethic-neutral term for whatever is considered good/holy/of ultimate value on any given view, then I would want to say that the Reformation theologies, with their new stress on the calling, made ordinary life the significant locus of the issues which distinguish the good life. *Euzên* now occurs within *zên*. And modern culture has continued this.

This I believe, is an important part of the background to modern humanitarianism. Because with the ethics of ordinary life arises the notion that serving life (and with later, more subjectivist variants, avoiding suffering) is a paradigm goal in itself, while at the same time the supposed higher ends which previously trumped life – aristocratic honour, the sustaining of cosmic order, eventually even religious orthodoxy itself – are progressively discredited.

The perspective would make one envisage the change in philosophies of punishment since the seventeenth century as a gain; perhaps in other respects also a loss, but at least in this one respect as a gain. In other words, it seems to contain a critique of the older view as based on a mystification, in the name of which human beings were sacrificed, and terrible suffering was inflicted. At least that has been the enlightenment-inspired reaction.

But Foucault doesn't take that stance at all. Ultimately, as is well known, he wants to take a stance of neutrality. Here are just two systems of power, classical and modern. But at first blush, there seems to be a *value* reason for refusing the enlightenment valuation. This lies in a reading of modern humanitarianism as the reflection of a new system of domination, directed towards the maintenance and increase of 'biomass'. This is the second analysis, which I would like to look at briefly.

2

The picture is drawn, in both *Surveiller et punir* and volume 1 of *Histoire de la sexualité*, of a constellation combining modern humanitarianism, the new social sciences, and the new disciplines which develop in armies, schools and hospitals in the eighteenth century, all seen as the formation of new modes of domination. In an immensely rich series of analyses, Foucault draws the portrait of a new form of power coming to be. Where the old power depended on the idea of public space, and of a public authority which essentially manifested itself in this space, which overawed us with its majesty, and relegated the subjects to a less visible status, the new power operates by universal surveillance. It does away with the notion of public space; power no longer appears, it is hidden, but the lives of all the subjects are now under scrutiny. This is the beginning of a work we are familiar with, in which computerized data banks are at the disposal of authorities, whose key agencies are not clearly identifiable, and whose *modus operandi* is often partly secret.[6]

The image or emblem of this new society for Foucault is Bentham's Panopticon, where a single central vantage point permits the surveillance of a host of prisoners, each of whom is isolated from all the rest, and incapable of seeing his watcher. In a striking image, he contrasts ancient to modern society through the emblem structure of temple and panopticon. The ancients strove to make a few things visible to the many; we try to make many things visible to the few. 'Nous sommes bien moins grecs que nous ne le croyons.'[7]

The new philosophy of punishment is thus seen as inspired not by humanitarianism but by the need to control. Or rather, humanitarianism itself seems to be understood as a kind of stratagem of the new growing mode of control.[8] The new forms of knowledge serve this end. People are measured, classed, examined in various ways, and thus made the better subject to a control which tends to normalization. In particular, Foucault speaks of the medical examination, and the various kinds of inspection which arose on its model, as a key instrument in this. The examination he says, is at once 'le déploiement de la force et l'établissement de la vérité'.

Far from explaining the rise of this technology of control in terms of the modern identity of man as an individual, Foucault wants to explain the modern notion of individuality as one of its products. This new technology brings about the modern individual as an objective of control. The being who is thus examined, measured, categorized, made the target of policies of normalization, is the one whom we have come to define as the modern individual.[9]

There is another way of contrasting modern power with the classical. Foucault touches on it in *Surveiller et punir* but sets it out more explicitly in later work.[10] The classical understanding of power turned on the notions of sovereignty and law. Much of early modern thought was taken up with definitions of sovereignty and legitimacy. In part these intellectual efforts were deployed in the service of the new centralized royal governments, which built up towards their apogee in the 'absolute' monarchies of the seventeenth century. In part they were concerned with the opposite movements, a definition of the limits of rightful sovereignty, and hence the rights of resistance of the subject. At the limit, this line of thought issues in the post-Rousseauian definitions of legitimate sovereignty as essentially founded on self-rule.

But in either case, these theories present an image of power as turning on the fact that some give commands and others obey. They address this question in terms of law or right. Foucault's thesis is that, while we have not ceased talking and thinking in terms of this model, we actually live in relations of power which are quite different, and which cannot be properly described in its terms. What is wielded through the modern technologies of control is something quite different, in that it is not concerned with law but with normalization. That is, it is above all concerned with bringing about a certain result, defined as health or good function, whereas, relative to any such goal, law is always concerned with what Nozick calls 'side constraints'. In fact, what has happened is a kind of infiltration of the process of law itself by this quite alien species of control. Criminals are more and more treated as 'cases' to be 'rehabilitated' and brought back to normal.

This change goes along with two others. First, where the old law/power was concerned with prohibitions, with instructions requiring that we in some way restrict our behaviour to conform to them, the new kind of power is *productive*. It brings about a new kind of subject and new kinds of desire and behaviour which belong to him. It is concerned to form us as modern individuals.[12] Second, this power is not wielded by a *subject*. It is essential to the old model that power presupposes a location of the source of command. Even if no longer in the hands of the king, it will now be located in a sovereign assembly, or perhaps in the people who have the right to elect it. In any case, the orders start from somewhere. But the new kind of power is not wielded by specific people against others, at least not in this way. It is rather a complex form of organization in which we are all involved.[13]

We still live in the theory of the old power, understood in terms of sovereignty/obedience. But the reality we have is the new one, which must be understood in terms of domination/subjugation.[14] In political theory, we still 'need to cut off the king's head'.[15]

Now this second analysis may remind us of another important theme of critical political theory, indeed, a central theme of Critical Theory (in capitals), that of the link between the domination of nature and the domination of man. This is set out in perhaps its clearest form, and in one of its most influential formulations, in Schiller's *Letters on the Aesthetic Education of Man* (1795).[16] But it was taken up and continued in a variety of ways, and emerges as an explicit theme in the writings of the Frankfurt School.

The basic notion is a critique of mainstream enlightenment humanism with its exaltation of instrumental reason and an instrumental stance towards nature, both within and without us. To objectify our own nature and to try to bring it under the control of reason is to divide what should be a living unity. It introduces a master within, in Schiller's language, a relation of domination internal to the person. The proper stance of reason to nature is that of articulator. In expression – in Schiller's formulation, in beauty – nature and reason come to reconciliation.

The relation of domination within man, which is part of a stance of domination towards nature in general, cannot help engendering a domination of man by man. What goes on within must also end up happening between men. Schiller's account of this connection is via the breakdown of a true consensual community among atomic individuals which necessitates a regime of enforced conformity to law. But Foucault seems to offer to the Schillerian perspective another connection (supplementing, not replacing the first). The objectifying and domination of inner nature comes about in fact not just through a change of attitude but through training in an interiorization of certain disciplines. The disciplines of organized bodily movement, of the employment of time, of ordered dispositions of living/working space – these are the paths by which objectification really takes place, becomes more than a philosopher's dream, or the achievement of a small elite of spiritual explorers, and takes on the dimensions of a mass phenomenon.

But the disciplines which build this new way of being are social; they are the disciplines of the barracks, the hospital, the school, the factory. By their very nature they lend themselves to the control of some by others. In these contexts, the inculcation of habits of self-discipline is often the imposition of discipline by some on others. These are the loci where forms of domination become entrenched through being interiorized.

Seen in this way, Foucault offers the Frankfurt School an account of the inner connection between the domination of nature and the domination of man which is rather more detailed and more convincing than what they came up with themselves. It is the measure of the great richness of his work that this 'gift' is not at all part of his intentions. On the contrary, Foucault will have nothing to do with this Romantic-derived view of the oppression of nature and our 'liberation' from it.

Once again this seems ultimately to be a matter of his Nietzschean refusal of the notion of truth as having any meaning outside a given order of power. But once again, there looks to be a more immediate, value-related reason. This comes out in the third analysis, which is the subject of the *Histoire de la sexualité*.

3

Central to the Romantic notion of liberation is the notion that the nature within us must come to expression. The wrong stance of reason is that of objectification, and the application of instrumental reason; the right stance is that which brings to authentic expression what we have within us. In accordance with the whole modern rehabilitation of ordinary life, of which the Romantic movement is heir, one of the crucial aspects of this inner nature which must be articulated is our nature as sexual beings. There is a truth of this: an authentic way for each of us to love. This is distorted by custom, or the demands of power external to us; in more modern variants, it is distorted by the demands of the capitalist work-ethic, or the disciplines of a bureaucratic society. In any case, whatever the distorting agent, it needs to be liberated, and coming to true expression is both a means and a fruit of this liberation.

Foucault aims to dismantle this whole conception, and show it to be thorough-going illusion. The idea that we have a sexual nature, and that we can get at it by speech, by avowal – perhaps with the help of experts – Foucault sees as an idea with deep roots in Christian civilization. It links together earlier practices of confession, through counter-reformation practices of self-scrutiny (and also reformed ones, naturally; but Foucault tends to be more familiar with French Catholic sources) to Freudian psychoanalysis, the 'talking cure'. We live in 'une société singuliérement avouante'.[17] But this idea is not the statement of a deep, culture-independent truth about us. It is rather one of these 'truths' which are produced by a certain regime of power. And in fact, it is a product of the same regime of power through the technology of control that we have just been examining.

Foucault's idea seems to be that the notion that we have a sexual nature is itself a product of those modes of knowledge designed to make us objects of control. Our acceptance that we have such a nature makes us an object of such control. For now we have to find it, and set our lives to rights by it. And finding it requires the 'help' of experts, requires that we put ourselves in their care, be they the priests of old or the psychoanalysts or social workers of today. And part of putting ourselves in their hands is our avowal, the requirement that we go on trying to *say* what we are like, what our experience is, how things are with us.

This whole idea turns out to be a stratagem of power. It helps the cause of control partly in that it presents us as enigmas who need external help to resolve ourselves; and partly in that it has created the very idea of sex. Not, of course, the desire, the instinct, but the understanding of sexuality as the locus of a crucial fulfilment for ourselves as human beings. This self-understanding in terms of an enigmatic nature requiring expression has made us into modern sexual beings, where a key element of the good life is some kind of sexual *fulfilment*. The question of the meaning of our life is bound up with the authentic nature of our sexual longing. 'La question de ce que nous sommes, une certaine pente nous a conduits, en quelques siècles, à la poser au sexe. Et, non pas tellement au sexe-nature (élément du système du vivant, objet pour une biologie), mais au sexe-histoire, au sexe-signification, au sexe-discours.'[18]

And this makes us objects of control in all sort of ways which we barely understand. The important thing to grasp is that we are not controlled on the old model, through certain prohibitions being laid on us. We may think we are gaining some freedom when we throw off sexual prohibitions, but in fact we are dominated by certain images of what it is to be a full, healthy, fulfilled sexual being. And these images are in fact very powerful instruments of control. We may think of the contemporary wave of sexual permissiveness as a kind of 'revolt of the sexual body'. But

> What is the response on the side of power? An economic (and perhaps also ideological) exploitation of eroticisation, from sun-tan products to pornographic films. Responding precisely to the revolt of the body, we find a new mode of investment which presents itself no longer in the form of control by repression but that of control by stimulation. 'Get undressed – but be slim, be good-looking, tanned!'[19]

The ruse is diabolic. The whole idea that we are generally too sexually repressed, and need above all liberation; that we need to be able to talk more freely; that we need to throw off taboos and enjoy our sexual nature – this is not just another of those illusions which makes us see power always in terms of prohibitions. In fact the self-experience whereby we have a sexual nature which is held down or confined by rules and taboos is itself a creation of the new kind of power/control. In going for liberation, we see ourselves as escaping a power understood on the old model. But in fact we live under a power of the new kind, and this we are not escaping; far from it, we are playing its game, we are assuming the shape it has moulded for us. It keeps us tied to the whole 'dispositif de sexualité'.[20]

The very idea of modern sexuality thus develops as part of technologies of control. It is at the hinge where two axes of such development join.[21] On one hand, it is related to the disciplines of the body; on the other, to the regulation of populations. It serves the preservation and extension of life as the 'bio-mass', which is the over-riding direction of much modern policy.

II

Let me try to sum up the discussion of the three analyses of Foucault. I have been trying through them to get to the point where we can see the break in Foucault's thought, the point which disconcerts, where he adopts a Nietzschean-derived stance of neutrality between the different historical systems of power, and thus seems to neutralize the evaluations which arise out of his analyses. In the first analysis, he opposes the classical liturgical idea of punishment to the modern 'humanitarian' one; and refuses to value the second over the first. But this refusal is over-determined, in a sense. It doesn't seem to depend only on the bottom-line Nietzschean stance of neutrality, but also on his concrete reading of this 'humanitarianism', which is seen as a growing system of control.

And so we have the second analysis, which seems to give us an *evaluational* reason for refusing the evaluation which issues from the first analysis. But the evaluation on which this depends would be something akin to the Schillerian/Critical Theory notion that modern discipline has repressed our own natures and constituted systems of domination of man by man, and this evaluation is also repudiated. Once again, though, we seem to have an over-determined judgement. It is not a pure case of Nietzschean neutrality. For there is another reason to refuse this whole Romantic-inspired notion of liberation from the domination of nature within and without. And that is that the ideology of expressive liberation, particularly in connection with sexual life, is itself just a strategy of power. This is the third analysis.

And so we come to the bottom line. What about the evaluation which seems to flow from the third analysis? This would offer us some idea of a liberation, but not via the correct or authentic expression of our natures. It would be a liberation from the whole ideology of such expression, and hence from the mechanisms of control which use this ideology. It would be a liberation which was helped by our unmasking falsehood; a liberation aided by the truth.

In short, it would be something which had certain parallels to the Romantic-originating notion. We would achieve a liberation from a system of control which operates in us largely through masks, disguises and false pretences. It operates by inducing in us a certain self-understanding, an identity. We can help to throw it off partly by unmasking this identity and the manner of its implantation, and thus cease to be accomplices in its control and shaping of ourselves.

This would be a notion of liberation through the truth, parallel to the Romantic-derived one, but different in that it would see the very notion of ourselves as having a true identity to express as part of the *dispositif* of control, rather than as what defines our liberation.

Now the official Nietzschean stance of Foucault would refuse this value-position as well. And here, at last, we would be at the pure case, where the refusal was not over-determined, but depended purely on the Nietzschean stance. But can he do it? Does he really do it? What does it mean to do it? These are the central questions which arise about Foucault's repudiation of the goods which seem implicit in his analyses. And this is the right place to pose these questions, where no extraneous considerations, no other possible value-positions muddy the waters.

Does he really do it? Even this is not so clear. There are moments where some notion of liberation seems to peek through. It is true (?) that he repudiates the notion of liberation through the truth: 'La vérité n'est pas libre, ni l'erreur serve.'[22] But later there is the hint of a possible *point d'appui* for at least a relative freeing: 'Contre le dispositif de la sexualité, le point d'appui de la contre-attaque ne doit pas être le sexe-désir, mais les corps et les plaisirs.'[23] What exactly this could mean I want to discuss later. But here, I just want to point to the implication that once one has rejected the false idea of a liberation through the truth of one's natural sexual desires (*le sexe-désir*), there remains something else it can be founded on. In this connection, we might also mention the passages where Foucault talks about the need for a kind of revolutionary practice which did not just reproduce the forms of control which exist in the structures against which they are rebelling.[24]

But the question I would like to explore here is: can he do it? By that I mean: what can be coherently said in this domain? Just how much sense does a Nietzschean position make?

Before I do this, I want just to mention another line of critique that one could take up against Foucault, but that I do not want to pursue here. Foucault's analyses are terribly one-sided. Their strength is their insightfulness and originality, in bringing usually neglected aspects to light. The weakness is that the other aspects seem denied altogether. We can see this with the three analyses above.

I already mentioned with the first analysis how Foucault reads the rise of humanitarianism exclusively in terms of the new technologies of control. The development of the new ethics of life is given no independent significance. This seems to me quite absurdly one-sided.

In the second analysis, the rise of new forms of discipline is seen exclusively in its relation to domination. Once again, I think there is a mine of valuable historical insights here. Foucault has filled in, as I mentioned above, some of the background which Critical Theory always supposed, but did not adequately work out. But Foucault has missed the ambivalence of these new disciplines. The point is, they have not only served to feed a system of control; they have also taken the form of genuine self-disciplines which have made possible new kinds of collective action characterized by more egalitarian forms of participation. This is not a new discovery. It is a truism of the civic humanist tradition of political theory that free participatory institutions require some commonly accepted self-disciplines. The free citizen has the *vertu* to give willingly the contribution which otherwise the despot would coerce from him, perhaps in some other form. Without this, free institutions cannot exist. There is a tremendous difference between societies which find their cohesion through such common disciplines grounded on a public identity, and which thus permit of and call for the participatory action of equals, on one hand, and the multiplicity of kinds of society which require chains of command based on unquestionable authority on the other.

Aside from the moral differences, there are also differences in efficacy, particularly military, which Machiavelli examined. Modern history has been shaped by striking examples of the citizen military, from the New Model Army to the Israeli Defence Forces. This is really too big a phenomenon to ignore.

The point is that collective disciplines can function in both ways, as structures of domination, and as bases for equal collective action. And they can also slide over time from one to the other. It can be argued that some of the disciplines which helped to found the societies based on contract and responsible government in earlier times, which represented a great leap forward in egalitarian politics, are now serving bureaucratic modes of irresponsible power which are sapping our democracy. I think that there is a lot in this. And undoubtedly the feeling that something like this is happening adds plausibility to Foucault's analysis, at first blush. But on reflection, we can see that Foucault's notion of modern power incapacitates us from understanding this process.

That is because we cannot understand modern bureaucratization unless we see how collective disciplines can function both for and against despotic control. The threatened degeneracy of modern mass democracies is a *slide* from one of these directions to the other. We will never see what is going on if we think of the disciplines as having their exclusive historical and social significance in forms of domination.

Foucault's attraction is partly that of a *terrible simplificateur*. His espousal of the reversal of Clausewitz's aphorism, which makes us see politics as war carried on by other means,[25] can open insights in certain situations. But to make this one's basic axiom for the examination of modern power as such leaves out too much.

Foucault's opposition between the old model of power, based on sovereignty/obedience, and the new one based on domination/subjugation leaves out everything in Western history which has been animated by civic humanism or analogous movements.[26] And that means a massive amount of what is specific to our civilization. Without this in one's conceptual armoury Western history and societies become incomprehensible, as they are for that reason to so many Russians (like Solzhenitsyn).

In the third analysis, Foucault is certainly on to something in the claim that sexual desire has been given exceptional importance in Western civilization, and that in the very attempts to control it, neutralize it and go beyond it. He is certainly right to point to the Christian roots of this. Again, we can appreciate the force of the point that we have somehow been led to place a tremendous weight of significance on our sexual lives and fulfilment in this culture, more than these can bear. But then to understand this simply in terms of technologies of control leaves out its roots in the theologies/ethics of ordinary life, in the Christian concern for the quality of the will, which Foucault himself rightly sees as basic to this.[27] And to reduce the whole Western, post-Romantic business of trying to save oneself to an artefact of such a technology of control approaches absurdity. That the aspiration to express one's true nature can *become* a mechanism of control is indeed true, and Foucault can offer insights on this. But just as in the case of bureaucratization above, you incapacitate yourself to understand this *becoming* if you conceive it from the beginning as essentially *being* control.

III

But I am less interested in hammering this line of critique than in seeing what can be coherently said in this area. I think Foucault's position is ultimately incoherent, but that this escapes detection because the points where it falls into contradiction are misidentified as new and deeper formulations of what many would recognize as valuable insights. I would like to explore this under three heads.

1

First, the idea of power without a subject. There are a number of interesting ideas here, of which two are especially important for this discussion. First, Foucault is setting aside the old model, where power is a matter of one person (group) exercising sovereign control over another; where some give orders and others obey, where some impose their wills on the others. This is usually conceived as a relation alongside the others – social, economic, familial, sexual, etc. – that people stand in with each other, conditioned by and conditioning the others, but distinct from them. On the contrary, the power Foucault is interested in is internal to, intrinsic to, these other relations. One could say that it is constitutive of them, that built in to the very understanding of the common activity, or goods sought, or whatever forms the substance of the micro-relation, are forms of domination.[28] Thus the doctor–patient relation is defined by a supposed common goal, constituted by a stance of helper on the part of the professional and a recognition of need on the part of the patient. But this coming together in a common goal is inseparable from a relation of power, founded on the presumption that one *knows* and that the other has an overwhelming interest in taking advice. The relation of force is integral to the common goal as defined.

This is a relation of power, but it cannot be conceived on the Hobbesian model. It is rare that a doctor can/wants to wreak his arbitrary and unrestrained will on his patient. Both parties are constrained in a sense by the common understanding, the common activity. But within this, there is a domination on the part of the doctor.

This helps us to understand another difference from the Hobbesian model: frequently, in this kind of situation, the dominated cooperate in their subordination. They often come to interiorize the norms of the common activity; they go willingly. They are utterly unaware of a relation of domination. Foucault's example is the ideology of sexual liberation, where we play along unwittingly with a technology of control, even as we are 'letting it all hang out'.

And we can see from this, also, how this kind of relationship can permit reversals. There is not necessarily a continuing identity of dominators and dominated over time. There was for instance an ensemble of father, mother, educator and doctor constituted in the nineteenth century around the control of the child's sexuality. The original relation puts the doctor on top, offering 'advice' to parents, who are in turn controlling their children. But later, the relation of psychiatrist to child is the basis on which the adult's sexuality is called into question.[29]

But Foucault is also putting forward a second thesis under the head of power without a subject, one about the relations of micro- to macro-contexts of power. It is not entirely clear what this thesis is, because it is stated somewhat differently in different places. But the baldest statement is perhaps this: 'que le pouvoir vient d'en bas'.[30] This seems to mean that we cannot hope to explain the local 'rapports de forces' in terms of some global relation of dominators and dominated. This is not to say that there may not be identifiable classes or groups of those who are 'on top', or 'on the bottom' at any given time. But we have to explain this division in terms of the combinations, alignments, mutual effects, oppositions, side-effects, etc, which the micro-contexts of domination produce on each other and with each other. Or, perhaps better, we have to allow for a circular relation, in which the grand alignments, which become concretized in, say, political or military institutions, both result from and have repercussions on the micro-'rapports de forces'.[31]

The grand strategies of the macro-contexts – state, ruling class, or whatever – form the context in which the micro-relations come to be, modify or reproduce themselves, while reciprocally these provide the soil and point of anchorage for the grand strategies. Thus, more than saying that power comes from the bottom, we should say that there is endless relation of reciprocal conditioning between global and micro-contexts.

Foucault's target in this thesis is plainly Marxism, even as he rejects the Hobbesian model with the other. It is a mistake to take the relations of opposition at one level as explanatorily *basic*. That is what Marxism does. It is the global class struggle and its exigencies which are used to explain the way people square off in the micro-contexts, of family, factory, professional association and so on. There is a widely accepted view that we ought to explain, for example, the incarceration of the mad in the sixteenth century, or the repressive interest in infantile sexuality in the nineteenth century, in terms of the requirements of the rising bourgeois economy. Foucault rejects this. Rather the relation was that these contexts of domination developed in their own fashion, and were then taken up and used by the macro-context of domination. They 'came to be colonized and maintained by the global mechanisms and the entire state system', in which the bourgeoisie was hegemonic.[32]

So far, so clear. Indeed, we might be tempted to say: so far, so true. But now there is a third thesis under this head which Foucault also seems to be propounding. Perhaps this is a good statement of it: 'que les relations de pouvoir sont à la fois intentionnelles et non subjectives'.[33] What Foucault seems to be affirming here is that, aside from the particular conscious purpose which agents pursue in their given context, there is discernible a strategic logic of the context itself, but this cannot be attributed to anyone as their plan, as their conscious purpose. As he puts it in *Power/Knowledge*, talking of the kind of history he writes, 'the coherence of such a history does not derive from the revelation of a project, but from the logic of opposing strategies'.[34]

Strategies without projects; this would be a good formula to describe Foucault's historiography. Besides the strategies of individuals, which *are* their projects, there is a strategy of the context. The whole constitution and maintenance of the modern system of control and domination is an example. Foucault speaks of its growth and self-maintenance in strategic terms. He speaks of power using certain stratagems, or certain points of purchase. Thus in describing the reversals which occur as power and the resistance to it each take up each other's instruments, he gives this example:

> Power, after investing itself in the body, finds itself exposed to a counter-attack in that same body. Do you recall the panic of the institutions of the social body, the doctors and politicians, at the idea of non-legalized cohabitation [*l'union libre*] or free abortion? But the impression that power weakens and vacillates here is in fact mistaken; power can retreat here, re-organize its forces, invest itself elsewhere . . . and so the battle continues.[35]

This notion of global strategies is essential to Foucault's reverse Clausewitzian thesis that we are engaged in perpetual war. This is not just the banality that there is much strife and rivalry among individuals. It is the thesis that there is a continuing struggle traversing the context in which we are all caught up. The use of the term 'strategy' in Foucault recovers its full original etymological force.

It is this third thesis which makes no sense, in Foucault's version. I stress this last phrase, because it would be quite wrong to say that no thesis of this kind makes sense. On the contrary, we can think of good examples where it makes sense to attribute a 'purposefulness without purpose' to history, or at least a logic to events without design. Let us look at some models, in order to see what is required by this kind of explanation.

(a)   We can recognize a certain purposefulness in people's action where their motivation and goals are unacknowledged or perhaps unacknowledgeable. An example would be the (I think profound)

Dostoyevskian analysis of modern political terrorism in terms of projected self-hatred and the response to a sense of emptiness. These purposes are not only unacknowledged, they *could not* be acknowledged without undermining the whole enterprise, which depends crucially on the notion that one is acting out of purely political-strategic considerations. But they might explain certain systematic features of terrorism better than the overtly avowed goals.

(b) Then there are theories of unintended but systematic consequences, such as 'invisible hand' theories, that is, theories where the situation is so constituted that individual decisions are bound to concatenate in a certain systematic way. The best-known example is the (malign) invisible hand account of capitalism by Marx. The structure of a capitalist economy is that individual decisions have to concatenate towards an ever-greater polarization, immiseration of the masses, concentration of capital, falling rate of profit and so on.

(c) There are unintended consequences theories which touch on the results of collective action, and not just the combination of individual actions. As an example, we can perhaps see a certain pattern in Leninist politics whereby the possibilities of devolution and a move towards participation are more and more restricted. This is a consequence unintended by Leninist parties at the outset, but it could perhaps be shown that it follows ineluctably from their model of mass mobilization, which systematically ends up destroying the bases for devolved power. The tragedy would be that a movement aimed at liberation and radical democratization should end up destroying these more effectively than predecessor regimes.

I am citing these types and examples to illustrate my main point, which is that purposefulness without purpose requires a certain kind of explanation to be intelligible. The undesigned systematicity has to be related to the purposeful action of agents in a way that we can understand. This is a requirement which the above kinds of explanation try to fulfil. The reason for this requirement is that the text of history, which we are trying to explain, is made up of purposeful human action. Where there are patterns in this action which are not on purpose, we have to explain why action done under one description on purpose also bears this other, undesigned description. We have to show how the two descriptions relate. A strategic pattern cannot just be left hanging, unrelated to our conscious ends and projects.

It is a mistake to think that the only intelligible relation between a pattern and our conscious purposes is the direct one where the pattern is consciously willed. This is a hang-up which did come down to us from classical Cartesian-empiricist views of the mind. Foucault is right to ridicule it: 'ne cherchons pas l'état-major qui préside à sa rationalité' (sc. *du pouvoir*).[36] But this must not be confused with the explanatory requirement outlined above. It is certainly not the case that all patterns *issue* from conscious action, but all patterns have to be made *intelligible* in relation to conscious action.

Now Foucault not only does not meet this requirement; it is difficult to see how he could without abandoning some or other part of his declared position. We could explain the constitution of the growing system of technologies of control, if we could understand it (on model (a)) as meeting the (largely unacknowledged) purposes of some group. But this Foucault could not do without going back on his second thesis, that there is no priority here of explanation in terms of the interest of some dominant class. The system has to arise out of the micro-contexts in which people act and react. It would be even worse for his case if the 'group' whose interest or purposes was the motor of change was co-terminous with society at large, or at least widely distributed within it; for then the changes would be thought of as largely self-wrought, and a problem might arise about interpreting these as relations of *domination*. The same difficulty with Foucault's second thesis rules out explanations on model (c), in terms of the unintended consequences of collective action (which might itelf be motivated by partly unacknowledged purposes).

In order to stick by the second thesis in this case, we would need some account on model (b), where micro-reactions concatenate in this systematic way. I don't say something like this cannot be found, but I am at a loss to say even where one should start looking for it. And Foucault doesn't even feel the need to start looking.

This is not to say that there is a difficulty with Foucault's second thesis in principle. On the contrary, there are obviously lots of aspects of social life in which this reciprocal play of micro-practice and global structures, each producing (largely unintended) consequences for the other, is the right explanatory model. The problem arises only when one combines this with Foucault's very strong claims to systematicity, in the idea that there are pervasive *strategies* afoot which condition the battle in each micro-context, that 'power' can 'retreat' or 're-organize its forces'. These can only be combined via some account of how actions concatenate systematically some model of type (b). But Foucault doesn't even try. He leaves us with a strange kind of Schopenhauerian will, ungrounded in human action.[37]

One of the most important reasons why Foucault doesn't feel a need to offer an account here is the confusion which has afflicted the republic of letters during these last decades about the supposed 'death of subjectivity'. This had its epicentre in Paris. Foucault took part in it.[38] Hacking praises Foucault for having stepped beyond the old conception of subjectivity, which required all purposefulness in history to have a purposer.[39]

The confusion lies in not seeing that there not only can be but *must* be something between total subjectivism, on the one hand, holding that there are no undesigned patterns in history, and the strange Schopenhauerianism-without-the-will in which Foucault leaves us. Much play is made of the discovery (which structuralists did a lot to put in vogue) that any act requires a background language of practices and institutions to make sense; and that while there will be a particular goal sought in the act, those features of it which pertain to the structural background will not be objects of individual purpose. That my declarations in this paper are all made with uninflected words has nothing to do with what I have decided, and everything to do with the fact that the medium of my thought is English (and I didn't really choose *that* either).

No one can deny that this is an invaluable point to have in mind in studies of power. The utter sterility of the view popular a while ago in American political science, that one could analyse power in terms of A's ability to make B do something he otherwise would not, or some such thing, illustrates this. The approach is sterile, just because acts of power are so heterogeneous; they absolutely do not admit of being described in such a homogeneous medium of culturally neutral makings and doings. The power of the audience over the star craving approval is utterly incommensurable with the power of the general, which is incommensurable with the power of the elected minister, and that in turn with the power of the guru, and so on. Power can only be understood within a context; and this is the obverse of the point that the contexts can only in turn be understood in relation to the kind of power which constitutes them (Foucault's thesis).

But all this does not mean that there is no such thing as explaining the rise and fall of these contexts in history. On the contrary, this is one of the major tasks of historiography. And that is the issue we were talking about in connection with Foucault's system of modern technologies of control. How does it arise? *Of course*, you don't explain it by some big bad man/class *designing* it (who ever suggested anything so absurd?), but you do need to explain it nevertheless, that is relate this systematicity to the purposeful human action in which it arose and which it has come to shape. You cannot evade *this* question by talking of the priority of structure over element, of language over speech act. What we want to know is why a language *arises*.

Indeed, for purposes of such diachronic explanation, we can question whether we ought to speak of a priority of language over act. There is a circular relation. Structures of action or languages are only maintained by being renewed constantly in action/speech. And it is in action/speech that they also fail to be maintained, that they are altered. This is a crashing truism, but the fog emanating from Paris in recent decades makes it necessary to clutch it as a beacon in the darkness. To give an absolute priority to the structure makes *exactly as little sense* as the equal and opposite error of subjectivism, which gave absolute priority to the action, as a kind of total beginning.

This helps explain why Foucault feels he can be evasive on this issue; but not why he feels the need to be. Here we touch the question of his motivations, which I would like to adjourn till later (if I dare take it up at all). Meanwhile, I turn to the second head under which there is incoherence.

2

'Power' without 'freedom' or 'truth': can there really be an analysis which uses the notion of power, and which leaves no place for freedom, or truth? I have already raised the question whether Foucault *really* does away with freedom (section II above). But this uncertainty of utterance is just the symptom, I believe, of a deeper problem. The Nietzschean programme on this level does not make sense.

This is because of the very nature of a notion like 'power', or 'domination'. True, they do not require that we have one agent who is imposing his will on another. There are all sorts of ways in which power can be inscribed in a situation in which both dominators and dominated are caught up. The first may see himself largely as the agent of the demands of the larger context; the second may see the demands on him as emanating from the nature of things. Nevertheless, the notion of power or domination requires some notion of constraint imposed on someone by a process in some way related to human agency. Otherwise the term loses all meaning.

'Power' in the way Foucault sees it, closely linked to 'domination', does not require a clearly demarcated perpetrator, but it requires a victim. It cannot be a 'victimless crime', so to speak. Perhaps the victims also exercise it, also victimize others. But power needs targets.[40] Something must be being imposed on someone, if there is to be domination. Perhaps that person is also helping to impose it on himself, but then there must be an element of fraud, illusion, false pretences involved in this. Otherwise, it is not clear that the imposition is in any sense an exercise of *domination*.[41]

But now something is only an *imposition* on me against a background of desires, interests, purposes, that I have. It is only an imposition if it makes some dent in these, if it frustrates them, prevents them from fulfilment, or perhaps even from formulation. If some external situation or agency wreaks some change in me which in no way lies athwart some such desire/purpose/aspiration/interest, then there is no call to speak of an exercise of power/domination. Take the phenomenon of imprinting. In human life, it also exists after a fashion. We generally come to like the foods which have assuaged our hunger, those we are fed as children in our culture. Is this an index of the 'domination' of our culture over us? The word would lose all useful profile, would have no more distinctiveness, if we let it roam this wide.

Moreover, the desire/purposes, etc., have to be of some significance. The trivial is not relevant here. If something makes it impossible for me to act on the slight preference that I have for striped over unstriped toothpaste, this is not a serious exercise of power. Shaping my life by 'imposition' in this respect would not figure in an analysis of power.

This is recognized by Foucault in his thesis that there is no power without 'resistances'.[42] Indeed, Foucault is sometimes dramatically aware of the force and savagery of the imposition. Take this passage, about knowledge, but illustrating its close connection to power: '. . . its development [sc. of knowledge] is not tied to the constitution and affirmation of a free subject: rather it creates a progressive enslavement to its instinctive violence. Where religions once demanded the sacrifice of bodies, knowledge now calls for experimentation on ourselves, calls us to the sacrifice of the subject of knowledge.'[43]

But this means that 'power' belongs in a semantic field from which 'truth' and 'freedom' cannot be excluded. Because it is linked with the notion of the imposition on our significant desires/purposes, it cannot be separated from the notion of some relative lifting of this restraint, from an unimpeded fulfilment of these desires/purposes. But this is just what is involved in a notion of freedom. There may, indeed, be all sorts of reasons why in certain situations certain impositions just cannot be lifted. There are empirical obstacles, and some very deep-lying ones in man's historical situation. But that is not Foucault's point. He wants to discredit as somehow based on a misunderstanding the very idea of liberation from power. But I am arguing that power, in his sense, *does not make sense* without at least the idea of liberation. It may then be shown that the specific liberation, defined in a given context as the negation of the power wielded therein, is not realizable for this or that reason. But that is another, quite different issue, into which Foucault doesn't even enter.

The Foucaultian thesis involves combining the fact that any set of institutions and practices form the background to our action within them, and are in that sense unremovable while we engage in that kind of action, with the point that different forms of power are indeed constituted by different complexes of practice, to form the illegitimate conclusion that there can be no question of liberation from the power implicit in a given set of practices. Not only is there the possibility of frequently moving from one set of practices to another; but even within a given set, the level and kind of imposition can vary. Foucault implicitly discounts both these possibilities, the first because of the fundamentally Nietzschean thesis which is basic to his work: the move from one context to another cannot be seen as a liberation because there is no common measure between the impositions of the one and those of the other. I want to address this in the next discussion (section 3 below). And he discounts the second, because of his over-simple and global notion of the modern system of control and domination, which I have already touched on above.

So 'power' requires 'liberty'. But it also requires 'truth' – if we want to allow, as Foucault does, that we can collaborate in our own subjugation. Indeed, that is a crucial feature of the modern system of control, that it gets us to agree and concur in the name of truth, or liberation of our own nature. If we want to allow this, then 'truth' is an essential notion, because the imposition proceeds here by foisting illusion on us; it proceeds by disguises and masks; it proceeds thus by falsehood. 'C'est à la condition de masquer une part importante de lui-même que le pouvoir est tolérable. Sa réussite est en proportion de ce qu'il parvient à cacher de ses mécanismes. Le pouvoir serait-il accepté s'il était entièrement cynique? Le secret n'est pas pour lui de l'ordre de l'abus: il est indispensable à son fonctionnement.'[44] Mask, falsehood makes no sense without a corresponding notion of truth. The truth here is subversive of power: it is on the side of the lifting of impositions, of what we have just called liberation. The Foucaultian notion of power not only requires for its sense the correlative notions of truth and liberation, but even the standard link between them, which makes truth the condition of liberation. To speak of power, and to want to deny a place to 'liberation' and 'truth', as well as the link between them, is to speak incoherently. That is, indeed, the reason why Foucault seems to be contradicting himself in the passages I quoted above (section II). He doesn't just slip into these formulations, which seem to allow for the possibility of a liberation and, indeed, one founded on a puncturing of illusions, a defence founded on 'les corps, les plaisirs, les savoirs, dans leur multiplicité et leur possibilité de résistance'.[45] He is *driven* into them by the contradictory position he has adopted.[46]

3

In the end, the final basis of Foucault's refusal of 'truth' and 'liberation' seems to be a Nietzschean one. This is not all of Nietzsche; there is more, and not all of it compatible with this part. But at least in the *Fröhliche Wissenschaft* we have a doctrine which Foucault seems to have made his own; there is no order of human life, or way we are, or human nature, that one can appeal to in order to judge or evaluate between ways of life. There are only different orders imposed by men on primal chaos, following their will-to-power. Foucault espouses both the relativistic thesis from this view, that one cannot judge between forms of life/thought/valuation, and also the notion that these different forms involve the imposition of power. The idea of 'régimes of truth',[47] and of their close intrication with systems of dominance, is profoundly Nietzschean. In this relationship Foucault sees truth as subordinated to power. Let me quote that passage again more fully:

> Each society has its régime of truth, its 'general politics' of truth; that is, the types of discourse which it accepts and makes function as true; the mechanisms and instances which enable one to distinguish true and false statements, the means by which each is sanctioned; the techniques and procedures accorded value in the acquisition of truth; the status of those who are charged with saying what counts as true.[48]

If this is so (true?) in general, it is even more emphatically so in our society:

There can be no possible exercise of power without a certain economy of discourses of truth which operates through and on the basis of this association. We are subjected to the production of truth through power and we cannot exercise power except through the production of truth. This is the case for every society, but I believe that in ours the relationship between power, right and truth is organized in a highly specific fashion . . . I would say that we are forced to produce the truth of power that our society demands, of which it has need, in order to function: we *must* speak the truth; we are constrained or condemned to confess to or discover the truth. Power never ceases its interrogation, its inquisition, its registration of truth; it institutionalizes, professionalizes and rewards its pursuit. In the last analysis, we must produce truth as we must produce wealth . . .[49]

This regime-relativity of truth means that we cannot raise the banner of truth against our own regime. There can be no such thing as a truth independent of its regime, unless it be that of another. So that liberation in the name of 'truth' could only be the substitution of another system of power for this one, as indeed the modern course of history has substituted the techniques of control for the royal sovereignty which dominated the seventeenth century.

This position is easy enough to state baldly, but difficult – or impossible – actually to integrate into the logic of one's analytical discourse, as I have just been trying to show in section 2 above. The 'truth' manufactured by power also turns out to be its 'masks' or disguises and hence untruth. The idea of a manufactured or imposed 'truth' inescapably slips the word into inverted commas, and opens the space of a truth-outside-quotes, the kind of truth, for instance, which the sentences unmasking power manifest, or which the sentences expounding the general theory of regime-relativity themselves manifest (a paradox).

There has to be a place for revolt/resistance aided by unmasking in a position like Foucault's, and he allows for it. But the general relativity thesis will not allow for liberation through a transformation of power relations. Because of relativity, transformation from one regime to another cannot be a *gain* in truth or freedom, because each is redefined in the new context. They are incomparable. And because of the Nietzschean notion of truth imposed by a regime of power, Foucault cannot envisage liberating transformations *within* a regime. The regime is entirely identified with its imposed truth. Unmasking can only destabilize it; we cannot bring about a new, stable, freer, less mendacious form of it by this route. Foucault's Nietzschean theory can only be the basis of utterly monolithic analyses; which is what we saw above in his failure to recognize the ambivalence of modern disciplines, which are the bases both of domination and self-rule.

And so, for him, unmasking can only be the basis for a kind of local resistance within the regime. In chapter 5 of *Power/Knowledge*, he speaks of rehabilitating subjugated and local knowledges against the established dominant truth. He uses the expression 'insurrection of subjugated knowledges'.[50] The term bespeaks his basic idea: there is no question of a new form, just a kind of resistance movement, a set of destabilizing actions, always local-specific, within the dominant form. One of Foucault's historical paradigms seems to be the popular riots and uprisings which occurred in the former regimes at some of the execution scenes. Plebeian resistance is a kind of model.

> No doubt it would be mistaken to conceive the plebs as the permanent ground of history, the final objective of all subjections, the ever smouldering centre of all revolts. The plebs is no doubt not a real sociological entity. But there is indeed always something in the social body, in classes, groups and individuals themselves which in some sense escapes relations of power, something which is by no means a more or less docile or reactive primal matter, but rather a centrifugal movement, an inverse energy, a discharge. There is certainly no such thing as 'the' plebs; rather there is, as it were, a certain plebeian quality or aspect. There is plebs in bodies, in souls, in individuals, in the proletariat, in the bourgeoisie, but everywhere in a diversity of forms and extensions, of energies and irreducibilities. This measure of plebs is not so much what stands outside relations of power as their limit, their underside, their counter-stroke, that which responds to every advance of power by a movement of disengagement.[51]

We can see at least some of the motivation for this espousal of local insurrections. Foucault is deeply suspicious of 'global, totalitarian theories'[52] which claim to offer the overall solution to our ills. The target, as it must be in the world Foucault inhabits, is of course principally Marxism. And one can have a great deal of sympathy for this reaction, in face of the destruction wrought by such global revolutionary schemes. There is a great deal to be said on the Left for a politics which stays close to the local, to lived experience, to the aspirations which groups spontaneously adopt. But this by itself does not determine one to adopt the Nietzschean model of truth, with its relativism and its monolithic analyses. Just because some claims to truth are unacceptable, we do not need to blow the whole conception to pieces.

Something else drives Foucault to Nietzscheanism. I think it will come out if I try to grapple with the central issue around this position. What does this combination of relativism between forms and monolithism of forms leave out? It leaves out – or better, it blocks out – the possibility of a change of life-form which can be understood as a move towards a greater acceptance of truth – and hence also, in certain conditions, a move towards greater freedom. But in order to conceive a change in these terms we have to see the two forms as commensurable; the form before and the form after the change cannot be seen as incommensurable universes. How can this come about?

Biographically, we see examples all the time. After a long period of stress and confusion, I come to see that I really love A, or I really don't want to take that job. I now see retrospectively that the image of myself as quite free and uncommitted had a merely superficial hold on me. It did not correspond to a profound aspiration. It just stood in the way of my recognizing the depths of my commitment to A. Or, the picture of a career which that job instantiated, which seemed before so powerful, so non-gainsayable, turns out to be a model which my entourage was pressing on me, but which I cannot really endorse.

What makes these biographical changes of outlook/life possible, which seem to be steps towards the truth? Our sense of ourselves, of our *identity*, of what we are. I see this change as a discovery of what I am, of what really matters to me. And that is why I do not see this as a kind of character change, what a lobotomy might produce, for instance. Rather I see it as a step towards truth (or perhaps better put, it is a step out of error), and even in certain conditions as a kind of liberation.

Is there nothing comparable in politics/history? There is. There are changes which turn on, which are justified by, what we have become as a society, a civilization. The American revolutionaries called on their compatriots to rise in the name of the liberties which defined their way of life (ironically as Englishmen). This kind of claim is always contested (there were Tories, there were Loyalists, as is well known where I come from). But is it by its nature unacceptable? Is it always sham? Foucault would have us believe so.

But it seems clear to me that there is a reality here. We have become certain things in Western civilization. Our humanitarianism, our notions of freedom – both personal independence and collective self-rule – have helped to define a political identity we share; and one which is deeply rooted in our more basic, seemingly infra-political understandings: of what it is to be an individual, of the person as a being with 'inner' depths – all the features which seem to us to be rock-bottom, almost biological properties of human beings, so long as we refrain from looking outside and experiencing the shock of encountering other cultures. Of course, these elements of identity are contested; they are not neatly and definitely articulated once and for all, but the subject of perpetual revisionist strife. And worse, they are not all easily compatible – the freedom of independence is hard to combine with that of self-rule, as we constantly experience – and so we fight among ourselves in the name of incompatible weightings. But they all count for us. None of them can be simply repudiated in the political struggle. We struggle over interpretation and weightings, but we cannot shrug them off. They *define* humanity, politics, for us.

This means that we can look at the kind of change Foucault described, from seventeenth-century punishments to our own, in a way which renders them partly commensurable. It is not for nothing that we are the descendants and heirs of the people who so tortured Damiens. The makings of our present stress on the significance of life were already there, in that Christian civilization. One of the important features of their world, which made them act so differently, was their sense of belonging to a cosmic order in which the polity was set. But *this* difference cannot be seen purely in a relativist light. One of the reasons why we can no longer believe in this kind of order is the advance in our civilization of a scientific understanding of the natural world, which we have every reason to believe represents a significant gain of truth. Some dimensions at least of the 'disenchantment' which helps shape modern culture represent an advance in the truth. To the extent that this change is operative, we can understand our difference from them as a change that denizens of Western Christendom have undergone under the impact of a stronger dose of truth.

Of course, this is not *all*. We can also discern losses. Indeed, Foucault ought perhaps best to be interpreted as having documented some of these losses. The growth of modern control has involved in some respects a dehumanization, an inability to understand and respond to some key features of the human context, those which are suppressed in a stance of thorough-going instrumental reason. That is why there is such a malaise in our civilization: so much groaning and travailling to recover what is lost, all the way from the Romantic period down to the most recent battles over ecology. But the point is that the sense both of gain and of loss depends on comparability, on our understanding of our identity, of what we now realize more fully, or are betraying and mutilating.

Gains and losses do not tell the whole story. There are also elements of incomparability. The reality of history is mixed and messy. The problem is that Foucault tidies it up too much, makes it into a series of hermetically sealed, monolithic truth-regimes, a picture which is as far from reality as the blandest Whig perspective of smoothly broadening freedom. Monolithism and relativism are two sides of the same coin. One is as necessary as the other to create this total incomparability across the changes of history. .

Foucault's monolithic relativism only seems plausible if one takes the outsider's perspective, the view from Sirius; or perhaps imagines oneself a soul in Plato's myth of Er. Do I want to be born a Sung dynasty Chinese, or a subject of Hammurabi of Babylon, or a twentieth-century American? Without a prior identity, I couldn't begin to choose. They incarnate incommensurable goods (at least prior to some deep comparative study, and conceivably even after this). But this is not my/our situation. We have already *become* something. Questions of truth and freedom can arise for us in the transformations we undergo or project. In short, we have a *history*. We live in time not just self-enclosed in the present, but essentially related to a past which has helped define our identity, and a future which puts it again in question.

And indeed in his major works, like *The Order of Things* and *Discipline and Punish*, Foucault *sounds* as though he believed that, as an historian, he could stand nowhere, identifying with none of the *epistemai* or structures of power whose coming and going he impartially surveys. But there were signs that this was not to be his last word. It would appear that Foucault was going to elaborate in forthcoming publications his own conception of a good life.

From certain indications,[53] this would seem to be based, as one would expect, on a rejection of the whole idea that we have a deep self or nature which we have to decipher. Foucault thinks that Christianity introduced this false turn into Western culture. Where the ancient 'care of the self' was concerned with self-making and self-mastery, Christian spirituality was preoccupied rather with purity and self-renunciation. 'From that moment on the self was no longer something to be made but something to be renounced and deciphered.'[54]

Foucault's project seems to be to return to these ancient sources, not in order to revive them – even if this were possible, he believes there is lots to criticize in ancient culture on other grounds – but as the point of departure for a different line of development. This would bring us to a conception of the good life as a kind of self-making, related in this way to the ancient 'aesthetic of existence'[55] that one would make one's own life a work of art. '. . . the principal work of art one has to take care of, the main area to which one has to apply aesthetic values is oneself, one's life, one's existence.'[56]

It is understandable how Foucault, from the standpoint of an ethic of this kind, should want to distance himself from the banners of 'freedom' and 'truth', since these have been the key terms in the view he is repudiating, that we ought to bring to light our true nature or deep self. And the affinity with Nietzsche in the stress on self-making is very understandable also. But this in no way lessens the paradox involved in the attempt to avoid these terms altogether. Indeed, in offering us a new way of re-appropriating our history, and in rescuing us from the supposed illusion that the issues of the deep self are somehow inescapable, what is Foucault laying open for us, if not a truth which frees us for self-making?

Perhaps Foucault was moving, before his sudden and premature death, to free his position from this paradox, seemingly linked with the impossible attempt to stand nowhere. Perhaps we can see the last work as a step towards and acknowledgement of his own sources, an identification of the moments when these sources were lost or obscured (the rise of Christian spirituality), and a definition of what we have to undo to rescue what needs saving.[57] At that point, the really interesting debate can begin, on the issues which count, which Foucault's mode of expression up to now has obscured.

There are two such issues, which it is worth tabling for future discussions.

(1)   Can we really step outside the identity we have developed in Western civilization to such a degree that we can repudiate all that comes to us from the Christian understanding of the will? Can we toss aside the whole tradition of Augustinian inwardness?
(2)   Granted we really can set this aside, is the resulting 'aesthetic of existence' all that admirable?

These questions are hard to separate, and even harder to answer. But they are among the most fundamental raised by the admirable work of Michel Foucault.

Notes

1 Foucault, *Power/Knowledge* (New York: Pantheon, 1980), p. 131.
2 Foucault, *Surveiller et punir* (Paris: Gallimard, 1975); *Histoire de la sexualité*, vol. 1 (Paris: Gallimard, 1976).
3 Foucault, *Surveiller et punir*, p. 53.
4 Ibid., p. 47.
5 Ibid., pp. 59–60.
6 Cf. the ancient idea of tyranny as power *hiding* itself, as in the myth of Gyges.
7 Foucault, *Surveiller et punir*, p. 219.
8 Thus in explaining the unplanned rise of this new form, Foucault says: 'Take the example of philanthropy in the early nineteenth century: people appear who make it their business to involve themselves in other people's lives, health, nutrition, housing; then, out of this confused set of functions there emerge certain personages, institutions, forms of knowledge: public hygiene, inspectors, social workers, psychologists' (*Power/Knowledge*, p. 62). Foucault is precisely *not* claiming that there was a plot laid by anyone. The explanatory model of history here seems to be that certain things arise for a whole host of possible reasons, and then get taken up and used by the emerging constellation. But what is clear is that the dominating thrust of the constellation which uses them is not humanitarian beneficence but control. I will discuss this understanding of historical change below.
9 Cf. Foucault, *Power/Knowledge*, p. 98.
10 E.g. in ibid., chap. 5.
11 Foucault, *Surveiller et punir*, p. 224. Cf. 'society of normalization', Foucault, *Power/Knowledge*, p. 107.
12 Cf. the referencees to Marcuse in *Power/Knowledge*, pp. 59, 120.
13 In *Power/Knowledge*, p. 140, Foucault points out the close link between these two changes.
14 Ibid., p. 96.
15 Ibid., p. 121.
16 Esp. letter 6.
17 Foucault, *Sexualité*, p. 79.
18 Ibid., p. 102.
19 Foucault, *Power/Knowledge*, p. 57.
20 Cf. the reference to Wilhelm Reich in Foucault, *Sexualité*, p. 173. This analysis obviously has parallels to Marcuse's about 'repressive de-sublimation', and this just underlines the point above about the possible utility of Foucault's analysis for critical theory. But the crucial difference remains, that Critical Theory stays within the notion of liberation through true expression, while Foucault denounces this. Hence his critique of Marcuse (*Power/Knowledge*, p. 59) for thinking of power still purely in terms of repression.
21 Foucault, *Sexualité*, p. 191.

22   Ibid., p. 81.
23   Ibid., p. 208.
24   Foucault, *Power/Knowledge*, pp. 60, 61.
25   Ibid., p. 90; see also Foucault, *Sexualité*, p. 123.
26   The sovereignty model is *meant* to cope with the rebellion against
     despotic power and the rise of representative institutions. But in fact it
     can only illuminate its Lockean aspect. The civic humanist aspect
     precisely cannot be put in terms of who is giving orders to whom. The
     concept of sovereignty cannot be integrated without strain in this form
     of thought.
27   *London Review of Books* (21 May–3 June 1981), p. 5.
28   Foucault, *Sexualité*, pp. 123–4.
29   Ibid., p. 131.
30   Ibid., p. 124.
31   Ibid., pp. 131–2.
32   Foucault, *Power/Knowledge*, pp. 99–101.
33   Foucault, *Sexualité*, p. 124.
34   Foucault, *Power/Knowledge*, p. 61.
35   Ibid., p. 56.
36   Foucault, *Sexualité*, p. 125.
37   Hacking, *New York Review of Books* (14 May 1981), has already
     pointed out the Schopenhauerian overtones of the title of volume 1 of
     Histoire de la sexualité, La Volonté de savoir (see above, p. 34). But
     even Schopenhauer would not do as a theoretical background for
     Foucault, for that would give an account in our 'nature'. He has to be
     more evasive than this.
38   This set of doctrines is sometimes called 'structuralist', or 'post-
     structuralist', but the aspiration to overcome subjectivity goes well
     beyond people who hold some structuralist model or other. Foucault is
     a case in point.
39   *New York Review of Books*, p. 35.
40   Foucault, *Power/Knowledge*, p. 98: '[Individuals] are not only its [sc.
     power's] inept or consenting target: they are also the elements of its
     articulation.' But this means that they *are* targets.
41   I indicated above how heedless Foucault is of this boundary, in which
     the self-disciplines of freedom are distinguished from the disciplines of
     domination. This all turns on whether and how they are *imposed*.
42   Foucault, *Sexualité*, pp. 125–7; *Power/Knowledge*, p. 142.
43   Foucault, *Language, Counter-Memory, Practice* (Oxford, 1977), p.
     163; quoted in an unpublished paper by Mark Philp.
44   Foucault, *Sexualité*, p. 113.
45   Ibid., p. 208.
46   Of course, there is a question whether Foucault isn't trying to have it
     both ways with his notion of a resistance founded on 'les corps et les
     plaisirs', on something quite inarticulate, not on an *understanding* of
     ourselves, or an *articulation* of our desires/purposes. But does this make
     sense? Can we 'faire valoir contre les prises du pouvoir les corps et les

plaisirs . . .' (ibid.) without articulating them for ourselves, and affirming the truth of that articulation against the specious claims of the system of control? I don't see how. Foucault seems to be talking here out of both sides of his mouth.

47 Foucault, *Power/Knowledge*, p. 131.
48 Ibid.
49 Ibid., p. 93.
50 Ibid., p. 81.
51 Ibid., pp. 137–8. This idea of political resistance without a positive new vision is parallel to the notion of resistance to the dominant sexuality based on the essentially unarticulated 'bodies and pleasures'. In both cases, the question very much arises whether Foucault can have it both ways. Is there a plebeian resistance which does not at least *point* to an alternative model, even if it may for some reasons be unrealizable in practice? Or if there is, if we can find really mindless insurrections in history, do they really offer us models for our political action?
52 Ibid., p. 80.
53 See the new chapters in the second edition of Hubert Dreyfus and Paul Rabinow, *Michel Foucault: Beyond Structuralism and Hermeneutics* (University of Chicago Press, 1983).
54 Ibid., p. 248.
55 Ibid., p. 251.
56 Ibid., p. 245.
57 Foucault, *Histoire de la sexualité* (Paris: Gallimard, 1984): vol. 2, *L'Usage des plaisirs*, and vol. 3, *Le Souci de soi*.

Taking Aim at the Heart of the Present

JÜRGEN HABERMAS

Foucault's death came so unexpectedly and suddenly that one can scarcely resist thinking that its circumstantiality and brutal contingency document the life and teachings of the philosopher. Even from a distance, the death of the 57-year-old man seems an untimely event affirming the merciless power of time – the power of facticity, which, without sense or triumph, prevails over the painstakingly constructed meaning of each human life. For Foucault, the experience of finiteness became a philosophical incitement. He viewed the power of contingency, which he ultimately identified with power *per se*, more from a stoical perspective than from the Christian frame of reference. And yet in Foucault the stoic attitude of the observer who keeps his precise distance, obsessed with objectivity, was combined with the opposite element of passionate self-consuming participation in the reality of the historical moment.

I met Foucault only in 1983, and perhaps I did not understand him well. I can only relate what impressed me: the tension, which resists easy categorization, between the almost serene scientific reserve of the scholar striving for objectivity on the one hand, and, on the other, the political vitality of the vulnerable, subjectively excitable, morally sensitive intellectual. I imagine that Foucault dug through archives with the dogged energy of a detective in hot pursuit of evidence. In March 1983, Foucault suggested that we meet with some American

Translated by Sigrid Brauner and Robert Brown, assisted by David Levin. © 1984 by the Regents of the University of California. Reprinted from *University Publishing*, No. 13, Summer 1984, pp. 5–6, by permission of the Regents.

colleagues for a private conference in 1984 to discuss Kant's 200-year-old essay, 'Answering the Question: What Is Enlightenment?' At the time I knew nothing of a lecture Foucault was preparing on this very subject. Naturally, I understood his invitation as a call for a discussion (together with Hubert Dreyfus, Paul Rabinow, Richard Rorty, and Charles Taylor) of various interpretations of modernity – based on a text which, in a sense, initiated modern philosophical discourse. However, this was not exactly Foucault's intention in this proposal, as I only realized in May 1984, when an excerpt from his lecture was published.

Here we do not encounter the Kant familiar from Foucault's *The Order of Things*, the epistemologist whose analysis of finiteness forced open the gateway to the age of anthropological thought and human sciences (*Humanwissenschaften*). In this lecture one meets a different Kant – Kant as the predecessor of the Young Hegelians, as the first to break seriously with the metaphysical heritage, withdrawing philosophy from the True and Eternal and instead concentrating on what philosophy until then had considered the meaningless and non-existent, the merely accidental and transitory. Foucault discovers in Kant the contemporary who transforms esoteric philosophy into a critique of the present to answer the challenge of the historical moment. Foucault sees in Kant's answer to the question 'What is enlightenment?' the origin of an 'ontology of actuality' leading through Hegel, Nietzsche, and Max Weber to Horkheimer and Adorno. Surprisingly, in the last sentence of his lecture, Foucault adds himself to this tradition.

Foucault relates the text of 1784 to 'The Dispute of the Faculties' (published fourteen years later), where Kant reflects on the events of the French Revolution. The dispute between the Faculty of Philosophy and the Faculty of Law deals, of course, with the question of whether the human race is steadily progressing. In his *Philosophy of Ethics* (*Rechtsphilosophie*), Kant clarified the endpoint in relation to which such progress could be measured. A republican constitution would guarantee the rule of law (*Rechtzustand*) internally as well as externally, the autonomy of citizens under self-made laws as well as the elimination of war from the arena of international relations. Kant searches for an empirical foothold to ground these postulates of 'pure practical reason', to show that they are actually supported by an historically observable 'moral tendency' of the human race. He seeks an 'event of our time' indicating a disposition of human nature toward moral improvement; and, as is well known, he finds this 'historical indicator' not in the French Revolution itself but, rather, in the openly expressed enthusiasm with which a broad public had fearlessly greeted these events as an attempt at a realization of principles of natural law. Such a phenomenon, Kant believes, cannot be forgotten, 'for this event is too great, too interwoven with the interests of mankind not to be remembered by the peoples of the world and not to stimulate renewed attempts of this kind whenever conditions are propitious'.

Foucault cites the famous sentences not entirely without, on his own part, 'desire for doing moral good'. In the earlier text on the enlightenment, Kant emphasized that revolution can never produce that 'true reform in thinking' which, as he asserts in 'The Dispute of the Faculties', emerges precisely in the enthusiasm for the revolution that had since taken place. Foucault relates the two texts in such a way that a synopsis emerges. From this perspective, the question 'What is enlightenment?' merges with the question 'What does this revolution mean for us?' Philosophy is successfully merged with thinking stimulated by contemporary historical actuality. The outlook schooled in eternal truths submerges in the detail of the given moment, which is pregnant with decision and bursting under the pressure of anticipated possibilities.

Thus, Foucault discovers Kant as the first philosopher, an archer who aims his arrow at the heart of the most actual features of the present and so opens the discourse of modernity. Kant leaves behind the classical dispute over the exemplary pre-eminence of the ancients and the comparable stature of the moderns. Instead he involves diagnostic thought – which acquires for him a new function – in that turbulent process of self-assurance that forms the horizon of a new historical consciousness which has kept modernity in constant motion until the present. A philosophy now engaged with actuality is concerned with the 'rapport "sagittal à propre actualité"', with the relationship of modernity to itself. Hölderlin and the young Hegel, Marx and the Young Hegelians, Baudelaire and Nietzsche, Bataille and the Surrealists, Lukács, Merleau-Ponty, the precursors of Western Marxism in general, and, not least of all, Foucault himself all contribute to the honing of that modern consciousness of contemporaneity which made its appearance in philosophy with the question 'What is enlightenment?' The philosopher turns contemporary; he emerges out of the anonymity of an impersonal endeavour and reveals himself as a flesh-and-blood human being toward whom every clinical investigation of each individual contemporary period that confronts him must be directed. Even in retrospect, the period of enlightenment is still presented by the description it gave itself: it designates the entry into a kind of modernity which sees itself condemned to creating its self-awareness and its norms out of itself.

If this is even a paraphrase of Foucault's own train of thought, the question arises: how does such a singularly affirmative under-standing of modern philosophizing, always directed to our own actuality and imprinted in the here-and-now, fit with Foucault's unyielding criticism of modernity? How can Foucault's self-understanding as a thinker in the tradition of the enlightenment be compatible with his unmistakable criticism of this very form of knowl-edge of modernity?

Kant's philosophy of history, the speculation about a state of freedom, about world-citizenship and eternal peace, the inter-pretation of revolutionary enthusiasm as a sign of historical 'progress toward betterment' – must not each line provoke the scorn of Foucault, the theoretician of power? Hasn't history, under the stoic gaze of the archaeologist Foucault, frozen into an iceberg covered with the crystals of arbitrary formations of discourse? (This, at least, is the view of his friend Paul Veyne.) Doesn't this iceberg, under what appears as the cynical gaze of the genealogist Foucault, have a much different dynamic than the actualizing thinking of modernity cares to acknowledge – namely, a senseless back-and-forth of anonymous processes of subjugation in which power and nothing but power appears in ever-changing guises? Using Kant as an example, didn't Foucault reveal in *The Order of Things* the peculiar dynamic of that will-to-truth which is stimulated anew by each frustration to an increased and in turn failed production of knowledge? The form of knowledge of modernity is characterized by the following aporia: the cognitive subject, having become self-referential, rises out of the ruins of metaphysics in order to take on, in full awareness of its finite powers, a project that would demand unlimited power. As Foucault demonstrates, Kant transforms this aporia into the structural principle of his epistemology; he reinterprets the limits of our finite apparatus of cognition into the transcendental conditions for infinitely progressing knowledge. A subject, thus structurally strained to the limits, is enmeshed in an anthropocentric mode of knowledge. And this whole field is now occupied by the 'sciences of man', which Foucault perceives as an insidiously operating disciplinary power. In any case, what it has achieved with its pretentious, in no way resolved, claims is a dangerous façade of universally valid knowledge behind which in reality is hidden the facticity of domination of knowledge rooted in the will-to-power. Only in the wake of this boundless will-to-knowledge arise the subjectivity and self-consciousness with which Kant begins.

If we return to the text of Foucault's lecture with these considerations in mind, we note certain precautionary measures against all-too-striking contradictions. To be sure, the enlightenment, which inaugurates modernity, does not imply for us just an arbitrary period in the history of ideas. However, Foucault explicitly warns against the pious attitude of those who are out merely to preserve the remains of the enlightenment. Foucault explicitly (if only parenthetically) establishes the connection to earlier analyses. Today, he notes, it can no longer be our task to maintain enlightenment and revolution as ideal models. Much more important is an investigation into the particular historical motivating forces which have simultaneously prevailed and concealed themselves in universalistic thought since the late eighteenth century. Foucault rejects those thinkers who, in pursuit of an abstract order, proceed from Kant's epistemological question; still in search of the universal conditions by which propositions can be really true or false, they are captives of an 'analysis (*Analytik*) of truth'. Despite these precautions, one is surprised that Foucault presents those subversive thinkers who try to interpret their own contemporaneity as the legitimate heirs of Kantian critique. They repeat that fundamental diagnostic question, first posed by Kant, of a modernity in search of self-assurance, under the altered conditions of their own time. Foucault sees himself as carrying on this tradition. For Foucault, the challenge of the Kant texts he has chosen is to decode that will once contained in the enthusiasm for the French Revolution, namely, the will-to-knowledge, which the 'analysis of truth' was unwilling to concede. Up to now, Foucault traced this will-to-knowledge in modern power-formations only to denounce it. Now, however, he presents it in a completely different light, as the critical impulse worthy of preservation and in need of renewal. This connects his own thinking to the beginnings of modernity.

Within the circle of the philosophers of my generation who diagnose our times, Foucault has most lastingly influenced the *Zeitgeist*, not least of all because of the seriousness with which he perseveres under productive contradictions. Only a complex thinking produces instructive contradictions. Kant entangled himself in an instructive contradiction when he declared revolutionary enthusiasm to be an historical indicator that reveals an intelligible arrangement of mankind in the world of phenomena. Equally instructive is another contradiction in which Foucault becomes enmeshed. He contrasts his critique of power with the 'analysis of truth' in such a fashion that the former becomes deprived of the normative yardsticks that it would have to borrow from the latter. Perhaps the force of this contradiction caught up with Foucault in this last of his texts, drawing him again into the circle of the philosophical discourse of modernity which he thought he could explode.

What Is Maturity?
Habermas and Foucault on
'What Is Enlightenment?'

HUBERT L. DREYFUS AND PAUL RABINOW

Two hundred years ago, in 1784, Kant responded to the question posed by a Berlin newspaper: 'What is enlightenment?', by equating enlightenment with the attainment of maturity through the use of reason. Since then the meaning of this claim has been debated periodically. Today the question has again been raised in the public arena by the two thinkers who could legitimately be called the heirs to this debate, because they embody two opposed but equally serious and persuasive ways of reinterpreting the philosophic life through understanding the relation between reason and the historical moment. The question also lies behind the writing of those anti-thinkers who, in the name of post-enlightenment and postmodern discourse, question seriousness in general.

The bulk of this paper will be concerned with the confrontation about 'seriousness' which has opposed Michel Foucault and Jürgen Habermas on the legacy of the enlightenment. Foucault's untimely death cut short this important emerging debate cast in terms of the relation between society, critical reason and modernity. But even had Foucault lived, this debate was unlikely to have become a true dialogue because each of these thinkers understands these terms and their relationship in incompatible ways. Both see society as in some way primary but they differ profoundly as to what a modern society is and could be. They both acknowledge that an understanding of critical reason is an essential task of contemporary philosophy but they understand critique and reason in radically different ways. And finally both agree with Kant that *maturity* is the task of the modern age, but Habermas's and Foucault's concepts of *modernity* and *maturity* stand in clear opposition. And both stand in opposition to the anti-thinkers.

Foucault and Habermas agree with Kant that critical reason begins with the rejection of the Western project of developing a theory which mirrors substantive universal truths about human nature. Foucault and Habermas also agree with Kant that the problem of moral action and social bonds must be faced anew once revealed religion and metaphysics have lost their authority. Both accept that *maturity* consists in man's taking over responsibility for using his critical rationality, and that critical rationality consists in the unflinching examination of our most cherished and comforting assumptions. Thus Kant was able to articulate a fundamental change taking place in Western understanding which still gives his philosophy contemporary relevance.

From here on Foucault's and Habermas's interpretation of the significance of critical reason, society and modernity and their relation diverge dramatically. For Habermas, Kant's *modernity* consists in his recognition of the limits of reason, i.e., in his rejecting reason's dogmatic claim to provide truths about transcendent reality. Kant's *maturity* consists in showing us how to save the critical and transcendental power of reason and thus the triumph of reason over superstition, custom, and despotism – the great achievement of the enlightenment.

Habermas's updated version of Kant's philosophy claims that a pre-critical attempt to offer a metaphysical grounding can be replaced with an analysis of the conditions in which the ideal speech community presupposed in all uses of language can be realized. Habermas argues that this analysis of the conditions for validating truth is the way to unify critical reason and social concerns, and thereby answer Kant's challenge. This account of the communicative use of language is essentially intellectualist. One must be able to reach agreement about valid claims on the basis of the reasons offered in the justification of the propositional content, the truthfulness or sincerity of the intentional expression and rightness or appropriateness of the speech act. The analysis of these universal social conditions necessary for the undistorted use of language provides the procedural normative criteria by which one can evaluate social organizations. Immaturity for Habermas is the failure to recognize and advance the increasing explicitness of the 'assumptions' underlying communicative practice. It leaves us open to the dangerous seductions of *phronesis*, art and rhetoric – ways of communicating and reaching agreement which, according to Habermas, our culture has outgrown. Maturity consists in clarifying the form social organizations take in a given epoch, judging their adequacy for promoting human community, and assuming responsibility both for the way they are and for making them more adequate.

For Habermas, then, the problem of modernity, a unique historical problem, consists in preserving the primacy of reason articulated most recently and fully in Kant's enlightenment critique while facing up to the loss of metaphysical ground of our substantive beliefs. Maturity is the discovery of the quasi-transcendental basis of community as all we have and all we need, for philosophy, and human dignity.

Foucault like Habermas holds that our modernity begins with Kant's attempt to make reason critical, i.e., to establish the limits and legitimate use of reason. But Kant's attempt to show that this critical use of reason is its true universal nature is not what is original and important for Foucault. Foucault does not deny that Kant is attempting to preserve the normative role of reason in the face of the collapse of metaphysics. But rather than seeing Kant as announcing a universal solution, Foucault uses Kant's essay as a diagnostic of a particular historical conjuncture. What Foucault finds distinctive and insightful in Kant's essay is a philosopher qua philosopher realizing for the first time that his thinking arises out of and is an attempt to respond to his historical situation. In Kant's terms one assumes one's place as a 'cog in the machine' and one's responsibility for thinking about current social and political issues, only one thinks of these issues not in terms of their content, but by determining to what extent current proposals promote universal procedural or critical rationality. Thanks to this transcendental turn one could heroically give up dependence on religion and/or metaphysics as a basis for justifying and criticizing the practices of the epoch, thus maintaining the possibility of universal, ahistorical, normative judgements concerning the form of one's society while appreciating Frederick's well-disciplined armies.

Foucault reinterprets Kant's linking of the historical moment, critical reason and society as a challenge to develop a radically new version of what it means to lead a philosophical life.

The critical ontology of ourselves has to be considered not, certainly, as a theory, a doctrine, nor even as a permanent body of knowledge that is accumulating; it has to be conceived as an attitude, an ethos, a philosophical life in which the critique of what we are is at one and the same time the historical analysis of the limits that are imposed on us and an experiment with the possibility of going beyond them.[1]

This critical ontology has two separate but related components: work on oneself and responding to one's time.

As a modern example of work on oneself, Foucault points to Baudelaire's advocacy of 'the asceticism of the dandy who makes of his body, his behaviour, his feelings and passions, his very existence, a work of art'. Foucault writes: 'Modern man, for Baudelaire, is not the man who goes off to discover himself, his secrets and his hidden truth; he is the man who tries to invent himself. This modernity does not "liberate man in his own being"; it compels him to face the task of producing himself'.[2] Like the dandy and the existentialist, Foucault proceeds from an ethos which renounces the guidance of religion and law and science, while renouncing as well the dedication to realizing the deep truth of the self which these, each in their own way, foster.

For Foucault an ethics does not seek to save the whole culture or, like existentialism, to save the individual from what Kierkegaard thought of as the irreversible levelling of the present age. Nor like early Heidegger does Foucault think that the deep truth about human existence is that there is no deep truth, so that maturity consists in facing up to the groundlessness of our being-in-the-world. And, despite overtones of the Sartrean ideal of the meaning-giving subject authentically facing up to its own nothingness, Foucault never read our current situation into the human condition and then tried to base an ethics on authentically living in terms of presumed universal human reality. This project, shared by early Heidegger, Sartre and Habermas, identifies maturity with the acceptance of universal structures of human existence revealed by Western philosophy and so rules out dialogue on equal terms with other ways of being human until they reach maturity by acknowledging that these conditions are universal. This is obviously not a position Foucault shares.

For Baudelaire and early Sartre inventing one's self doesn't change society but at most affronts it. Foucault, however, is not seeking to make his life an outrage, nor is he seeking to provide an example for direct imitation; rather he seeks to be responsive to what is intolerable in his current situation so as to frame both a general problem and to embody a style of action which allows us to see, through a test of limits, that there are meaningful differences in the kinds of society we can have and there are ways of being human worth opposing and others worth strengthening.

But, Habermas asks, how can Foucault legitimately make such normative judgements once he has defined maturity as the relinquishing of dependence on the authority of law, religion and science as well as formal universal claims put forward by philosophers? From Habermas's point of view, Foucault's propounding a political theory without justification must be pure decisionism.

Habermas highlights this seemingly arbitrary position in his lectures on Foucault.[3] He points out what he takes to be an unresolved tension between Foucault's intense ethical and political commitments, on the one hand, and his ability, qua archaeologist, to view the most meaningful concerns of our society with bemused indifference, on the other. Foucault's subtle, sophisticated, but not well-conceptualized ironic stance towards the present is bound to look paradoxical to anyone who agrees with Kant in identifying maturity with the acceptance of limits on reason in order to preserve traditional philosophical seriousness. This is an issue we discussed with Foucault on a number of occasions, and it is one which is so close to the centre of his work and life that he was not often clear about it. However, as we will seek to show, the interpretation of Foucault as making normative but unjustified theoretical claims, as well as taking unargued-for political positions, although plausible (and sometimes echoed in Foucault's interviews and conversations) is not consistent with Foucault's general approach.

While the heirs of German philosophy attack Foucault for being arbitrary and ungrounded, the French post-philosophers (and their American literary critical followers) attack him for not being arbitrary enough. From this perspective, Foucault once understood the subversive role of language and desire, but when he turned to the investigation of non-discursive practices and the productive role of power relations, both the form and the content of his work seem to come dangerously close to accepting traditional norms of clarity and analysis. Habermas is right, however, Foucault is not following in the philosophical tradition of using language to represent reality, nor is he using language as a vehicle for undistorted communication. But, *pace* Habermas, neither is Foucault prepared to abandon himself to the free play of self-referential signifiers. To those who believe that language speaks only to itself and only about itself through us, it is bound to seem, as Leo Bersani put it recently in language typical of this tendency, 'as if he were seeking a new, desexualized austerity in the very act of writing, to elude the exuberant despair of being had, of being penetrated, and possessed, by a language at once inescapably intimate and inescapably alien'.[4] True, rather than deconstructing texts to reveal their attempt to conceal their self-reference to their own textuality, Foucault uses texts as clues to other social practices. Indeed, like the pre-Platonic rhetoricians, Foucault uses language to articulate an understanding of our situation which moves us to action.

Already in *The Order of Things*, in analysing the cogito and the unthought, Foucault showed how a philosophical belief in an autonomous, meaning-giving subject finds itself necessarily involved in the infinite task of making sense of its own unthinkable foundations. He was clear that this infinite task called into question the cogito. But at the time of *The Order of Things* Foucault suggested that what resists representation offers hope of a way out of the analytic of finitude. He shared the Lacanian interpretation of Freudian psychotherapy as the discovery of '. . . the region where representation stands in suspense . . .' and where 'conflicts and rules [find] their foundation in the naked opening of Desire'.[5] But he devoted the last decade of his life to rethinking this position.

Once Foucault turned his attention to the productive dimension of power relations and formulated the repressive hypothesis as part of the problem, he reinterpreted the analytic of finitude genealogically, not merely as an epistemic structure, but also as a stage in the constitution of Western man as subject/object. Thus Foucault sought to 'free himself from a schema of thought which was quite current then'.[6] He began to construct an interpretation in which the opposition of law and meaningless desire was understood as an historical phenomenon that had shaped him and everyone else. This is what made the Lacanian view that there was a structure of the human subject seem plausible, even true. Which for Foucault '. . . revient à mettre hors champ historique le désir et le sujet du désir . . .'[7] Inverting the relation of question and answer, Foucault began to investigate how it came to be taken for granted that subjects, desires and interdictions were given as concepts for explaining history and society. The central interpretative problem for Foucault became the constitution of ourselves as men of desire from Christian confessional practices through the Freudian hermeneutic of sexuality.

Foucault is not trying to construct a general theory, nor deconstruct the possibility of any metanarrative; rather, he is offering us an interpretive analytic of our current situation. It is Foucault's unique combination of genealogy and archaeology that enables him to go beyond theory and hermeneutics and yet to take problems seriously. The practitioner of interpretive analytics realizes that he himself is produced by what he is studying; consequently he can never stand outside it. The genealogist sees that cultural practices are more basic than any theory and that the seriousness of theory can only be understood as part of a society's on-going history. The archaeological step back that Foucault takes in order to see the strangeness of our society's practices does not mean that he considers these practices meaningless. Since we share cultural practices with others, and since these practices have made us what we are, we have, perforce, some common footing from which to proceed, to understand, to act. But that foothold is no longer one which is universal, guaranteed, verified, or grounded.

Foucault does not propound a normative theory, yet as Habermas points out, Foucault's work certainly has a normative thrust. Quite consistent with his interpretive stance, Foucault has, like Richard Rorty and Robert Bellah, abandoned the attempt to legitimate social organization by means of philosophical grounding. Foucault goes even further and refuses to articulate normative principles. Building on Heidegger and Wittgenstein, he uses language to shift what we see as our social environment. And he positively embraces what Austin would call the perlocutionary effect of language as a means for moving us to concerted action. What makes one interpretive theory better than another on this view has yet to be worked out, but it has to do with articulating common concerns and finding a language which becomes accepted as a way of talking about social situations, while leaving open the possibility of 'dialogue', or better, a conflict of interpretations, with other shared discursive practices used to articulate different concerns.

Foucault's interpretive approach consists in identifying what he takes to be our current problem, describing with detachment how this situation arose and, at the same time, using his rhetorical skills to reflect and increase shared uneasiness in the face of the ubiquitous danger as he extrapolated it. Thus the tension between Foucault's preferences and his insight into the impossibility and undesirability of offering a theory justifying his action only seems a contradiction; this very tension provides the elements for a coherent method.

As we attempted to show in our book, Foucault's approach is not as subjective nor as objective as it might seem. Already in his book on madness he was engaged in a project which started from the observation of social practices which he took to be a source of personal distress and social danger. After the book on madness he consistently repudiated hermeneutics as the revealing of nonrational forces making possible and thereby undermining rationality. He nonetheless, not unlike Nietzsche and Heidegger on some readings, was offering an interpretation. The shifting boundary between reason and unreason, health and disease, science and pleasure, while presented with detached objectivity (Foucault's happy positivism), could not be singled out as the basic issue of our time by any objective method, but neither could Foucault's interest in writing history from the perspective of these concerns be taken to express merely his personal situation.

Seen in this light Foucault as genealogist is anything but cynical. He would, indeed, be cynical if his aim were to attack every form of power and undermine every truth claim. He has, however, been at pains to criticize and distance himself from those who speak the truth against power as if truth and power were self-evidently external to each other, and from those who think that society has a single *telos* which has finally been exposed by the increasing rationalization of the life-world. Foucault has never taken this position. He sees the job of the intellectual as one of identifying the specific forms and specific interrelationships which truth and power have taken in our history. His aim has never been to denounce power *per se* nor to propound truth but to use his analysis to shed light on the specific dangers that each specific type of power/knowledge produces.

In his analysis of modern society Foucault has diagnosed 'bio-power' as the form of power/knowledge specific to our time. Bio-power can be defined as the way our current practices work so as to bring about an order in which Western men will be healthy, secure and productive. When one sees how bio-power works, one has a grid of intelligibility for understanding the sort of human beings we are today. Foucault does not claim that bio-power is the only thing going on with us. Rather he makes the interpretive claim that if you look at things this way a lot will fall into place.

Foucault has singled out the practices that produce modern objects and described them in *Discipline and Punish*. The *History of Sexuality* was to have traced the development of those practices of confession and self-mastery which have made us into self-interpreting, autonomous, meaning-giving subjects. These disciplinary and confessional practices, in Foucault's view, converged after the enlightenment to form a coherent form of life which we call modernity.

Modernity is not a specific historical event, but a historical conjuncture which has happened several times in our history, albeit with different form and content: for example, the breakdown of the traditional virtues in Athens at the time of Socrates and Aristophanes, the decline of the Hellenistic world, the end of metaphysics at the time of Kant. This breakdown results in a specific attitude toward reality which, to differentiate it from a subjective state, Foucault calls an *ethos*. In a modernity-crisis, a taken-for-granted understanding of reality ceases to function as a shared background in terms of which people can orient and justify their activity and the modernist response is heroically and lucidly to face up to the collapse of the old order. Such was the attitude of Thucydides and the Sophists in Greece, the Gnostics and Stoics in Alexandria and, of course, Kant.

This modern ethos, the lucid and heroic ability to face up to these crises, is not yet what Foucault calls maturity. Maturity consists in not only a *heroic* but what Foucault calls an ironic stance toward one's present situation.

What Foucault means by ironic is not simple, but understanding it will help us differentiate his view of maturity from those other contemporary candidates. It is an abandonment of traditional seriousness while preserving active engagement in the concerns of the present. It seeks to avoid preserving some special status for truth which grounds serious involvement, and also to avoid the frivolity which arises when one abandons all seriousness to dance on the grave of god, or *logos*, or phallo-centrism, etc.

The ironic stance results in seeking in the present those practices which offer the possibility of a new way of acting. For Baudelaire the modern attitude meant looking for moments of 'poetry within history', poetry within the ugly modern world just as it is and has to be: 'wherever the sun lights up the swift joys of the depraved animal'. Hölderlin, the poet Heidegger admires, knew like Baudelaire that the tradition was finished, and sought to preserve hints of other possible ways of being which might come together one day in a new cultural paradigm, which Heidegger, echoing Hölderlin, calls a new god.[8]

Foucault thinks that what he is doing is not poetry if poetry is what Baudelaire thought it was – an aesthetic transformation of our perceptions of our present world with an acceptance of its monotony and homogeneity. Like Heidegger, Foucault wants to change our world. But whereas Heidegger considered his effort a failure because it did not help bring about a new god, Foucault never lamented the default of god nor himself looked for a new one. Nor did he consider it his main task to offer alternative possibilities for acting. He was simply trying to diagnose the contemporary danger, and in his last works, providing the elements of a modern ethics.

On Foucault's reading Kant was modern but not mature. He heroically faced the loss of the grounding of human action in a metaphysical reality, but he sought to reground it in epistemology. He saw that a philosopher must bring his philosophy to bear on his present situation, but sought a way to reconcile human dignity with the current social arrangements rather than face their dangers. Not that it was too early for anyone to have the ironic maturity of a Baudelaire. Thucydides had faced the collapse of Athenian democracy, without denying his Athenian loyalty and without accepting the superiority of Spartan discipline. While not embracing any normative account of what would constitute an ideal society, he preserved a critical stance towards the present. While realizing that forms of the Athenian disaster would be endlessly repeated, he did not give up hope, and even noticed hints in the practices of the Athenians that their new constitutional democracy would preserve some of the best features of the Athenian and Spartan societies.[9]

The thesis of this paper is that maturity would consist in at least being willing to face the possibility that action cannot be grounded in universal, ahistorical theories of the individual subject and of writing, or in the conditions of community and speaking, and that, in fact, such attempts promote what all parties agree is most troubling in our current situation. On this interpretation our modernity begins with Kant's attempt to ground moral norms and theoretical truth claims in the empty formal structure of human finitude. But Kant's heroic break with natural law and the cosmic order, far from opening up the possibility for diversity, shifted the debate to the search for the structure of human finitude which would provide universal norms for human action. The latest versions of this attempt, now turned linguistic, continue to be universal and prescriptive. On the one hand, the anti-thinkers, on the basis of an ahistorical theory of the human subject as empty desire constituted by the arbitrary play of signifiers, condemn seriousness and insist that everyone be relentlessly ironic. On the other hand, the heroic defenders of seriousness, on the basis of a theory of communication, condemn what they consider irresponsible irony, and, in an exasperated tone, seek to remind everyone of his or her duty to conform to the universal imperative implicit in all speech acts. Foucault resisted both these philosophical universalizing positions. In his last interview he straightforwardly asserted: 'The search for a form of morality acceptable by everyone in the sense that everyone would have to submit to it, seems catastrophic to me.'[10]

Foucault has noted the tendency of the anti-thinkers to appeal to theory to defend their attack on seriousness:

> The whole relentless theorisation of writing which we saw in the 1960s was doubtless only a swansong. . . . it was precisely a matter of theory . . . that [the writer] needed scientific credentials, founded in linguistics, semiology, psychoanalysis. . . .[11]

Likewise, from this interpretive perspective, the defenders of philosophy look more sober than mature. If, for example, one looks back at the arguments by which Habermas arrives at his universal norms, we find him making two crucial interpretive moves disguised by the fact that they constitute the heart of our philosophical tradition. First he claims that 'understanding is the inner *telos* of language',[12] thereby privileging the communicative use of language without taking into consideration that other philosophers of language such as Heidegger and Charles Taylor have interpreted language as that which *first opens up* an arena for action and communication by letting things appear *as* something. A second more tenuous and consequential move occurs when, after equating the use of language with performing speech acts, he proceeds to exclude the perlocutionary effect of what is said and assert that ideally only the illocutionary content should play a role in reaching agreement. This move excludes rhetoric as well as authority based on accumulated experience, and thus further reduces language from its communicative to only its intellectualist function. Because they presuppose these two important interpretive reductions, Habermas's universal objective communicative norms turn out to be quite modern in their ungroundedness.

A further intellectualist implication of the claim that only illocutionary content should play a role in reaching agreement is that it leaves out of account the shared cultural meanings in the context of which agreement is reached. Habermas would surely agree with the observation that rational discussion takes place on the background of a shared understanding of what is important, what makes sense, what is in the true/false language game, what counts as a reason, etc. But in order to support his contention that no factors outside the explicit intentional content should be allowed to affect and perhaps distort communication, he needs to hold that our shared background understanding is in fact being made more and more explicit in late Western capitalistic culture, and that, wherever there is a problem, the background can be made sufficiently explicit so as to allow rational evaluation.

The difficulties this position encounters can be seen most clearly in the enlightenment's favourite case of rational activity, natural science. One of the current conflicts of interpretation concerning how scientific disciplines work is whether paradigms play an essential role in their practices. If Thomas Kuhn and his followers are right, normal science is a practice in which scientists argue by reference to shared exemplars. Moreover, agreement is possible precisely because no attempt is made to rationalize these paradigms as a set of shared assumptions, i.e., to make the paradigm part of the intentional content of the assertions being assessed. In such cases lack of concern with rational procedure makes possible rational communication about content.

While their insistence on frivolity makes the anti-thinkers immature, Habermas's refusal to admit his indebtedness to interpretation makes his position professorial. Neither position is mature and both, in the name of modernity, foreclose any possibility of dialogue with other acknowledged interpretive positions such as Foucault's. Taking up Kant's task two centuries later seems to require giving up any attempt to identify critical reason with universal objective grounding, and current social conditions as a step ahead of all other societies on the way to social maturity.

It would be more in keeping with Kant's task of using critical reason maturely and with Foucault's idea of an interpretive analytics: (1) to describe and interpret our current practices so as to understand what aspects of our modernity we have to accept as inescapable; (2) to characterize the sense, diffusely manifest in the practices of some epochs that in some pervasive way things have gone awry (Heidegger's 'distress' and Foucault's 'dangers' seem either too subjective or objective to capture this crucial dimension of interpretation); (3) to articulate further a widely shared sense that the promise of the enlightenment has yet to be fulfilled; (4) to go beyond thinkers and anti-thinkers in taking a stand toward the present that does not legislate empty universal norms but encourages conflicts of interpretation; (5) and to go beyond Foucault in rhetorically strengthening the post-enlightenment practices that are positive, such as many of our technological, legal and medical advantages, and in identifying and preserving pre-enlightenment practices which have so far escaped rationalization and normalization.

As Foucault showed us in his last books and in his life, there is a kind of ethical and intellectual integrity which, while vigorously opposing justifications of one's actions in terms of religion, law, science or philosophical grounding, nonetheless seeks to produce a new ethical form of life which foregrounds imagination, lucidity, humour, disciplined thought and practical wisdom.

Notes

1 Michel Foucault, 'What Is Enlightenment?', in Paul Rabinow (ed.), *The Foucault Reader* (New York: Pantheon, 1984), p. 50.
2 Ibid., pp. 41–2.
3 Jürgen Habermas, *Des philosophische Diskurs der Moderne* (Frankfurt: Suhrkamp, 1985).
4 Leo Bersani, 'Pedagogy and pederasty', *Raritan*, Summer 1985, p. 21.
5 M. Foucault, *The Order of Things* (New York: Random House, 1970), p. 374.
6 M. Foucault, *Histoire de la sexualité*: vol. 2, *L'Usage des Plaisirs* (Paris: Gallimard, 1984), p. 10.
7 Ibid.
8 Martin Heidegger, 'What Are Poets For?', in *Poetry, Language, Thought* (New York: Harper & Row, 1971), pp. 94–5.
9 *Peloponnesian War*, book 8, section 97.
10 M. Foucault, interview in 'Le Retour de la morale', *Les Nouvelles* (28 June 1984); p. 37.
11 Michel Foucault in *Power/Knowledge: Selected Interviews and Other Writings 1972–1977*, ed. Colin Gordon (New York: Pantheon), p. 127.
12 Jürgen Habermas, *Theorie des kommunikativen Handelns*, vol. 1 (Frankfurt: Suhrkamp, 1981). 'Verständigung wohnt als Telos der menschlichen Sprache inne', p. 387.

Power, Repression, Progress: Foucault, Lukes, and the Frankfurt School

DAVID COUZENS HOY

Power always has been and probably always will be contested. But it is less certain that the *concept* of power will always be contested by social scientists and philosophers. Although social philosophers may be fated to perpetual quarrelling, social scientists should be able either to define univocally central theoretical concepts like power or dismiss such concepts if they continue to elude quantifiable refinement.[1] Power appears to be a concept that, if not understood, would also make it impossible to understand what a society is. Conflicting political views of what society is and ought to be could not even be compared and disputed if they involved different and incommensurable understandings of the meaning of central terms like society and power.

However, debates in current social theory about what social forms of power are legitimate appear to involve different conceptions of what legitimation and power mean. The problematic character of these concepts has been increased by Michel Foucault's efforts to rethink the concept of power, especially in terms of its connection with the social forms that *knowledge* takes. In this paper I situate Foucault's conception of 'power/knowledge' (*pouvoir/savoir*) in relation to other attempts to clarify the nature of power, particularly by comparing it with the procedure of 'ideology criticism' as developed by the Frankfurt School and more recently by the Oxford social theorist Steven Lukes. I will show that although Foucault's notion of power is nontraditional, it is not incommensurable with more

© 1981 by David Couzens Hoy. Reprinted from *Tri Quarterly*, vol. 52, Fall 1981, pp. 43–63.

traditional social theory (of both the Marxian and liberal types). Seeing power from another perspective and modifying the concept accordingly allows Foucault to reassess our understanding of power, repression, and progress in modern society.

Power

If social scientific models use different conceptions of power, their findings are likely to diverge and there may be no neutral way to assess which model is correct. In *Power: A Radical View* Steven Lukes attempts to show that the social sciences are in fact relativistic in this respect, and to identify the conflicting models of power currently in use. He assumes that Talcott Parsons was justified in lamenting that 'unfortunately the concept of power is not a settled one in the social sciences'.[2] In order to evaluate the debate between Parsons and C. Wright Mills, the elite theorist, about the question, 'which kind of conception of power offers a superior basis for theorizing about American society?'[3] Lukes argues that power is a concept that is 'ineradicably value-dependent' and 'essentially contested'.[4] To say that basic scientific concepts are essentially contested is to say, with the philosopher W. B. Gallie, that they 'inevitably involve endless disputes about their proper uses on the part of their users'.[5] As Lukes states (more strongly), their very definition and any given use are 'inextricably tied to a given set of (probably unacknowledged) value-assumptions which predetermine the range of [their] empirical application'.[6]

If Lukes were right about the use of the concept of power in the social sciences, his point would illustrate the general thesis of other philosophers of science who believe the sciences do not conform to the traditional empiricist conception of scientific method. Mary Hesse is one of these, and she maintains that theory choice in the social sciences is even more relativistic than in the natural sciences, since the principles used to select social theories would be guided by a variety of values. Unlike a natural scientist's explanation, which relies on the pragmatic criterion of predictive success, a social scientist's evaluation of the data in terms of a commitment to a social theory would be more like taking a political stand.[7]

Lukes similarly holds that to engage in disputes about social scientific concepts like power 'is itself to engage in politics'.[8] It is not surprising, then, that he labels his own model for the study of power 'a radical view'. Lukes does not mention the perhaps too obvious fact that his model differs from the other two models he identifies by incorporating what the Frankfurt School came to call 'ideology criticism'. The distinguishing feature of the radical view of power is that it insists on a distinction between subjective and real interests, as well as a related difference between observable (whether overt or covert) and latent conflicts of interests. Observable conflicts would be acknowledged by those involved in the conflict, but latent ones would not be readily admitted due to ideological distortion of the agents' perception of their real self-interest.

To explain how this difference arises in the study of power, we must begin with a definition of power. To Lukes, power is essentially 'power over', which is to say that power is exercised by A over B when A affects B in a manner contrary to B's interests. The social scientific question is, then, how to study the exercise of power-over when so defined. The first model Lukes identifies relies on an obvious answer: identify a conflict of interest between A and B, and study the decision-making process involved in A's success in getting B to do something B would not do otherwise. However, a second model recognizes that power is exercised, not only in making a decision that goes against B, but in the 'nondecision' or 'nonevent' that keeps the questions that are in B's interests, but not in A's, from even arising. So conflicts of interest can be not only overt but covert, and both can be studied.

These two models are overly 'behaviourist' from Lukes's point of view insofar as they restrict their observations to actual behaviour and conscious decisions. More significantly, they assume that B's interests are what B takes them to be. Lukes believes the behaviourist models are inevitably inadequate because, although 'A may exercise power over B by getting him to do what he does not want to do, . . . he also exercises power over him by influencing, shaping or determining his very wants'.[9]

Lukes's view is thus similar to the Frankfurt School's notion of domination, since Critical Theory also assumes that what B's interests really are may be different from what B consciously takes them to be, whether B is an individual or a social group. The concept of ideology relies on the assumption that if socially oppressive conditions had not forced a social group, B, to have certain interests, B would see that its real interests were different from the interests it appears to have as a result of oppression. The effects of power are often repressed: both the dominating group and the dominated may be unconscious of the exercise of power. Therefore, the study of power must also identify what Lukes calls latent conflicts of interest, which are presumably the result of ideological distortion of real interests.

Lukes and the Critical Theorists are fully aware of the central difficulty with the radical model. What the model postulates as the real interests are not readily identifiable or justifiable as such, especially since B is not likely to assent to them. Lukes follows Antonio Gramsci in thinking that some evidence can be obtained through the contrast between what an oppressed social group does in normal times, when it is submissive, and what it does in abnormal times of social unrest and upheaval. Lukes goes further, though, and maintains that evidence can be found even in normal times:

> We are concerned to find out what the exercise of power prevents people from doing, and sometimes even thinking. Hence we should examine how people react to opportunities – or, more precisely, perceived opportunities – when these occur, to escape from subordinate positions in hierarchical systems. In this connection data about rates of social mobility can acquire a new and striking theoretical significance.[10]

The neo-Marxian justification of the counterfactually postulated 'real' interests tends to be a priori, or at least not simply an empirically verifiable matter from within a given ideology. In contrast, Lukes suggests that such justification can appeal to evidence, and is an empirical as well as a philosophical matter. Given this insistence on verifiability, however, his central thesis that power is an essentially contested concept, and his related contention that the social sciences are relativistic, can be misleading. His presentation indicates that the third model is not a more encompassing model that could incorporate the other models as special cases. The models are incompatible. Given this incompatibility and the relativistic appeal to the inability to resolve the contest between the various conceptions, one might assume that Lukes believes there are no grounds for deciding between the apparently incommensurable theories. Lukes himself would then appear to be making his own radical model an exception. He would be committing what Maurice Mandelbaum aptly dubs the self-excepting fallacy,[11] since Lukes could not believe both in the truth of the results of his model and in relativism.

Lukes clearly believes, however, in the inadequacy of the behaviourist models and the superiority of the radical model. Reasons can be given, he thinks, for one view rather than another, and in particular, for the claim that one view enables one to see further and deeper than another. Such a claim can only be made out by bringing out both the implications of alternative views and their unacceptability. That they are unacceptable can always be denied: hence essential contestability. But the contending positions are not incommensurable: the contests are real ones.[12]

So the radical theorist can argue that limiting the conception of power as the behaviourist theorists do is unacceptable, and that the radical view is in fact acceptable, at least in part because it is *not* empirically vacuous. Thus, the radical theorist can claim to be discovering truths missed by the other theorists while recognizing that they will read the data differently, perhaps even 'misconstruing' it altogether. He is thus not claiming the essential incontestability of theories in the manner that Paul Feyerabend does in *Against Method* or that Foucault seems to in his earlier works.[13]

Whether Lukes's response is satisfactory, however, depends on another feature of the problem and of his theory. When Bertrand Russell defines power as 'the production of intended effects', he fails to capture Marx's thought that power is not reducible to individuals' intentions.[14] The familiar point is that although history happens as a result of individuals' wills, it does not happen as they will it. The debate in the social sciences is thus between those who see power as exercised by (individual *or* institutional) *agents* and those who see it as a result of structural factors within systems. This debate is not between methodological individualists and methodological holists, but between voluntarist and structuralist theories. For Marx the economic structure of society is independent of and not reducible to agents' willed intentions. Subsequent theorists, from Weber to Parsons and from Lévi-Strauss to Althusser, stress structure rather than agency. Lukes includes Foucault with the structuralists in contrast to Lukes's own emphasis on agency,[15] and we shall see shortly whether that assessment is correct.

The larger question is, then, whether the historical, human subject still has an explanatory role – 'an issue,' says Lukes, 'very much alive within contemporary Marxism, dividing so-called Hegelian "historicists" and "humanists" from their structuralist adversaries'.[16] Lukes sides with those who link power to human agency. His reason is that to talk about an *exercise* of power is necessarily 'to assume that it is *in the exerciser's or exercisers' power* to act differently'.[17] Structuralists, he thinks, are necessarily determinists and could not allow this counterfactual. They would thereby lose the ability to attribute responsibility for certain consequences to identifiable agents. Since in Lukes's view an attribution of power is at the same time an attribution of (partial or total) responsibility for certain consequences, he believes the emphasis on structure to the exclusion of subjects and agents fails to capture the meaning of 'power', or at least of the locution 'power over' (as opposed to 'power to').

The question he does not address is why a theory rejecting the concept of the subject and the voluntarist view Lukes prefers must be so strictly deterministic. While, in fact, the structuralists Lukes is opposing (Althusser, Balibar, and Poulantzas) do seem to be determinists, the controversy about free will and determinism is different from the question whether structural systems or human agents are to be used as the basic explanatory units in the social sciences. The claim that a structural system restricts what an agent *can* do does not entail the claim that such a system determines what an agent *will* do. Correlatively, the system itself need not remain unaffected by what agents in fact do. Furthermore, the sense of 'power over' is not stretched by attributing responsibility to a system (and to the individuals who perform strategic functions within it). The social scientist or historian could still ask, what if the system were different in this or that respect? This counterfactual would appear to satisfy Lukes's requirements.

In fact, whatever the merits of the historiographical studies themselves, Michel Foucault's books on power are interesting precisely for the reason that he appears to be working out a method for the historical study of power (what he calls an 'analytics of power') without relying either on the concept of the subject or on the assumption that the structural relations he is identifying are not subject to change. Foucault thinks of power as intentionality without a subject, such that power relations are intentional and can be described without being attributed to particular subjects as their conscious intentions. Power is for him an explanatory concept, but not all explanations are causal. So without attributing power either to conscious agency or to underlying forces like the modes of production, Foucault thinks he can explain contemporary society by mapping the network of power relations that have evolved historically. Before evaluating Foucault's projected model in contrast to the other models, we must ask whether his view can be stated without paradox and with sufficient detail to satisfy Lukes's demands on a model of power.

Repression

'Nietzsche, Freud, Marx' is not only the title of an essay by Foucault, but also an indication of the intersection at which his own conception of power can be located. Nietzsche is particularly important, for the uniqueness of Foucault's work is that it develops and applies Nietzsche's method of genealogy. A central hypothesis of the genealogical explanation of phenomena in terms of will-to-power is that 'knowledge is power'. Of course, Bacon had asserted this before Nietzsche, but he meant something different. For Nietzsche and Foucault the 'is' connecting knowledge and power does not indicate that the relation of knowledge and power is one of predication such that knowledge leads to power. Rather, the relation is such that knowledge is not gained prior to and independently of the use to which it will be put in order to achieve power (whether over nature or over other people), but is already a function of human interests and power relations.

Nietzsche indicates this stronger claim by identifying the will-to-knowledge with the will-to-power, and Foucault accordingly labels what he is studying 'power/knowledge'. The slash suggests that *for his purposes* power and knowledge are not to be studied separately. From his perspective there is little point in speaking even about the relation between knowledge and power, since these are not so readily distinguishable.

A certain caution is in order here, however. Just as Nietzsche claims that the will-to-power is only a hypothesis or an interpretation and not a fact, Foucault's power/knowledge should be regarded as a heuristic device, a pragmatic construction to be tested in terms of its value in reconstructing the history of the sciences of man and of society. Foucault's enterprise is neither epistemological nor ontological, for he is not making claims about what knowledge and power are ultimately. Rather, his project is historical, and his construction of the concept of power/knowledge is a device for studying the social and scientific practices that underlie and condition the formation of beliefs. He is offering an interpretation of how what counts as knowledge and power has historically come to be so counted. His question is not the epistemological one: whether given pieces of what is taken as knowledge are, in fact, true. If his historical account is illuminating, however, it would indicate that there would be no context-free, unhistorical way to decide that epistemological question.

The hint of relativism in this last point indicates a certain affinity with Lukes's position. Foucault's history of the prison, translated as *Discipline and Punish*, illustrates Lukes's point that historians and social scientists using similar data but relying on different conceptions of power will arrive at different and perhaps even competing understandings and explanations. In fact, Foucault himself suggests in *Discipline and Punish* that his major competitor is Kirchheimer and Rusche's *Punishment and Social Structure*, published in 1939 through the exiled Frankfurt School.[18] His attitude toward that book is echoed in his attempt, during an interview, to distance his own thinking from that of another member of the Frankfurt School, Herbert Marcuse:

> I would also distinguish myself from para-Marxists like Marcuse who give the notion of repression an exaggerated role – because power would be a fragile thing if its only function were to repress, if it worked only through the mode of censorship, exclusion, blockage and repression, in the manner of a great Superego, exercising itself only in a negative way ... Far from preventing knowledge, power produces it ... The fact that power is so deeply rooted and the difficulty of eluding its embrace are effects of all these connections. That is why the notion of repression which mechanisms of power are generally reduced to strikes me as very inadequate and possibly dangerous.[19]

Whereas Marxians think of power negatively – as domination, coercion, manipulation, authority, or, in short, repression – Nietzscheans think of power as producing positive as well as negative effects. Nietzsche does not completely condemn the ascetic will-to-truth-and-knowledge that is the other side of the will-to-power, for instance, but on the contrary commends the self-discipline that leads to the great variety of its achievements. Foucault's need to rewrite Kirchheimer and Rusche's book is prompted, then, by the inadequacy of their conception of power and their one-sided focus on repression. Foucault objects to those who use the infrastructure–superstructure model of materialist explanations, and who would see the change from one system of punishment to another as being correlated with and required by the change from one system of production to another. Foucault challenges their historiography by suggesting, first, that they achieve these correlations only by failing to explain the persistence of an extreme degree of torture and thus of the earlier style of punishment, and, second, that they omit altogether an account of how it is possible for the human body even to be constituted as labour power.[20]

Concerning the first point, Foucault thinks that accounts like Kirchheimer's and Rusche's are correct to see torture as an effect of a system of production in which labour power has a low utility and commercial value. He also thinks that torture is more likely in a society with a more casual attitude toward death than in subsequent times as a result of superstructural factors like Christian values, but also of factors like frequent plagues, famines, and high child mortality rates. The inadequacy of base–superstructure explanations is that they explain neither how the older forms of punishment can persist so long after the older order is gone nor why there is such a variety of practices of punishment.

This criticism leads Foucault to the second point: explanations based on the merely negative conception of power as repression will fail to see that what also needs to be explained is how the kinds of knowledge necessary for controlling the human body and labour power have emerged. His history is intended to show that the human body could have been constituted as labour power only if there were a technology or a 'knowledge' of the body that made it possible to organize and subjugate bodies into docile, useful roles. Furthermore, this subjugation is not something imposed on one class (the oppressed workers) by another (the dominant class); it increasingly permeates and characterizes all aspects of society. Foucault is concerned to chart what he calls the process of 'normalization' – the increasing rationalization, organization, and homogenization of society in modern times.

Foucault's own conception of the importance of his studies of power configurations is, then, that they show the inadequacy of and provide an alternative to the Frankfurt School's still too traditional conception of the relation of power and knowledge. The very ideas of false consciousness and of the critique of ideology imply the possibility of nonideological thinking or of *true* consciousness. Ideology is the result of distortion introduced by the oppressive exercise of power by the dominant class. Only if such distortions were seen through and the repression dispelled would true consciousness be possible.

The concept of ideology, Foucault thinks, thus implies the traditional view that knowledge must be disinterested, that truth can be ascertained only in the absence of distorting power relations. Of course, he may be wrong in ascribing this view of the independence of power and knowledge to all Critical Theorists. Adorno calls his project *negative* dialectics, and refrains from making positive claims about what ought to be. More recently, Jürgen Habermas began a defence of the procedure of ideology criticism with an explicit rejection of the traditional view that 'the *only* knowledge that can truly orient action is knowledge that frees itself from mere human interests'.[21] Habermas goes on to develop an account of knowledge not as disinterested, but as always conditioned by human interests. A closer inspection of Habermas's conclusions, however, may well vindicate Foucault's thesis, for finally Habermas thinks that *emancipation* from power is a fundamental interest of knowledge-acquisition.[22] This freedom would be gained when knowledge reflects back on itself and sees through false authority to the true consensus that could be achieved only in a totally emancipated society of autonomous, responsible persons.[23] Foucault may also be right, to some extent, even about the earlier Critical Theorists. Adorno and Horkheimer do say in their introduction to the *Dialectic of Enlightenment* that their 'critique of enlightenment is intended to prepare the way for a positive notion of enlightenment which will release it from entanglement in blind domination'.[24] They thereby hold out the traditional hope for progress away from coercive social power by freeing knowledge and reason from ideologically coerced distortion.

The notion of real interests Lukes and other social scientists appeal to is different from what Habermas has constructed. For Lukes, as for the early Frankfurt School, the question is, how to determine that A is affecting B contrary to B's real interests if, as a result of ideological coercion, B is not actually aware of these interests. Furthermore, except when there is a conspiracy, the critique of ideology could show that if B is affected contrary to B's real interests, then it is also contrary to A's real interests for A to coerce B. So A acts against both A's and B's real interests when exercising power over B. Given knowledge of the real interests, the exercise of coercion would be counterproductive, and perhaps even self-contradictory, so power ought to disappear.

Lukes does not explicitly link his model to this conception of *Ideologiekritik*. Nevertheless, his model requires that the investigator be able to reason counterfactually that, being rational agents, the exercisers of power would have acted differently knowing the real interests of all concerned.

While structuralist determinists are committed to the assumption that agents are not true causes of events, and therefore cannot say the agent could have acted differently, Foucault is not similarly restricted. The technology of power does not causally determine particular actions;

only makes them probable. So A could have options open, and, similarly, both A and B would have different interests if they were not caught up in this net of ideological coercion. As Foucault says, 'Another power, another knowledge'.[25]

This close a connection between power and knowledge challenges, however, the appeal to real interests – if by real interests one means a set of interests existing independently of some social organization or set of purposes. Like Nietzsche, Foucault does not think there are any givens that remain constant. Even the human body, the lowest common denominator throughout all historical change, is transformed over time by various technologies of power. In volume 1 of *The History of Sexuality*, for instance, Foucault suggests that sex is not a biological given, but a complex construct resulting from a certain way of conceiving human beings, namely, as personalities totally permeated by one of several modes of sexuality.[26] His playful suggestion that there has been 'sex' only since the nineteenth century (and that we would be better off not wanting to 'have sex') probably comes down to the claim that physical acts are always construed under a particular mode of description, and over a period of time these modes of description (or forms of knowledge) come into and go out of cultural and even scientific fashion.

For Foucault, then, the project of *Ideologiekritik* deludes itself if it posits the possibility of knowledge emancipated from power relations, or if it thinks that it could decide what our interests would necessarily be in the absence of any social coercion. Consider the only case Lukes supplies of what he calls a 'clear-cut' instance where real interests can be specified using the counterfactual reasoning his radical model requires. He cites Matthew Crenson's study of the factory town of Gary, Indiana, whose citizens did not lobby against severe air pollution until 1962.[27] Their sociologically similar neighbours in East Chicago had taken action against comparable air pollution in 1949. Lukes comments, 'The empirical hypothesis that those citizens, if they had the choice and fuller information, would prefer not to be poisoned is more than plausible (on the assumption that such an alternative did not entail increased unemployment).'[28] While of course it seems to be in everyone's real interest not to be poisoned, assumptions like that in parentheses work toward vitiating the empirical character of the hypothesis. Adding *ceteris paribus* clauses empties the counterfactual hypothesis about the real interests people would have had. Many workers would probably choose to risk an unhealthy environment (which is not exactly equivalent to being poisoned) if the rewards were sufficient. Furthermore, Gary was a one-company town, so any individual who actively worked against pollution was working against the company, and would have risked being fired (although unemployment might not have increased, since someone could have been hired to replace him).

Foucault's approach has an advantage if, in making knowledge relative to interests or power configurations, it also can criticize without assuming an external standpoint outside the power configuration in order to specify the real interests of the parties involved. In order to accomplish this, Foucault must revise the concept of power. He takes an initial step by revaluing power, insisting that power is positive and productive, not simply repressive; it is, he reminds us, not always suffered but sometimes enjoyed. We cannot understand this revaluation, however, without recognizing the other conceptual revisions he introduces. Like Lukes, Foucault wants to describe how power is *exercised*, and he sees that there would be no power if it were not exercised by agents. Foucault even uses the phrase 'exercise of power' frequently, as in the title of his essay, 'How is Power Exercised?'[29] There he says explicitly that power is exercised by individuals or groups of individuals. This statement should show that he is neither arguing against methodological individualism nor attributing ontological status and causal efficacy to historical forces or to institutions or ideologies as opposed to individuals. He denies that power is a mysterious *substance* with a nature, essence, and origin. By his own admission Foucault is nominalistic about power, even willing to say that 'power' does not exist (only local exercises of power are real) – thereby affirming that he is not offering a metaphysics of power.

Unlike Lukes and the Frankfurt School, however, Foucault does not think of power as something possessed by those who exercise it. In *Discipline and Punish* he remarks that he wants to describe how 'power is exercised rather than possessed'.[30] This implies that power is not a property, possession, or privilege. Power is not simply what the dominant class has and the oppressed lack. Power, Foucault prefers to say, is a strategy, and the dominated are as much a part of the network of power relations and the particular social matrix as the dominating. As a complex strategy spread throughout the social system in a capillary fashion, power is never manifested globally, but only at local points as 'micro-powers'. Power is not something located in and symbolized by the sovereign, but permeates society in such a way that taking over the state apparatus (through a political revolution or coup) does not in itself change the power network.[31]

Including the background network of social practices in the definition of power in this way may appear to be simply stipulative. Lukes, for instance, wants to locate power more specifically so that empirical inquiry can determine the answer to the question, *who* exercises power over whom? Foucault, given his pragmatic nominalism, could admit that his definition is stipulative, but he would also have to show that it is informative. His analytics of power is not intended to tell us what power really is, but only where to look. He is interested in a slightly different question from Lukes's. He wants to explain how it is possible for A to affect B when who A happens to be is arbitrary (the 'subject' being itself an effect of the historical transformations of power/knowledge).[32]

Foucault hears the question about how power is exercised (in his essay with that title) as what he calls the 'flat and empirical' question, 'how does it occur?' This asks both where power actually has been exercised (an empirical question for historians and social scientists) and how individuals can have power over others. This latter question does involve matters of social theory that are not strictly empirical, and it also points to a further difference between Foucault and Lukes. Whereas for Lukes power is exercised by one agent over another, Foucault, who wishes to avoid suggesting that power is possessed by subjects, sees power exercised in the effect of one action on another action. As the effect of 'une action sur des actions', power can be explained only by understanding the 'field of possible actions' in which the action occurs. The description of this field would presumably include an account, not only of the way that action inhibits some other possible actions, but also of the manner in which that action increases the probability of other actions. Power is not, Foucault says, like two adversaries confronting each other; it is comparable to 'government' in a broad sense, where to govern means 'to structure the field of the eventual actions of others'.

To offer an analogy, to which Foucault does not appeal explicitly (although his explanation of what *strategy* means in 'How is Power Exercised?' approaches it), consider a game of chess. Power in a game of chess is paradigmatically exercised, according to Lukes's model, by one piece over another at the moment of capture. On Foucault's model, the capture is indeed a 'micro-power', but it is also the effect of the overall arrangement of the pieces at the time as well as of the strategy leading up to and including the capture.

Two of Foucault's points are illustrated here. First, power is not a function only of the capturing set of pieces, but is a result also of the possible resistance by the opposed set. To program a computer for chess, presumably one must include some considerations about counter-attacks. Second, notice that the strategy explains why the one piece can or ought to capture the other, but it does not *determine* that the piece must capture the other (unless the game is at a point where no other move is possible without, for instance, checkmate). Opportunities are sometimes deliberately delayed for larger future gains, as well as simply overlooked. In fact, the notion of a real interest could be introduced here as an interest relative to a strategy: B might believe it is in B's interest to sacrifice a piece but, given B's strategy, the sacrifice would be a mistake.

There is nothing a priori, metaphysical, or reductive about 'real' as opposed to 'apparent' interest here, but the distinction can still be used to point out the difference between what people think about what they are doing and what might actually be occurring. Thus, just as the Frankfurt School criticizes the belief in enlightenment – that is, the belief in the possibility of the acquisition of knowledge and self-understanding undistorted by coercion – and argues that the desire for enlightenment conceals a desire for control, Foucault maintains that modern 'humane' punishment is not what it seems. The shift from 'atrocious' torture to humane 'correction' may look like increased humanitarianism and progressive recognition of the autonomy of the individual. However, Foucault argues that what looks like a new respect for humanity is, rather, a more finely tuned mechanism of control of the social body, a more effective spinning of the web of power over everyday life. Whereas reformists thought the objective of the juridical and penal systems was to punish less atrociously, Foucault thinks that the real point of the penal system is 'not to punish less, but to punish better; to punish with an attenuated severity perhaps, but in order to punish with more universality and necessity; to insert the power to punish more deeply into the social body'.[33]

While Foucault might think that models based on a conception of power as repression do not explain enough about power, by expanding his own notion of power to include the background network of social practices he opens himself up to the charge that his notion of power is so broad as to be indeterminate and empty. This charge against Foucault is frequently heard, but it is often advanced for two quite different reasons. Some readers think Foucault's approach to power is too philosophical, or even metaphysical, and not empirical enough. Others find Foucault's studies too empirical and historiographical, and not sufficiently theoretical.

These stylistic objections are connected with two conceptual problems. First, one might think that since Foucault does not view power as something that some possess and others lack, there is no contrast class for his concept of power – a concept without a contrast class being vacuous. However, Foucault could reply to this charge through his pragmatic nominalism. He could maintain he is not claiming that power is everything, as Nietzsche, for instance, sometimes implies that everything, including the material universe, is will-to-power. Foucault's indication that his concept of power is not metaphysical suggests that he is looking at social relations with the purpose of studying power/knowledge configurations, without claiming that social relations could not be studied under different descriptions for different purposes (although his position would imply that there is no such thing as a purposeless social description). Furthermore, the concept of power as he uses it is necessarily differential. Just as for Nietzsche there is no one thing that will-to-power is, and thus different will formations require different genealogical analyses, for Foucault the contrast class for one power/knowledge configuration is another such configuration (for instance, an earlier one, like the model of punishment before the French Revolution in comparison with the one after it).

A second problem about the potential vacuity of power concerns Foucault's apparent inability to think beyond the present and to speculate about whether future power configurations might be better or worse than the present one. Foucault holds the quite plausible view that to live socially is to be involved in power relations, and that the notion of society without power relations is only an abstraction. Beyond power there is only more power, so one could easily slip into fatalism and accept the injustices of the present in favour of possibly greater injustice in an unknown, future power configuration.

Foucault can argue against this fatalism, but his view does risk being interpreted that way, just as Nietzsche's attempt to overcome nihilism is often interpreted as another version of nihilism. Because he combines power and knowledge, Foucault also must abstain from the traditional tendency to think of the overcoming of repression as progress. The antithesis to power is usually thought to be freedom. Progress thus occurs when power gives way to freedom, with uncoerced knowledge being a crucial instrument in this transition. Recognizing Foucault's reasons for breaking with the traditional identification of power and repression, we must now examine the consequences of also abandoning the notion of progress.

Progress

Foucault's histories are not only histories of the past, but also critical analyses of power configurations persisting in the present. He is writing, he says in *Discipline and Punish*, a 'history of the present'.[34] The historiographical knowledge presented in his studies is not assumed to be untouched by power relations. He does not exempt his own knowledge from the claim that knowledge is always produced by power configurations and is tied to interests and purposes (and not necessarily those one explicitly acknowledges). Yet Foucault criticizes the present without suggesting how the future could be better. He maintains, for instance, that the technology of power used in prisons has spread to all aspects of society. The problem is not the prison *per se*, but the increasing normalization of modern culture. The whole society has become 'carceral', and there is no outside.[35] Are we then irrevocably trapped in the prison of the present? Can we even dream of escape if there is no outside?

The language of liberation usually implies that criticism of a society involving repression is possible only from the envisioned liberated standpoint transcending that society. According to the traditional liberal theory, criticism would have no point unless progress were possible, and progress means liberation. Marxian theories speak similarly. Ideology, for instance, is frequently construed as thought distorted by oppressive power relations, such that genuine, nonideological knowledge could be attained only in a nonoppressive society. Thus, the early Lukács infers that in a society characterized by the class struggle, all thinking would be ideological. Even the proletariat could not claim to have 'true consciousness', since its outlook would be coerced by the circumstances.[36] Power thus produces false consciousness – what Foucault would call a 'regime of falsity' – and true consciousness would occur only in a classless society, liberated from repressive power.

For Foucault, the repressive hypothesis overlooks the Nietzschean hypothesis that power makes possible not only falsity but also truth. Since there is no knowledge that is not also describable as part of a power network, the concept of ideology is misleading in hypothesizing progress toward a nonideological knowledge freed from power struggles.

Foucault's critique of the identification of power and repression may be put as the inverse of the charge that his conception of power is vacuous because it lacks a contrast. Foucault could counter that both liberal and Marxian theories tend to use an empty and abstract notion of freedom. From his claim that a society without power relations would be an abstraction, it follows that freedom in the absence of power would be equally abstract. Construing progress as liberation from repression and positing a completely liberated, unrepressed society leaves freedom without a genuine contrast.

Whether or not this countercharge is, in fact, valid, there is no doubt that it is mistaken to think Foucault's notion of power is idiosyncratic because it is not contrasted in the traditional way with liberty. Foucault makes clear in 'How Is Power Exercised?' that he does continue to think of liberty as the opposite of power. Rather than think of the logical, conceptual opposition between power and freedom when concretely instantiated in social relations as an antagonism, however, Foucault prefers to think of it as an 'agonism' – a reciprocal contest, where each incites and struggles with the other in a 'permanent provocation'.

Freedom is both the condition and the effect of power. It is a condition because power is only exercised on free beings, and it is an effect since the exercise of power will invariably meet with resistance, which is the manifestation of freedom. Foucault illustrates this point by suggesting, contrary to ordinary parlance perhaps, that because a slave in chains has no real options of alternative action or escape, such a degree of slavery could not be called a power relation, especially since it would not make sense to think of anyone desiring to be a slave in this sense. While this claim about slavery is not convincing, it does emphasize that power for Foucault requires the deployment of a field of possible actions, such that why one particular action occurs rather than another becomes the focus of empirical investigation.

This last point brings out again that Foucault's interest in power is really not that of a metaphysician who wants to believe freedom is progressively replacing power. Rather, his perspective is that of the historian or social scientist who wants to understand why one action rather than others occurred, so that a series or set of actions can be described without imposing on it a teleological evaluation about whether or not it was essentially for the better. Foucault's abjuration of the rhetoric of progress must be understood, then, as a methodological consequence of his pragmatic nominalism. If power is to be taken nominalistically – not as a real substance or as a property, but simply as a name for a complex strategy or grid of intelligibility –

then, admittedly, this grid could be mapped in different ways, and there is no final, privileged, or foundational mapping. Foucault's own work takes place in the indeterminate boundary between general history and the history of science, and his theory is sketched only insofar as it provides a useful recommendation to historians about how to write histories, and how to look at both the past and the present. Thus, when Foucault was asked in an interview about his claim in an earlier book that we must 'free historical chronologies and successive orderings from all forms of progressivist perspective', he responded,

> This is something I owe to the historians of science. I adopt the methodical precaution and the radical but unaggressive scepticism which makes it a principle not to regard the point in time where we are now standing as the outcome of a teleological progression which it would be one's business to reconstruct historically: that scepticism regarding ourselves and what we are, our here and now, which prevents one from assuming that what we have is better than – or more than – in the past.[37]

When the interviewer then suggested to him that science has always postulated that man progresses, Foucault insisted,

> It isn't science that says that, but rather the history of science. And I don't say that humanity doesn't progress. I say that it is a bad method to pose the problem as: 'How is it that we have progressed?' The problem is: how do things happen? And what happens now is not necessarily better or more advanced, or better understood, than what happened in the past.[38]

This exchange shows that Foucault is not giving up all hope for emancipation, but only the belief that emancipation necessarily results from the growth of knowledge. His philosophical stance is not that of the epistemologist who, like Kant, models progress on the development of modern science. Even if science is still our best example of knowledge, scientific knowledge also has a history. Whereas the Kantian epistemologist assumes that the growth of knowledge is progress toward the goal of unified science, the historian has another option. Rather than simply assuming we now understand better what our predecessors were trying to do (as Kant claims about his relation to Plato),[39] the historian may have to hypothesize that we do not understand better, only differently. Another historian of science, Thomas Kuhn, also operates on the principle that 'there are many ways to read a text, and the ones most accessible to a modern are often inappropriate when applied to the past'; he therefore offers his students the following hermeneutical maxim: 'When reading the works of an important thinker, look first for the apparent absurdities in the text and ask yourself how a sensible person could have written them. When you find an answer, I continue, when those passages make sense, then you may find that more central passages, ones you previously thought you understood, have changed their meaning.'[40] French historians such as Canguilhem made similar points, and thus Foucault is not being original when he tries to write history without imposing a 'progressivist perspective'. Rather, he is following a sensible procedure in demurring from the 'Whiggish' assumption that *we* know better *now*, for otherwise we could not have reached as far as we have.

Where Foucault's histories get their radical effect is precisely through their ironic reversal of the common Whiggish outlook. In *Discipline and Punish*, for instance, we read a story of progress, but it is the progress of the spread of the discipline of the prison throughout the whole society. Reading such a history of supposed progress is not, then, as the Whig would expect, reassuring and edifying, but frightening and disturbing. Progress is not necessarily for the better, Foucault intends us to realize, and, indeed, no one welcomes news about the progress of a cancer.

Thus, Foucault's writings do not eliminate the use of teleological narrative in historiography, but, like Nietzsche's genealogies, his histories question the tendency of the present to evaluate its own progressiveness positively. In contrast to standard Marxian *Ideologiekritik*, Foucault can challenge the supposed superiority of the present without postulating an ideology-free understanding that transcends current power relations. While believing in the inevitability of free resistance to the imposition of power, and thus while not despairing about the possibility of some successful emancipation, Foucault can avoid the illusion that his own thinking is itself necessarily progressive and free of desires constituted by power relations.

While Foucault's view may be free of paradox, it is still subject to other objections. Social criticism is also empty if it is not efficacious. A post-Marxian conception of power must nevertheless remember that the goal is not only to comprehend the world, but to change it. In the absence of some standard (such as universal freedom) by which to measure social progress, is Foucault's shrill attack on the increasingly carceral society only *ressentiment*, a bitter but ineffectual rage? Nietzsche's analyses of other cultural forms of *ressentiment*, such as the priestly or the scholarly asceticism, show that *ressentiment* quickly leads to resignation, fatalism, and nihilism. In fact, Nietzsche's lack of a plausible social theory is often taken as a sign that his own thinking is bourgeois, and that theoretical denunciation lacking practical goals is ineffectual.

Foucault's probable response to this objection must be constructed without obscuring the difference between his notion of power and the 'para-Marxist' notion of domination he rejects. He accepts the Marxian critique of the theory that power is held by the sovereign, or a political elite, and then forced on the rest of society from above. He agrees that power does not spread from the top down, but rather rises from the bottom. Thus, the study of the modes of production will be more revealing than a history that is merely political. His critique of Kirchheimer and Rusche shows, however, that the modes of production constitute only one factor, and that there are others that are consubstantial.[41] In fact, the top–bottom metaphor is unusable, for there is no absolute top or bottom, but rather a grid or network. A linguistic model comes closer to capturing Foucault's conception than a causal, materialist model. Foucault tends to think of the network as being like a grammar, which conditions what can be uttered in a language but does not determine which actual utterances emerge (and when).

Both the sovereignty and the materialist conceptions of power are akin in thinking of change and progress as taking place *totally*. Foucault resists this totalizing or, as he sometimes says, 'totalitarian' thinking, maintaining that there is no such thing as power as a whole, and no standpoint from which the totality can be viewed or evaluated. In 'How Is Power Exercised?' he asserts that 'there is no first and fundamental principle of Power which dominates society down to the least detail'. We experience power only in diverse and multiple ways at the 'micro-level' when we find ourselves subjected to particular exercises of power (or more rarely, and perhaps without understanding our own facility or authority, when we exercise power over others).

For Foucault, then, neither comprehending the world nor changing it depends on grasping (in either the theoretical or the practical sense) the totality, since the concept of totality is not applicable to his understanding of power as an open-ended network or grid. Rather, his 'micro-physics' of power depends on comprehending power by first studying the everyday practices where individuals continually experience micro-powers, the particular confrontations with and resistances to impositions of power. Charting these micro-powers will then reveal the more general terrain of the larger social battles taking place. Change does not occur, however, by transforming the whole at once but only by resisting injustices at the particular points where they manifest themselves. To continue the military metaphor, which Foucault uses frequently, the battle can be won only by the continued efforts of the individual combatants.

This response is consistent with Foucault's desire to develop a notion of power that avoids political theory, but it is not sufficient to rebut the charge of vacuity entirely. Calling for change for its own sake, without specifying the appeal of one direction of change over others, is not genuinely efficacious. This point has been made before, but its importance is far from clear. As a criticism of Foucault it may well be off-target. Foucault may be able to write his histories in such a way that the question of determining the ultimate basis of social progress does not even arise. A historian who is interested only in showing that change occurs and what the changes involved actually are (how, for instance, a discipline spread itself throughout society so quickly) need not invoke the progressivist perspective. The problem of explaining progress may also drop away for a historian who does not think the question *why* change occurred could ever be answered sufficiently.

It may not be Foucault but his readers who are inconsistent when they want him to avoid causal and teleological explanations of historical changes and then expect him to appeal to causal or teleological principles for progressive social change. His project is probably too limited to justify the strident polemical tone of his criticism of the carceral society. His polemics have led perceptive reviewers like Clifford Geertz to speculate that in *Discipline and Punish* Foucault has abandoned the Whiggish or progressivist perspective only to take up a reverse Whiggism: 'We seemed to be faced,' says Geertz, 'with a kind of Whig history in reverse – a history, in spite of itself, of The Rise of Unfreedom.'[42]

There is no doubt that Foucault's negative assessment of normalization and his hasty elevation of Bentham's Panopticon to the predominant social paradigm of our society warrant this reading. His conception of power, however, is as incompatible with the reversed Whiggish stance as with the traditional Whiggish one. Foucault's voice may sound like that of the prisoner who wants out and cannot get out, but since Foucault is talking about our inability to get out of our own place in history, he is surely correct in this regard. Although his history may sound like a Rousseauean story of the rise of unfreedom, it could not be, for there is in Foucault no hint of an age of innocence. The contrast between earlier and later ages can only show them to be different in detailed respects, not better or worse on the whole. We can also certainly regret what is bad for us now without knowing either that things were better before or that proposed ways to mend things will not actually produce other injustices.

Foucault's notion of power does not necessarily entail the fatalism that his critics perceive. The historical subjugations that Foucault portrays are real enough, and will be resisted even as they are experienced. Foucault's genuine contributions to social praxis, like anyone else's, can therefore only be at the micro-level. But he can also make a contribution at the philosophical level by calling into question the belief in progress and the complacent Whiggish insistence on the necessary superiority of the present.

Foucault's own denial in 'How is Power Exercised?' that his conception entails fatalism emphasizes the 'agonism' between freedom and power, the contest between them being an 'incessant political task' that is 'inherent in all social existence'. In other words, he, like Lukes, is probably suggesting that it is part of the power struggle in society to decide how power itself should be conceived (in order to achieve the best outcome in this struggle). Power will thus be an essentially contested concept because it will rely on political judgements; but this fact should not obscure the agonistic contest that makes it important to challenge alternative models of power. Fatalism will result only if one believes dogmatically that one's knowledge of the nature of social power is itself not conditioned by power relations.

Both Lukes's and Foucault's models of power have an advantage over their rivals in being self-reflective and thus capable of not exempting themselves from their own claims. But Foucault's model differs from neo-Marxian models in his insistence that the network of practices makes particular actions possible and significant, but not dialectically necessary. Rejecting the dialectic of contradiction, Foucault insists that saying there is no social existence without power relations does not entail that particular, oppressive power relations are necessary. The field of possibilities that gave rise to such current injustices as Foucault perceives in the carceral society also contained, historical analysis brings out, alternatives that were not acted upon. Whether these alternatives, if pursued, would have been better or worse, the historian cannot say. All the historian can point out is that the landscape of action is littered with many events that do not fit into the materialistic account of the necessary progression of history.

Foucault's critique of progress cuts against liberal notions as well as dialectical ones. The Whiggish or even Pragmatist belief that things are, on the whole, getting better all the time is also too general to be confirmed empirically, and is therefore not part of Foucault's concern. Although he gives up the notion of universal progress, his programme need not abandon the hope for emancipation, if by that one means the resistance at particular points to local exercises of power.

This reply will not satisfy those who want global solutions to injustice, but it still represents a plausible critique of the rhetoric of progress, and of the traditional intellectual's desire to have a total understanding before engaging in concrete action. Foucault's *theory*, then, is a form of critical theory, since it does not construct a new, systematic set of principles, including a 'primary and fundamental principle of Power', but settles for counterattacking the remnants of holistic, metaphysical assumptions in other social theories. Foucault's praxis is essentially that of the historian, but not the disengaged historian. Showing historically that the belief in progress has actually had the effect of increasing repression would itself be a concrete and productive achievement. Whether Foucault has, in fact, succeeded in either of these respects is still an open question, but we can at least avoid confusing his social vision with those it contests.

Notes

1 Rom Harré, for instance, argues that what sociologists call power is reducible to other factors and is thus simply a dramatic fiction. See *Social Being: A Theory for Social Psychology* (Totowa, N.J.: Littlefield, Adams, 1980), pp. 233–5.
2 Steven Lukes, *Power: A Radical View* (London: Macmillan, 1974).
3 Steven Lukes, 'On the Relativity of Power', in S. C. Brown (ed.), *Philosophical Disputes in the Social Sciences* (Atlantic Highlands, N.J.: Humanities Press, 1979), p. 272.
4 Lukes, *Power*, p. 26.
5 W. B. Gallie; cited by Lukes, *Power*, p. 26.
6 Lukes, *Power*, p. 26.
7 Mary Hesse, 'Theory and Value in the Social Sciences', in Christopher Hookway and Philip Pettit (eds), *Action and Interpretation: Studies in*

the Philosophy of the Social Sciences (Cambridge University Press, 1978), pp. 1–16. Further, see D. C. Hoy, 'Hermeneutics', *Social Research*, vol. 47 (Winter 1980), pp. 649–71.

8 Lukes *Power*, p. 26.
9 Ibid., p. 23.
10 Ibid., p. 48.
11 Maurice Mandelbaum, 'Subjective, objective, and conceptual relativisms', *Monist*, vol. 62 (October 1979), p. 405; see his earlier essay, 'Some instances of the self-excepting fallacy', *Psychologische Beiträge*, vol. 6 (1962), pp. 383–6.
12 Lukes, in Brown (ed.), *Philosophical Disputes*, p. 272.
13 Paul Feyerabend, *Against Method* (London: New Left Books, 1975).
14 See Lukes, *Power*, p. 22.
15 Lukes, 'Power and Structure', in his *Essays in Social Theory* (New York: Columbia University Press, 1977), pp. 8 and 199, n. 30.
16 Ibid., p. 3. I would argue that Hegel himself is not a 'Hegelian' in this controversy if *Geist* can be interpreted as the name for a structural system and not a particular subject.
17 Lukes, *Power*, p. 55 (italics added).
18 Michel Foucault, *Discipline and Punish: The Birth of the Prison*, trans. Alan Sheridan (New York: Vintage 1979), p. 24. See Colin Gordon's 'Afterword' in Michel Foucault, *Power/Knowledge: Selected Interviews and Other Writings, 1972–1977* (New York: Pantheon, 1980), pp. 234ff.
19 Foucault, *Power/Knowledge*, p. 59.
20 See Foucault, *Discipline and Punish*, pp. 24–30 and 54f.
21 Jürgen Habermas, *Knowledge and Human Interests*, trans. Jeremy J. Shapiro (Boston: Beacon Press, 1971), p. 301.
22 Ibid., p. 287.
23 Ibid., p. 314.
24 Adorno and Horkheimer, *Dialectic of Enlightenment* (New York: Seabury Press, 1972), p. xvi.
25 See Foucault, *Discipline and Punish*, pp. 27–30.
26 Michel Foucault, *The History of Sexuality, vol. 1: An Introduction*, trans. Robert Hurley (New York: Pantheon, 1978).
27 Matthew A. Crenson, *The Un-Politics of Air Pollution: A Study of Non-Decisionmaking in the Cities* (Baltimore: Johns Hopkins Press, 1971). Cited by Lukes, *Power*, pp. 42–6.
28 Lukes, *Power*, p. 46.
29 Unpublished at the time of the writing of the present essay, Foucault's 'How Is Power Exercised?' appeared in translation as an 'Afterword' to *Michel Foucault: Beyond Structuralism and Hermeneutics*, Hubert Dreyfus and Paul Rabinow (University of Chicago Press, 1982).
30 Foucault, *Discipline and Punish*, p. 26.
31 Ibid., p. 27.
32 Ibid., p. 28.
33 Ibid., p. 82.

34 Ibid., p. 31.
35 Ibid., pp. 228, 301.
36 Georg Lukács, *History and Class Consciousness*, trans. R. Livingstone (Cambridge, Mass.: MIT Press, 1968), p. 228.
37 Foucault, *Power/Knowledge*, p. 49.
38 Ibid., p. 50.
39 Immanuel Kant, *Critique of Pure Reason*, A314/B370.
40 Thomas S. Kuhn, *The Essential Tension: Selected Studies in Scientific Tradition and Change* (University of Chicago Press, 1977), p. xii.
41 See Foucault, *Power/Knowledge*, pp. 159–60.
42 Clifford Geertz, review of *Discipline and Punish*, *New York Review of Books* (26 January 1978), p. 6. Compare Richard Rorty, 'Beyond Nietzsche and Marx', *London Review of Books*, vol. 3; and Ian Hacking, 'The Archaeology of Foucault', *New York Review of Books* (14 May 1981), reprinted here.

Foucault and the Imagination
of Power

EDWARD W. SAID

By the time power had become an explicit and central theme in his work in the early seventies, Foucault had already spelled out his theory of discourse and discourse analysis in *L'Ordre du discours* and *L'Archéologie du savoir*. While they looked forward to what he would later write, both of these works built and elaborated upon still earlier work, his archaeological studies in *Histoire de la folie*, *Les Mots et les choses*, and *Naissance de la clinique*. What is, I think, deeply compelling about the continuity of Foucault's early with his middle works is his highly wrought presentation of the order, stability, authority, and regulatory power of knowledge. For him *les choses dites* are objects placed on the registers of knowledge much as formations of soldiers are located tactically and strategically on fields of battle. When Borges says, 'I used to marvel that the letters in a closed book did not get mixed up and lost in the course of a night', it is as if he were providing Foucault with the start of a historical quest, to understand how statements acquired not only their social and epistemological status, but their specific density as accomplished work, as disciplinary convention, as dated orthodoxy.

Thus Foucault's view of things was, as he implied to the journal *Hérodote* in 1976,[1] spatial, which makes it somewhat easier to understand his predilection for the analysis of discontinuous, but actual spaces, territories, domains, and sites – libraries, schools, hospitals, prisons – rather than, as one would expect in a historian, a tendency to talk principally about continuities, temporalities, and absences. It is probable that Foucault's admirably un-nostalgic view of history and the almost total lack in it of metaphysical yearning, such as one finds in heirs to the Hegelian tradition, are both ascribable to his geographic bent. So marked is this in Foucault, and so deeply linked to his vision of statements as carefully fashioned extensions of institutions and instruments of governance, that it is usefully elucidated by someone who, although in a different and much earlier tradition than Foucault, resembles him in many ways, Ibn Khaldun, the great fourteenth-century Arab historiographer and philosopher. In the *Muqadimah* Ibn Khaldun says that the science of history is unique because while related to rhetoric and civil politics it is different from both. He thus sees the historian's task as work taking place between rhetoric, on the one hand, and civil politics, on the other. This, it seems to me, describes Foucault's analytical attitude uncannily well: statements for him carry more weight than ways merely of speaking either convincingly or not, and these statements are also somewhat less in authority than the direct pronouncements of someone in governmental power.

The difference between Ibn Khaldun and Foucault is no less instructive. Both men – Ibn Khaldun more – are worldly historians who understand, and perhaps even appreciate, the dynamics of secular events, their relentless pressure, their ceaseless movement, their elusive complexity which does not permit the luxury of easy moral classification. And both are unlike Hobbes in that they respect and suspiciously admire the drive towards coherent order which characterizes human discourse as well as the historian's craft. Ibn Khaldun's vision of social order is what he calls '*asabiyah* (usually translated as 'group solidarity'); Foucault's is 'the order of discourse', *l'ordre du discours*. Yet Ibn Khaldun's perspective is such that history for him is composed of social life cycles describing movements from origin, to ascendancy, to decline, and rise again that occur within various polities, each of which is organized around the greater or lesser degree of '*asabiyah* within it. Foucault's perspective, however, is that in the modern period to which he belongs there is an unremitting and unstoppable expansion of power favouring the administrators, managers, and technocrats of what he calls disciplinary society. Power, he writes in his last phase, is everywhere. It is overcoming, co-opting, infinitely detailed, and ineluctable in the growth of its domination. The historical tendency that seems to me to have held Foucault in its grip intellectually and politically in his last years was one he perceived – incompletely, I think – as growing ever more coherent and unidirectional, and it is this tendency that carried him over from the differentiations and subtleties within power in *L'Ordre du discours* and *L'Archéologie du savoir* to the hypertrophied vision of power in later works like *Surveiller et punir* and volume 1 of *L'Histoire de la sexualité*.

Many of the people who admire and have learned from Foucault, including myself, have commented on the undifferentiated power he seemed to ascribe to modern society. With this profoundly pessimistic view went also a singular lack of interest in the force of effective resistance to it, in choosing particular sites of intensity, choices which, we see from the evidence on all sides, always exist and are often successful in impeding, if not actually stopping, the progress of tyrannical power. Moreover Foucault seemed to have been confused between the power of institutions to subjugate individuals, and the fact that individual behaviour in society is frequently a matter of following rules and conventions. As Peter Dews puts it: '[Foucault] perceives clearly that institutions are not merely imposed constructs, yet has no apparatus for dealing with this fact, which entails that following a convention is not always equivalent to submitting to a power . . . But without this distinction every delimitation becomes an exclusion, and every exclusion becomes equated with an exercise of power.'[2]

Although we shouldn't indulge ourselves in the practice of saving Foucault from himself in order to make self-interested use of him, there is some value in trying to understand why he went as far as he did in imagining power to be so irresistible and unopposable. I shall suggest that there are other images of power, contemporary with Foucault's, that do much to modulate and complement his. But it is sensible to begin by asking the beginning questions, why imagine power in the first place, and what is the relationship between one's motive for imagining power and the image one ends up with. Consider these four possibilities. You think about power (1) to imagine what you could do if you had power; (2) to speculate about what you would imagine if you had power; (3) to arrive at some assessment of what power you would need in order to vanquish present power, and instate a new order or power; (4) to postulate a range of things that cannot be imagined or commanded by any form of power that exists at present.

It seems to me that Foucault was mainly attracted to the first and second possibilities, that is, to thinking about power from the standpoint of its actual realization, not of opposition to it. The third and fourth possibilities are insurgent and utopian. Foucault's emphasis, for example, upon the productivity of power, its provocative inventiveness and generative ingenuity, invigorated his analyses of how disciplines and discourses get things done, accomplish real tasks, gather authority. Similarly, his descriptions of lonely prophetic figures like de Sade and Nietzsche are interesting because of the way their outrageous and even preposterous pressures on rationality are absorbed and institutionalized almost routinely by the very structure one might have thought they had permanently disabled.

In short Foucault's imagination of power is largely *with* rather than *against* it, which is why the third and fourth possibilities do not seriously interest him as matters either of moral choice or rationalized political preferences. I wouldn't go as far as saying that Foucault rationalized power, or that he legitimized its dominion and its ravages by declaring them inevitable, but I would say that his interest in domination was critical but not finally as contestatory, or as oppositional as on the surface it seems to be. This translates into the paradox that Foucault's imagination of power was by his analysis of power to reveal its injustice and cruelty, but by his theorization to let it go on more or less unchecked. Perhaps this paradox is rooted in the extreme isolation one senses in Foucault's efforts, the discomfort both with his own genius and with an anonymity that does not suit him, as he gives voice to both in the effacements of self that accompany the brilliant rhetorical display occasioned by his self-presentation (an inaugural *leçon* at the Collège de France) that opens *L'Ordre du discours*.

Still there is no doubt at all that Foucault is nevertheless extraordinarily brilliant as a visionary of power who calls forth in his reader a whole gamut of responses testifying not so much to the rightness of Foucault's reports but to alternative visions of power not entirely suppressed or obliterated by his work, but stimulated and enlivened by it. Against the heedless impersonal efficiency of power there is, first of all, the inflection introduced by C. Wright Mills whose attack on the banality and irresponsibility of corporate managers will not be silenced by the notion that a micro-physics of power has eliminated classical ideas about ruling classes and dominant interests:

> In so far as there is now a great scatter of relatively equal balancing units, it is on the middle levels of power, seated in the sovereign localities and intermittent pressure groups, and coming to its high point within the Congress. We must thus revise and relocate the received conception of an enormous scatter of varied interests, for, when we look closer and for longer periods of time, we find that most

of these middle-level interests are concerned merely with their particular cut, with their particular area of vested interest, and often these are of no decisive political importance, although many are of enormous detrimental value to welfare. Above this plurality of interests, the units of power – economic, political, and military – that count in any balance are few in number and weighty beyond comparison with the dispersed groups on the middle and lower levels of the power structure . . .

 . . . Those having real power in the American state today are not merely brokers of power, resolvers of conflict, or compromisers of varied and clashing interest – they represent and indeed embody quite specific national interests and policies.[3]

Secondly, to the extent that modern history in the West exemplifies for Foucault the confinement and elision of marginal, oppositional and eccentric groups, there is, I believe, a salutary virtue in testimonials by members of those groups asserting their right of self-representation within the total economy of discourse. Foucault is certainly right – and even prescient – in showing how discourse is not only that which translates struggle or systems of domination, but that for *which* struggles are conducted, 'le pouvoir dont on cherche à s'emparer.'[4] What he seemed not quite as willing to grant is, in fact, the relative success of these counter-discursive attempts first to show the misrepresentations of discursive power, to show, in Fanon's words, the violence done to psychically and politically repressed inferiors in the name of an advanced culture, and then afterwards to begin the difficult, if not always tragically flawed, project of formulating the discourse of liberation.

We may finally believe with Foucault and Lyotard that the great narratives of emancipation and enlightenment are over, but I think we must remember more seriously what Foucault himself teaches, that in this case, as in many others, it is sometimes of paramount importance not so much *what* is said, but *who* speaks. So that it can hardly pass muster that having once declared the 'assujettissement du discours', the same source that does so erases any opportunity for adversarial responses to this process of subjugation, declaring it accomplished and done with at the start. The work of Fanon himself, Syed Alatas, Abdallah Laroui, Panikkar, Shariati, Mazrui, novelists like Ngugi and Rushdie – all these as well as the enormously powerful adversarial work of feminists and minority cultures in the West and in the Third World, amply record the continuing attraction to libertarian struggle, for which I have gathered Foucault and others in his camp felt either resignation or spectatorial indifference after the Iranian revolution. I must also mention that to describe these counter-discursive efforts simply as non-systemic in Wallerstein's phrase is, I think, to negate precisely the force in them that I am certain Foucault would have understood, the *organized and rationalized* basis of their protest. So that while granting their non-systemic force on one level, we would have to grant on another level the limits of our imagination of *their* power and organizing principles, and thus that they imagine things that we have no easy way of grasping.

Finally – to return to more familiar arenas of struggle – Foucault's unmodulated minimization of resistance provokes allusion to the formation in writers like Gramsci and Raymond Williams of an emergent or alternative consciousness allied to emergent and alternative subaltern groups within the dominant discursive society. I mention them because their work and the work of the Frankfurt School theorists, like Foucault's, accords a paramount place to ideology and culture critique, although they place a quite different, altogether more positive emphasis upon the vulnerability of the present organization of culture. For Gramsci and Williams, the analysis of discursive power is made coeval with an image of what we could describe as contingent power, the principle of whose constitution is that, since it is constructed by humans, it is therefore not invincible, not impervious to dismantling, not unidirectional. Even if we leave aside the complexities of Gramsci's philosophy and the political organization it entails, as well as what he calls 'the conquest of civil society', there is the theoretical insistence, against Foucault, of a guaranteed insufficiency in the dominant culture towards which it is possible to mount an attack. Williams says that 'however dominant a social system may be, the very meaning of its domination involves a limitation or selection of the activities it covers, so that by definition it cannot exhaust all social experience, which therefore always potentially contains space for alternative acts and alternative intentions which are not yet articulated as a social institution or even project.'[5]

I wouldn't want to conclude simply by appearing to turn these comments and others against Foucault's notions of power. For in fact the great invigoration of his work, in its extremism and its constant savaging of limits and reifications, is its disquieting recollection of what, sometimes explicitly but often implicitly, it leaves out, neglects, circumvents, or displaces. The problematic of the relationship between subjectivity and ideas of justice, for example, or the category of the aesthetic as a negation of power, or of genealogical and critical history as interventionary activities within the network of discourses of knowledge – all these are suggested through a kind of antithetical engagement, by Foucault's imagination of power. But nowhere is this engagement more gripping than in the conflict between Foucault's archaeologies and social change itself, which it must remain for his students, like ourselves on such occasions, to expose and if possible to resolve.

Notes

1 'Question à Michel Foucault sur la géographie', *Hérodote*, no. 1, Jan.–March 1976.
2 Peter Dews, 'The *Nouvelle Philosophie* and Foucault', *Economy and Society*, vol. 8, p. 147.
3 C. Wright Mills, *The Power Elite* (Oxford University Press, 1956), pp. 266–7.
4 *L'Ordre du discours* (Paris: Gallimard, 1971), p. 12.
5 Raymond Williams, *Politics and Letters: Interview with* New Left Review (London: New Left Books, 1979), p. 252.

The Politics of Truth and the Problem of Hegemony

BARRY SMART

The works of Michel Foucault have been interpreted in a number of different ways. Readings of the major texts and studies have identified parallels with 'field-theory' physics, the presence of structuralist conceptions and assumptions, residues of phenomenological philosophy, a hermeneutic interest, as well as evidence of the influence of a number of classic intellectual forebears, the most prominent of which are probably Nietzsche, Marx, and Freud.[1]

The intellectual and socio-political milieu of postwar France in which Foucault's analytic approach formed and developed, the centrality in the 'post-'68' writings of questions of power/knowledge and objectification/subjectification, and the controversy aroused by the forms of political analysis and action associated with the author's work have provided a compelling context for a number of comparisons and contrasts with other forms of analysis, but above all with the established radical theory and politics of Marxism. Although no sustained discussion of Marxist theory and politics is to be found in Foucault's corpus, the analytic focus, methodological orientation, and political thrust of the work may as a number of key references and observations in the texts imply, be read as a response to, or in effect as a critique of fundamental elements of both Marxist analysis and socialist political strategy.

The question of the character of Foucault's work and its relation to Marxist theory and politics has generally been addressed in one of the following three ways. From within the analytic and political parameters of the Marxist tradition there have been two responses. One, relatively predictable, has been to dismiss the work because of its transgression of the central tenets of a Marxist problematic that is deemed to be beyond question; such a reading neither requires nor allows serious consideration of the 'truths' on which it is founded.[2] An alternative has been to consider Foucault's work as offering both a clarification and a development of understanding of a region within the field of Marxist analysis, to be more precise as providing necessary insights into the process of individualization and the operation of particular forms of power relation in modern capitalist societies.[3] Thus Foucault's work, or at best certain parts of it, is deemed to make sense and be of value when read in terms of the general parameters of Marxism. In contrast to both of the above readings, the work has been interpreted as a radical departure from or even as a critique of many of the methodological and political assumptions and substantive preoccupations and findings of Marxism – quite literally as 'beyond Marxism'. In such readings Foucault has been credited with the formation of a new mode of critical analysis.[4]

A related address of Foucault's work in relation to issues central to Marxist theory and political practice is to be found in the readings of theorists concerned with the construction, extension, or development of a 'non-reductionist' analysis of politics and power from the writings of Gramsci. Such readings tend to present Foucault's analyses of the politics of truth or the relations of power and knowledge articulated in discourse as substantially in accord with and necessarily subordinate to Gramsci's attempted reformulation or reconstruction of Marxist analysis through a theorization of the problem of hegemony. For example, Foucault's analyses of relations of power and knowledge have been described as both similar to Gramsci's observations on the relations central to the establishment of hegemony and as 'anticipated on several points' by the latter.[5] Once again it has been assumed that the general parameters and founding assumptions of an existing Marxist problematic are not in question, and that an alternative form of analysis may simply be subsumed or incorporated. However, it may be argued that such an assumption is unwarranted, for the appropriation and attempted absorption of elements of Foucault's work within a Gramscian problematic has not so much re-affirmed the continuing influence and topicality of the latter but has instead effectively underlined the necessity of reconceptualizing a set of analytic issues at the very heart of Gramsci's work, notably those concerning the constitution of hegemony. In short Foucault's work may be read as providing a radically different approach and a new set of concepts through which to develop analysis and understanding of the exercise of power and the associated effects of hegemony in modern societies.

The Problem of Hegemony

The principal reference for the concept of hegemony in Gramsci's work is the nature and mechanisms of bourgeois class rule in stable capitalist societies.[6] The concept of hegemony serves for Gramsci as the appropriate term for describing one form of relationship between a leading group or social class and subordinate groups or classes, a relationship structured in terms of consent rather than force or domination. However, Gramsci is far from consistent in his employment of the term hegemony or for that matter the related concepts of the state and civil society. In some passages in *The Prison Notebooks* hegemony (viz. direction/leading) refers to a relationship of consent in civil society achieved through 'so-called private organizations, like the Church, the trade unions, the schools etc.'[7], in contrast to a relationship of domination achieved through the 'State-as-force'. Elsewhere in the notebooks both civil society and the state are conceived to exercise hegemony, which by implication appears therefore to be an effect of relations of force *and* consent. Subsequently the state is presented as encompassing not only 'the apparatus of government, but also the "private" apparatus of "hegemony" or civil society.'[8] The texts clearly confirm Anderson's view that the interrelated concepts of '"state", "civil society", "political society", "hegemony", "domination" and "direction" all undergo a persistent *slippage*' in Gramsci's work.[9]

It is evident that the concept of hegemony requires clarification and reformulation, a task which in my view takes us beyond the basic conceptual categories of Marxism to be found in Gramsci's work to a consideration of events, phenomena, and techniques embodied in the figure of 'the social' and effectively outlined in Foucault's studies of objectivizing and subjectifying practices. The concept of 'the social' refers not to that global abstraction 'society' but to a series of methods, techniques, and practices which have effected a particular form of social cohesion.[10] It is in the analysis of such methods, techniques, and practices through which power has been exercised in modern Western societies that the complex constitution of hegemony has begun to be effectively addressed. As Donzelot has commented, if we are to achieve an understanding of the basis of 'social cohesion' it is necessary to move beyond conceptions and strategies derived from the nineteenth century to an analysis of the various measures,

> which allow social life to escape material pressures and politico-moral uncertainties; the entire range of methods which make the members of a society relatively safe from the effects of economic fluctuations by providing a certain security – which give their existence possibilities of relations that are flexible enough, and internal stakes that are convincing enough, to avert the dislocation that divergences of interests and beliefs would entail.[11]

It is in the work of Foucault that an analysis of the various complex social techniques and methods fundamental to the achievement of a relationship of direction, guidance, leadership, or hegemony is to be found.

Hegemony contributes to or constitutes a form of social cohesion not through force or coercion, nor necessarily through consent, but most effectively by way of practices, techniques, and methods which infiltrate minds and bodies, cultural practices which cultivate behaviours and beliefs, tastes, desires, and needs as seemingly naturally occurring qualities and properties embodied in the psychic and physical reality (or 'truth') of the human subject. It is by virtue of a dual analytic focus upon forms of knowledge and relations of power through which the human subject has been objectivized and upon techniques of the self and related discourses in terms of which human beings 'have learned to recognize themselves as subjects' respectively that Foucault's work has revealed the complex multiple processes from which the strategic constitution of forms of hegemony may emerge. The corollary of the expressed objective of Foucault's various analyses, namely to 'create a history of the different modes by which in our culture human beings are made subjects',[12] is a revelation of the forms of government and self-government to which human beings have been subject, where the concept of government refers to 'the way in which the conduct of individuals or groups might be directed',[13] that is an action or practice synonymous with the achievement or exercise of hegemony.

The Politics of Truth

The principal analytic reference for Gramsci's work is the discourse of Marxism, one consequence of which is that discussion of hegemony is necessarily situated in relation to the problem of economism and the theorization of ideology. Although it may be argued that Gramsci was sensitive to the limits and limitations of Marxist analysis arising from the cornerstone principle of economic-determination-in-the-final-instance and sought through the conception of hegemony to develop a new approach to the problem of politics and power, ultimately the analysis remains at best ambiguous on the problem of economism and virtually silent on the complex matter of the establishment of forms of hegemony.[14] In contrast, Foucault by virtue of his critical distance from the limits and limitations of the Marxist problematic has been able to transform the terms of debate from a preoccupation with the ambiguous concept of 'ideology' and its effects to a consideraton of the relations of 'truth' and 'power' which are constitutive of hegemony.

There are three interrelated elements or dimensions in Foucault's work which effectively transform the terms of reference through which the complex question of the constitution of forms of hegemony may be addressed. These may be differentiated as follows: (i) historical; (ii) analytical; (iii) political.

In Foucault's work on relations of power and knowledge a significant historical transition contemporaneous with the emergence of industrial capitalism is identified in which a shift of emphasis occurs from the primacy of sovereignty, law, and coercion or force; that is from the deployment of juridical forms of power literally 'to take life', to the emergence of new, more effective and complex technologies of power which are positive or productive and seeking to foster life. The emergence of forms of power exercised over life, notably the development of an anatomo-politics of the human body ('discipline') and a bio-politics of the population ('bio-power') constitutes a distinctive feature of modern societies. These two forms of power are directed respectively to the cultivation of more 'useful' and 'docile' individuals and to the administration or management of population(s), ultimately through 'measures described as social which since the end of the nineteenth century have centred on the issues of industrial accidents, unemployment, sickness and old age, on questions of assistance and prevention, on questions of workers' demands, of promotion (school) and leisure'.[15] The historical transition documented is conceived by Foucault not in terms of a reduction in the use of 'violence' in the exercise of power and a concomitant increase in 'consent', but in terms of a complex process of 'governmentalization' which has involved the emergence and development of new technologies of power targeted on individuals and populations, and the articulation of new forms of political rationality. This transition does not represent a shift from 'state' to 'civil society' but rather a progressive governmentalization of power relations in which 'apparatuses of security' and 'insurantial technologies' have predominated and become 'rationalized and centralized in the form of, or under the auspices of, state institutions'.[16] The implication of the above is not that power relations derive from the state form but rather that such relations have become more and more under state control and influence in modern societies.

The modern state does not constitute a monolith confronting individuals from above, but a 'matrix of individualization' which forms, shapes and governs individuality through the exercise of a new form of 'pastoral power' over the social, that is to say the deployment of various measures directed to the health, well-being, security, protection, and development of both the individual and the population by public institutions and 'private ventures, welfare societies, (and) benefactors'.[17] In short the 'State'/'civil society' dichotomy is displaced by an analytic focus upon the 'governmentalization' of power relations, that is the development of individualizing techniques and practices which are reducible neither to force nor to consent, techniques and practices which have transformed political conflict and struggle through the constitution of new forms of social cohesion.

Analytically Foucault's work pries open the problem of hegemony in so far as it de-centres the question of the state, introduces a non-reductionist conception of power, and displaces the concept of ideology, through which Gramsci sought to theorize questions of 'intellectual and moral leadership' central to the achievement of hegemony, with analyses of the relations of 'truth' and 'power' through which 'men govern (themselves and others)'. Furthermore, although the historical conjuncture at the centre of Foucault's discussion of relations of power and knowledge encompasses the emergence of industrial capitalism and the rise of the bourgeoisie, the technologies of power analysed (e.g. discipline, bio-power, pastoral power, etc.) are not conceived to originate in or with either the interests of capital or the intentions of the bourgeoisie. Foucault's genealogical approach is antithetical to both forms of global or totalizing theory and conceptions of power as a product or possession of a class subject, as is implied in the above. Instead, analysis is directed towards the multiple processes through which events are constituted, in particular to the study of technologies of power, their strategic deployment, and effect(s) respectively. For example, in Foucault's exploration of the history of sexuality the analytic focus falls upon the formation in modern Western societies of an 'experience' of sexuality, literally upon 'the methods by which individuals are led to recognize themselves as sexual subjects'.[18] The analysis offers a critique of essentialist conceptions of sexuality and the related hypothesis of sexual repression. Sex is conceived to have achieved importance as a political issue because it offered access to 'the life of the body and the life of the species'.[19] Furthermore, it is argued that in the first instance it was the bourgeois body and the bourgeois class that was subjected to the deployment of sexuality and that such a deployment served to constitute the distinctiveness or identity of the bourgeoisie by providing it with a 'body to be cared for, protected, and preserved'. It is in this context that Foucault explicitly addresses the matter of hegemony, arguing that emphasis on the sexual body

> should undoubtedly be linked to the process of growth and establishment of bourgeois hegemony: not, however, because of the market value assumed by labor capacity but because of what the 'cultivation' of its own body could represent politically, economically, and historically for the present and the future of the bourgeoisie. Its dominance was in part dependent on that cultivation; but it was not simply a matter of economy or ideology, it was a 'physical' matter as well. The works, published in great numbers at the end of the eighteenth century, on body hygiene, the art of longevity, ways of having healthy children and of keeping them alive as long as possible, and methods for improving the human lineage, bear witness to the fact.[20]

And in a series of more general comments on the development of industrial capitalism, Foucault notes that techniques of power, 'present at every level of the social body and utilized by very diverse institutions (the family and the army, school and the police, individual medicine and the administration of college bodies) . . . acted as factors of segregation and social hierarchization . . . guaranteeing relations of domination and effects of hegemony.'[21]

However, notwithstanding such explicit references to bourgeois hegemony in the study of sexuality it is in the analyses of relations of truth and power in general ('regimes of truth') and to a lesser extent in comments on the role of intellectuals that Foucault's work offers an analytical and political purchase on the problem of hegemony.

Foucault's studies of various 'experiences' (e.g. confinement, medicine, punishment, sexuality) have been concerned with the interrelationship between objectifying and subjectifying practices and 'true discourses' which rationalize and legitimate particular courses of action upon the actions of self and others. To the extent that the focus of study may be reformulated as analysis of the 'regimes of truth' through which people govern themselves and others, then Foucault's work can be considered to provide a reconceptualization of the problem of hegemony, shifting it away from the essentially humanist philosophy of action to be found in Gramsci's work to an examination of the production, transformation, and effects of the true/false distinction which has been at the centre of processes of government in modern Western societies. Central to Foucault's analyses of the political problem(s) of truth have been both a recognition of the importance of a scientific hierarchization of knowledges through which 'true' and 'false' have increasingly been distinguished in modern Western societies, an important consequence of which has been the disqualification of low-ranking, local, and popular forms of knowledge ('le savoir des gens'), and an appreciation of the politics of intellectual activity.

Intellectuals and Politics

Foucault presents a distinction between two types of intellectual, the 'universal' who speaks for and is the conscience of the collectivity and the 'specific' who has a particular expertise in a specialized field of knowledge. The distinction might seem to resemble that drawn by Gramsci between the 'traditional' and the 'organic' intellectual, the former term being used to describe established intellectual formations, for example the 'category of ecclesiastics', scholars, theorists, and philosophers, who put themselves forward as 'independent or autonomous of the dominant social group', the latter to refer to the intellectuals created 'organically' along with every new class or social group.[22] For Gramsci the principal concern was to theorize the role of intellectuals in relation to both dominant and subordinate groups and classes in order to develop the philosophy of praxis (Marxism) and thereby advance to construction of 'an intellectual–moral bloc which can make politically possible the intellectual progress of the mass'.[23] Implicit in this formulation is a conception of the necessity of an intellectual vanguard or elite '"specialised" in conceptual and philosophical elaboration of ideas' and able to organize or lead, the ultimate embodiment of which is the revolutionary party.

Although some of Foucault's ideas on intellectuals may initially seem to resemble those of Gramsci, there are important conceptual and political differences. To begin with, no 'leading role' is attributed to intellectuals by Foucault; on the contrary, it is argued that events have shown that the masses do not lack for knowledge, the problem is that their local and popular forms of knowledge have been steadily discredited, disqualified, or rendered illegitimate by the very institutions and effects of power associated with the prevailing 'regime of truth' within which the modern intellectual operates. Implicit here is the idea of a transformation in the intellectual function, in short an historical displacement of the 'universal' intellectual, the master of truth and justice upholding reason and revealing the truth to those unable to see or speak it, by the 'specific' intellectual. The argument is that the intellectual may no longer assume the traditional role of representing the universal or the 'just-and-true-for-all'. With the development of a series of offices, occupations, and subjects (e.g. school teachers, magistrates, probation officers, social workers, technicians, etc.) bearing forms of knowledge and techniques invested with scientific reason, modern intellectuals function or work 'within specific sectors at the precise points where their own conditions of life or work situate them' – hence the appellation 'specific'.[24] The change described by Foucault arising from an extension of 'technico-scientific structures in the economic and strategic domain', a growth and diffusion of forms of scientific rationality, and the associated emergence of new forms of intellectual activity and office constitutes nothing less than a 'global process of politicization of intellectuals'.

However, the figure of the intellectual, whether 'universal' or 'specific', effectively occupies a secondary place in Foucault's analysis, for the key issue is that of the relation of truth and power, the general politics or ' "political economy" of truth' characteristic of Western societies. In such societies truth is associated with the institutions and discursive form of science; subject to economic and political demand; produced and transmitted under the control of and diffused and consumed through particular apparatuses (e.g. 'university, army, writing, media' and 'education and information' respectively); and last but by no means least, it is the subject of political contest, confrontation, and debate. It is in this context that Foucault has suggested that the modern intellectual has a 'three-fold specificity', namely of class position, of conditions of life and work associated with intellectual activity, and of 'the politics of truth in our societies'; and it is in relation to the latter, that is, struggles and conflicts around the question of truth, that a politicization of intellectuals has become most apparent. In short, Foucault's position is that intellectuals are inextricably involved in a struggle over 'the status of truth and the economic and political role it plays' and that the option before radical intellectuals is not that of 'emancipating truth from every system of power (which would be a chimera, for truth is already power) but of detaching the power of truth from the forms of hegemony, social, economic and cultural, within which it operates at the present time.'[25] Thus the political thrust of Foucault's work has not been towards the clarification of a distinction between different types of intellectual activity, nor the delineation of an appropriate representative role or 'organic' class reference for the modern intellectual, but rather with the development of analyses which offer a critique of the politics of truth at the heart of the constitution of forms of hegemony in the present.

The Politics of Genealogy

Foucault's work has been subjected to criticism in relation to questions of historical accuracy, methodological rigour, and political effect or consequence, and it is to the latter that I should like to turn in conclusion.

The most common political criticism of Foucault's work has been that it removes 'all basis for a progressive political intervention' or, what amounts to much the same end, that it has a sterilizing or anaesthetizing effect and leaves 'no possible room for initiative'.[26] In short, what is considered to be missing from the work is a recommendation or direction for action, an answer to the question 'What is to be done?' The omission is a logical consequence of Foucault's method and associated analytic focus rather than a sign of political obduracy, both archaeology and genealogy standing in opposition to unitary bodies of theory or globalizing discourses which seek to integrate diverse 'local' events within a totalizing frame in order to prescribe particular practices and thereby realize specified effects. Indeed, it is the problematic or uneven character of the relations between such rational schemas or programmes, associated social and institutional practices and their 'unintended' or 'unprojected' effects that has constituted the focus of much of Foucault's work.

At the centre of Foucault's investigations there is an analysis of the social and human sciences, broadly conceived and including by implication their critical corollaries (e.g. Marxism). In Western culture the social and human sciences have increasingly constituted the 'true' discourses which have provided reasons, principles, and justifications for objectifying and subjectifying practices through which people have been classified, examined, trained, 'divided from others', and formed as subjects (e.g. class and political subjects) with a 'self' respectively. It is on the assumed scientificity of such discourses and the effects of power 'linked to the institution and functioning of an organized scientific discourse within a society such as ours'[27] that both 'conservative' and 'progressive' prescriptions and programmings of behaviour have been predicated. One of the principal objectives of Foucault's analysis is to contest 'the scientific hierarchisation of knowledges and the effects intrinsic to their power' implied in the above − not by constructing a higher, more general and more powerful theory, but by developing critiques of both objectifying and subjectifying forms of knowledge, action, and their respective effects, in order to reveal and thereby help reactivate the various forms of subjugated knowledge and local criticism of 'an autonomous, non-centralised kind . . . whose validity is not dependent on the approval of the established regimes of thought'.[28]

Aside from brief and enigmatic references to the possibility of a 'different economy of bodies and pleasures' and the prospect of 'constituting a new politics of truth', Foucault consistently refrained from the articulation of policy alternatives to the programmes and practices which were the object of critique in the respective genealogical analyses of the present. The objective of the latter was to identify strengths and weaknesses in the networks of power, to provide in short, tools or 'instruments for analysis' and to leave the question of tactics, strategies, and goals to those directly involved in struggle and resistance. A central political objective of the work has therefore been to assist in the creation of conditions in which particular subject groups, for example patients or prisoners, can express themselves and act, rather than to provide a theory about 'madness' or 'delinquency' from which specialized social agents or functionaries ('social' workers) may derive guidance for their acts of intervention. Indeed, in respect of the latter Foucault has argued that in effect his project has been to 'bring it about that they "no longer know what to do", so that the acts, gestures, discourses which up until then had seemed to go without saying became problematic'.[29]

The absence in Foucault's work of prescriptions for the guidance or direction of conduct derives not only from an opposition to global or totalizing forms of discourse and their effects but in addition from a radically different conception of the relationship between discourses, practices, and effects. The 'orthodox' or 'conservative' and 'radical' or 'critical' discourses of the social and human sciences have tended to contrast theory or discourse on the one hand with social practice or the 'real' on the other and to assume that a particular rational ordering of social life may be engineered through a realization in one form or the other of discourse (programmes or policies) in practice (action or conduct). Foucault, by contrast, acknowledging the play of dispersion, deviation, and contingency in history, has argued that discourses, programmes, or rational schemas are themselves fragments of reality in complex relations with other social and institutional practices and that the effects or ends which emerge generally fail to correspond with those programmed. Foucault's analyses document the complex interplay between the various elements referred to in the above, and in addition indicate the way in which 'failed' programmes (e.g. of penal incarceration) may be preserved, developed, and redeployed for strategic ends other than those initially proposed and promoted. However, although the issue of strategy is addressed in the context of analyses of relations of power, no consideration is given to the question of the formulation of conventional political strategy in general or those 'alternative' socialist forms which the analysis indirectly undermines. What the work achieves in relation to established forms of radical or critical analysis is a problematization of concepts and assumptions which have constituted an insecure foundation for both analysis and the formulation of political strategy. For example, the articulation of 'the social' as a series of measures, techniques, and practices through which a particular form of social cohesion has been achieved calls into question the assumed progressiveness of a socialist conception and strategy of 'social'-ization. Further, insofar as relations between programmes, practices and their respective effects are revealed to be both highly complex and unpredictable, conceptions of centralized social planning and policy formation intrinsic to socialist political strategy are open to question. Finally, not only does a criticism of 'representation' and 'universality' effectively undermine the idea of a leading role for a vanguard political party, but in addition a de-centring of class subjects and class struggle in the analysis of relations of power draws attention to the fact that with the emergence of 'the social' political subject groups may and do assume a different form to that implied in the conception of an historic binary division, a corollary of which is a questioning of the desirability of 'revolution' and a marginalization of related conceptions of political strategy.[30] In short, the classic discourse of socialism, including associated forms of political strategy, is rendered problematic.

Concluding Remarks

It does not follow from the above that Foucault is merely a 'dispassionate observer' rather than a 'concerned critic' of the existing order, that the work is 'neo-conservative' because it fails to provide either a political rationale or a direction for action, or that resistance is rendered impossible if we follow the terms of the analysis.[31] The various studies and texts together constitute a genealogical history of the present, the future form of which will be a complex consequence of the actions of subjects 'through which the real is transformed' rather than the outcome of any 'plan of reform'. In short, what is presented by Foucault is a critical analysis of the prevailing regime of truth and its effects of power, criticism which translates into political activity of a specifically delimited kind, namely assisting in the creation of conditions necessary to allow those directly involved in a struggle to speak out and act on their own behalf. To proceed in this manner does not signify 'indifference' or a lack of critical concern but rather that a political discourse promising 'emancipation' constitutes at best a form of rhetoric. In the final instance as Foucault notes,

> a society without power relations can only be an abstraction … [However,] to say that there cannot be a society without power relations is not to say either that those which are established are necessary, or, in any case, that power constitutes a fatality at the heart of societies, such that it cannot be undermined. Instead I would say that the analysis, elaboration, and bringing into question of power relations and the 'agonism' between power relations and the intransitivity of freedom is a permanent political task inherent in all social existence.[32]

Hence the concentration in the work upon particular instances and effects of the deployment of technologies of power and their associated rationalities.

It is clear therefore that in Foucault's terms there can be no power-free or power-less society, no millennial end of history towards which oppressed, exploited or dominated subjects may be led or guided, for relations of power, that is, ways of acting upon the actions of (other) acting subjects, are endemic in society. In consequence the objective of the work becomes not the development from on high of confrontation strategies through which relations of power might finally be undermined, but rather a critical analysis of how power is exercised. The emphasis placed upon the exercise of power and associated rationalities has led critics to argue that an important implication of Foucault's work is that forms of resistance are inevitably eroded or encompassed within relations of power. However, such criticism is misplaced, for whilst it might be argued that there is a relative neglect of resistance as an issue in the analysis, there is no sense in which it is presented as inevitably eroded or encompassed within relations of power; to the contrary, power is defined in such a way that resistance or 'freedom's refusal to submit' constitutes a condition of its very existence.

Far from reducing the analytical and political significance of forms of resistance and struggle, Foucault ultimately argued that they might well constitute the starting point of an analysis of power. Although the proposal for an investigation of resistances provoked by power receives only a brief address, it is clear that the struggles in question are those which have formed and developed in relation to the emergence of what Foucault has described as the 'government of individualization', that is, individualizing techniques of power deployed in everyday life and directed at individuals. It is through the exercise and effects of such techniques that forms of hegemony have been constituted and it is around the selfsame techniques that have emerged forms of struggle and resistance which may in turn become the basis of counter-hegemonic strategies.

Foucault's work has opened up the question of hegemony with analyses of the operation and effects of techniques of power and the associated rationales or regimes of truth through which forms of social cohesion are constituted, and to a lesser extent by belatedly placing on the agenda the question of an investigation of the forms of resistance provoked by relations of power, the very existence of which signify the presence of a potential for instability or confrontation in any situation of hegemony. Although the latter inquiry represents work to be done, at least the necessary conceptual and analytic means have been provided for an interrogation of the present that supersedes the limitations of analyses of social relations and practices in terms of an evaluative model of emancipation – repression in which an unrealistic promise of an end to power constitutes the focal point for both theorizing and political practice.

To be critical of the idea of an end to power does not mean that revolt, struggle, and protest is pointless. On the contrary, Foucault's position is that it is through such manifestations of resistance that

> subjectivity . . . introduces itself into history and gives it the breath of life. A delinquent puts his life into the balance against absurd punishments; a madman can no longer accept confinement and the forfeiture of his rights; a people refuses the regime which oppresses it. This does not make the rebel in the first case innocent, nor does it cure in the second, and it does not assure the third rebel of the promised tomorrow. One does not have to be in solidarity with them. One does not have to maintain that these confused voices sound better than the others and express the ultimate truth. For there to be a sense in listening to them and in searching for what they want to say, it is sufficient that they exist and that they have against them so much which is set up to silence them . . . it is due to such voices that the time of men does not have the form of an evolution, but precisely that of a history.[33]

The aim of the work is neither an endorsement nor a neutralization of domination or resistance, but rather an examination of their respectively complex forms and effects and of the ways in which historically constituted distinctions and divisions between 'true' and 'false' have rationalized or validated the implementation of particular courses of action upon the actions of others. The principal objective is not the preparation or formulation of strategy, the articulation of the views of a subordinate class, or a judgement of the competing claims to validity of different modes of programming behaviour, but a critical examination of the various ways in which we have come to govern ourselves and others through the articulation of a distinction between truth and falsity – in other words, the central issue is that of the complex constitution of forms of social hegemony.

Foucault's critical genealogical analyses of human experience, relations of power, and forms of knowledge effectively reveal that forms of social cohesion and hegemony have a precarious and complex history in human practice. The analyses not only disclose the fragile and complex character of the processes through which 'events' and 'experiences' have been formed and rationalized, but as a corollary signify that social phenomena may be transformed. In sum, the work constitutes a major contribution to the development of both a critical understanding of and a challenge to prevailing social, economic, and cultural forms of hegemony.

Notes

1 See for example the discussion of Foucault's work by P. Major-Poetzl, *Michel Foucault's Archaeology of Western Culture; Toward a New Science of History* (Brighton: Harvester Press, 1983); H. L. Dreyfus and P. Rabinow, *Michel Foucault: Beyond Structuralism and Hermeneutics* (Brighton: Harvester Press, 1982); M. Poster, *Foucault, Marxism and History* (Oxford: Polity Press, 1984); B. Smart, *Foucault, Marxism and Critique* (London: Routledge & Kegan Paul, 1983).

2 See for example the reading of Foucault's work in A. Callinicos, *Is There a Future for Marxism?* (London: Macmillan, 1982); B. Fine, 'Struggles against discipline: the theory and politics of Michel Foucault', *Capital and Class*, no. 9 (1979); J. Lea, 'Discipline and Capitalist Development' in B. Fine *et al.* (eds), *Capitalism and the Rule of Law: From Deviancy Theory to Marxism* (London: Hutchinson, 1979).

3 See for example N. Poulantzas, *State, Power, Socialism* (London: New Left Books, 1978).

4 See P. Patton and J. Allen (eds), *Beyond Marxism? Interventions After Marx* (Sydney: Intervention Publications, 1983); also Smart, *Foucault, Marxism and Critique* and Poster, *Foucault, Marxism and History*.

5 See respectively C. Mercer, 'Revolutions, Reforms or Reformulations? Marxist Discourse on Democracy' in A. Hunt (ed.), *Marxism and Democracy* (London: Lawrence & Wishart, 1980); C. Mouffe, 'Hegemony and Ideology in Gramsci' in C. Mouffe (ed.), *Gramsci and Marxist Theory* (London: Routledge & Kegan Paul, 1979).

6 For a discussion of the development of the concept of hegemony in the work of the Marxist tradition in general and Gramsci in particular see C. Mouffe and E. Laclau, *Hegemony and Socialist Strategy: Towards a Radical Democratic Politics* (London: Verso, 1985); P. Anderson, 'The Antinomies of Antonio Gramsci', *New Left Review*, no. 100 (1976/77).

7 See Q. Hoare and G. Nowell (eds), *Selections from the Prison Notebooks of Antonio Gramsci* (London: Lawrence & Wishart, 1976), p. 56, n.5.

8 Ibid., p. 261.

9 See Anderson, 'The Antinomies of Antonio Gramsci', p. 25.

10 Although Foucault and to a lesser extent Deleuze may be credited with outlining the figure of 'the social', the concept receives its most succinct and explicit address in the work of J. Donzelot in *The Policing of Families: Welfare Versus the State* (London: Hutchinson, 1980) and 'The poverty of political culture', *Ideology and Consciousness*, no. 5 (1979).

11 Donzelot, *The Policing of Families*, p. xxvi.

12 M. Foucault, 'The Subject and Power' in Dreyfus and Rabinow, *Foucault: Beyond Structuralism*, p. 208.

13 Ibid., p. 221.

14 The question of the relationship between Gramsci's conception of hegemony and the problem of economism and theory of ideology is a complex and controversial one. See for example papers by Bobbio, Texier and Mouffe in Mouffe, *Gramsci and Marxist Theory*.

15 Donzelot, *The Policing of Families*, p. 80.

16 Foucault 'The Subject and Power', p. 224.

17 Ibid., p. 215.

18 M. Foucault, *Histoire de la sexualité*, vol. 2, *L'Usage des plaisirs* (Paris: Gallimard, 1984), p. 11.

19 M. Foucault, *The History of Sexuality*, vol. 1, *An Introduction* (London: Allen Lane, 1979), p. 146.

20 Ibid., p. 125.

21 Ibid., p. 141.

22 See Hoare and Nowell (eds), *Prison Notebooks*, pp. 5–23.

23 Ibid., pp. 322–3.

24 M. Foucault, 'Truth and Power' in *Power/Knowledge: Selected Interview and Other Writings 1972–1977*, ed. C. Gordon (Brighton: Harvester Press, 1980), p. 126.

25 Ibid., p. 133.

26 See M. Foucault, 'Politics and the study of discourse', *Ideology and Consciousness*, no. 3 (1978), p. 8. and 'Questions of method', *I & C*, no. 8 (1981), pp. 11–13 respectively.

27 M. Foucault 'Two Lectures' in *Power/Knowledge*, p. 84.

28 Ibid., p. 81.

29 See 'Questions of method', p. 12.

30 The relevance of Foucault's work for socialist political stragegy is addressed in J. Minson, 'Strategies for socialists? Foucault's conception of power', *Economy and Society*, vol. 9, no. 1 (1980).

31 These views are expressed respectively by R. Rorty, 'Habermas and Lyotard on post-modernity', *Praxis*, vol. 4 (1984), p. 40; J. Habermas, 'Modernity versus postmodernity' and 'The entwinement of myth and enlightenment: re-reading *Dialectic of Enlightenment*', *New German Critique*, no. 22 (1981) and no. 26 (1982) respectively; and N. Poulantzas, *State, Power, Socialism*.

32 M. Foucault, 'The Subject and Power', pp. 222–3.

33 M. Foucault, 'Is it useless to revolt?', *Philosophy and Social Criticism*, vol. 8 (1981), p. 8.

In the Empire of the Gaze: Foucault and the Denigration of Vision in Twentieth-century French Thought

MARTIN JAY

If, as Michel Foucault has taught us, authorial originality pales before the constraints of epistemic or discursive determination, then the proper contextualizing of his own seemingly idiosyncratic work becomes a particularly intriguing task. Unfortunately, it has proved to be a no less troublesome one. For when the initial efforts to categorize Foucault as a structuralist or semiotician foundered, alternatives quickly proliferated. As a result, he has been variously described as a latter-day Nietzschean, a heterodox Heideggerian, a wayward Western Marxist, a postmodernist and, most frequently, a poststructuralist. With all the difficulties attending each and any of these categorizations, it may seem most prudent to accept the advice of two of his recent commentators and conclude that 'whoever wants to understand Foucault should not make him something he is not. Take him on his own, difficult terms.'[1]

And yet, to do so risks ignoring Foucault's own lesson of the power of discursive formations to undermine the alleged sovereignty of the creator subject. For his 'own terms' ironically imply that the terms can never be 'his own'. Foucault, to be sure, never argued that individuals could be reduced to mere instances of a larger unified field. 'In the proposed analysis,' he wrote in *The Archaeology of Knowledge*, 'instead of referring back to *the* synthesis of *the* unifying function of *a* subject, the various enunciative modalities manifest his dispersion. To the various statuses, the various sites, the various positions that he can occupy or be given when making a discourse. To the discontinuity of the planes from which he speaks.'[2] The partial truth of each of the rubrics under which he has been subsumed may thus be admitted without necessarily trying to force a reconciliation among them. Foucault should instead be seen as occupying the dynamic nodal point of a force-field of discursive impulses, which resist totalization into a coherent whole.[3]

It is therefore with no intention of providing a master key to unlock the mysteries of his heterogeneous *oeuvre* that I offer the following analysis. Rather, I hope to draw attention to only one of the intersecting planes, hitherto unexamined,[4] which can help us make sense of his remarkable work, in particular the source of its puzzling critical impulse. The plane in question can be called the anti-visual discourse of twentieth-century French thought or, more modestly, the interrogation of sight carried out by a wide and otherwise disparate number of French intellectuals beginning perhaps with Bergson.

Although I hope to explore its full ramifications at a later date, a few schematic remarks are necessary now to make clear the importance of the anti-ocular discourse in which Foucault can be situated. Long accounted the 'noblest' of the senses,[5] sight traditionally enjoyed a privileged role as the most discriminating and trustworthy of the sensual mediators between man and world.[6] Whether in terms of actual observation with the two eyes (often understood monocularly rather than in their true stereoscópic operations) or in those of internal mental speculation, vision has been accorded a special role in Western epistemology since the Greeks. Although at times more metaphorical than literal, the visual contribution to knowledge has been credited with far more importance than that of any other sense. A cursory and impressionistic 'glance' at such common English words and phrases as insight, perspective, overview, far-sighted, survey, point of view, demonstration, and synopsis reveal that there is more than an arbitrary choice of images in the question, do you see what I mean? As Richard Rorty has recently emphasized, modern thought at least since Descartes has generally privileged mental representations in 'the mind's eye' as mirror reflections of an external reality.[7]

The role of vision in the imaginative history of Western man is no less important, as students of religious and mythical symbols have convincingly demonstrated.[8] The visionary search for illumination, whether through mystical or mundane means, has generated a rich tradition of what Carlyle called 'spiritual optics'.[9] Here the resonance of related clusters of images surrounding the sun, the moon, the stars, fire, mirrors, and day and night show how basic visual experience has been in structuring our attempts to make sense of the sacred as well as the profane. In negative terms, the fear of being watched by an omniscient God or followed by the evil eye shows how highly ambiguous the role of sight has been, especially when it includes the experience of being the object instead of the subject of the look.[10] The complicated scopophilic-scopophobic dialectic of exhibitionism and paranoia that is evident in such figures as Rousseau shows the intimate linkages between vision and psychological phenomena.[11] Indeed, thinkers from the time of Augustine have recognized a fundamental relationship between ocular experience and desire, especially in its unfulfilled form.[12]

To detail the history of attitudes towards vision, including such anti-ocular moments as the Jewish prohibition of graven images, the iconoclastic controversy of the eighth century or the Protestant Reformation, is impossible here. Suffice it to say that with the rise of modern science, the Gutenberg revolution in printing and the Albertian emphasis on perspective in painting, vision was given an especially powerful role in the modern era.[13] In France in particular, the domination of visual experience and the discourse of sight seems to have been especially strong. Whether in the theatrical spectacle of Louis XIV's court, the emphasis on clear and distinct ideas in Cartesian philosophy, the enlightening project of the *philosophes*, or the visual phantasmagoria of the 'city of light', the ocularcentric character of French culture has been vividly apparent. So too has the French fascination with technical improvements in the capacity to see, evident from the time of Descartes' paean to the telescope in *La Dioptrique*, through Baudelaire's critique of photography, all the way to Barthes's ruminations on the camera and Deleuze's recent writings on the cinema.[14] Not surprisingly, one of the most striking aspects of twentieth-century French thought is the almost obligatory consideration of painting on the part of a wide variety of thinkers, such as Merleau-Ponty, Sartre, Derrida, Lyotard, Kofman, Lefort, Marin, Deleuze, Starobinski and, of course, Foucault himself.[15] And as a recent commentator on the poet Jean Tardieu's visual preoccupations remarks, 'a list of poet-art critics of the late nineteenth and twentieth centuries would be almost identical to a list of great poets of the era: Baudelaire, Valéry, Apollinaire, Reverdy, all the Surrealists, Ponge and Bonnefoy'.[16] One might add novelists like Robbe-Grillet, Tournier and Simon to hammer the point home even more firmly.

If the French obsession with vision has continued unabated to our own day, it has, however, taken a very different turn from its earlier direction. Beginning with Bergson's critique of the spatialization of time,[17] the French interrogation of sight has tended increasingly to emphasize its more problematic implications. The link between privileging vision and the traditional humanist subject, capable of rational enlightenment, has been opened to widespread attack. The illusions of imagistic representation and the allegedly disinterested scientific gaze have been subjected to hostile scrutiny. The mystifications of the social imagery and the spectacle of late capitalist culture have been the target of fierce criticism. And the psychological dependence of the ideological 'I' on the totalizing gaze of the 'eye' has been ruthlessly exposed.

Thinkers as different as Bataille and Sartre, Metz and Irigaray, Althusser and Levinas have all called into question the time-honoured nobility of sight. Even Merleau-Ponty, whose phenomenological exploration of perception can be seen in part as a celebration of embodied vision, was deeply suspicious of what he called *pensée au survol*, the high-altitude thinking which maintained the Cartesian split between a distant, spectatorial subject and the object of his sight. In short, although the reasons are still uncertain,[18] it is legitimate to talk of a discursive or paradigm shift in twentieth-century French thought in which the denigration of vision supplanted its previous celebration.

The degree of hostility has varied from thinker to thinker, as has the precise dimension of vision under attack; indeed, in certain cases, what is disliked by one critic is defended by another, and on occasion ambiguities arise within an author's *oeuvre*. How complicated the story actually is can, in fact, be discerned if we now turn to the special role played by Foucault in the anti-visual discourse. For although it is immediately evident that Foucault recognized important links between *voir* and both *savoir* and *pouvoir*, the nature of his fascination with the ocular is uncertain. One recent commentator, Allan Megill, has contended that in his earlier, more structuralist moments, Foucault was himself intent on portraying 'a lucent, Apollonian world'[19] within which ocularcentrism was neutrally accepted, although he abandoned this attempt in his later writings. Another, Michel de Certeau, has argued that throughout Foucault's work a tension can be discerned between his substantive critiques of the power of the gaze and his own 'optical style', which drew on visual astonishment to subvert that power.[20] There may, in fact, be justification for both these analyses in the labyrinthine, often highly ambiguous corpus of Foucault's writings. But the story is more complicated still, as a systematic consideration of his many references to aspects of vision will help us to understand.

That Foucault was fascinated with vision from the beginning of his career is not surprising in view of his early interest in Merleau-Ponty's phenomenology of perception, Ludwig Binswanger's existential psychoanalysis and Heidegger's phenomenological ontology. For in these thinkers the traditional Cartesian privileging of a detached, contemplative subject was decisively repudiated, as was Husserl's notion of an eidetic consciousness capable of intuiting essences through a *Wesensschau*. The humanist notion of a centred, rational subject, so Heidegger insisted in his influential essay, 'The Age of the World View', was rooted in scientific, pictorial subjectivism;[21] indeed, the very notion of *theoria* introduced by the Greeks was grounded in a technological appropriation of the world dependent on the same spectatorial split between subject and object. For Merleau-Ponty and Binswanger, the problematic distinction between consciousness and body was closely linked to the elevation of perspectival vision with its single point of view. More unmediated senses like touch were thus necessary to remedy the hypertrophied role of vision in Western experience.

In all of these cases, however, another, more attractive visual mode was also possible. Heidegger spoke of a type of circumscribed vision (*Umsicht*) in which the mediated distance of representation was abandoned in favour of a more primordial encounter with ontological reality. His celebrated, if somewhat fuzzy, evocation of a 'clearing' (*Lichtung*) in which Being might manifest itself expressed this hope for a more revelatory visual experience. For Binswanger and especially Merleau-Ponty, embodied vision, the reversible, chiasmic intertwining of the visible and invisible, the viewer and the viewed, in the 'flesh' of the world, could be the locus of positive meaning.

From the beginning, Foucault seems to have been less confident of the viability of their alternatives, even as he absorbed the phenomenological critique of Cartesian ocularcentrism. Although it may appear in hindsight that he overemphasized his own distance from phenomenology,[22] it is nonetheless striking that he would condemn the phenomenology of perception as a final variant of the very 'transcendental narcissism' that it claimed to overcome.[23] Unlike Merleau-Ponty, he never placed his faith in an ontology of vision that would replace the discredited epistemology derived from Descartes. Instead, he drew on earlier manifestations of the anti-visual discourse, most notably those evident in Bataille and Sartre, and combined them with others coming apparently from Nietzsche,[24] to probe far more thoroughly than the phenomenologists the dark side of the primacy of sight. Even in his most 'structuralist' moments, Foucault never endorsed the possibility of a transparent, fully visible and meaningful reality. Well before his celebrated and influential critique of panopticism in *Discipline and Punish*, he was aware of the costs of visual primacy. The writings of the early 1960s – *Madness and Civilization* (1961), *The Birth of the Clinic* (1963), *Raymond Roussel* (1963), and 'A Preface to Transgression' (1963) – demonstrate this awareness in numerous ways.[25]

Foucault's emphasis on the sinister implications of ocularcentrism is strikingly apparent in his analysis of the history of madness in 'the age of reason' or what he called 'the classical age' (roughly 1650 to 1800). The modern category of insanity, he contends, was predicated on the dissolution of the medieval and Renaissance unity of word and image, which liberated a multitude of images of madness deprived of any eschatological significance. As a result, madness became a pure spectacle, a theatre of unreason: 'During the classical period, madness was shown, but on the other side of bars; if present, it was at a distance, under the eyes of reason that no longer felt any relation to it and that would not compromise itself by too close a resemblance. Madness had become a thing to look at.'[26] For the 'classical' mind, the essence of madness was either blindness, a term which 'refers to the night of quasi-sleep which surrounds the images of madness, giving them, in their solitude, an invisible sovereignty',[27] or dazzlement, which means that 'the madman sees the daylight, the same daylight as the man of reason (both live in the same brightness); but seeing this same daylight, and nothing but this daylight, he sees it as void, as night, as nothing'.[28] For Foucault, the Cartesian distrust of the actual senses nonetheless betrayed an ocular bias that worked to exclude the insane:

> Descartes closes his eyes and plugs up his ears the better to see the true brightness of essential daylight; thus he is secured against the dazzlement of the madman who, opening his eyes, sees only the night, and not seeing at all, believes he sees when he imagines . . . Unreason is in the same relation to reason as dazzlement to the brightness of daylight itself. And this is not a metaphor. We are at the center of the great cosmology which animates all classical culture.[29]

There was, as well, an institutional expression of the visual definition of insanity in the birth of the asylum, where 'madness no longer exists except as *seen* . . . The science of mental disease, as it would develop in the asylum, would always be only of the order of observation and classification. It would not be a dialogue.'[30] For the main psychiatrist of the postclassical era, Pinel, the patient was not merely the object of another's scrutiny; he was turned instead into a self-reflective mirror so that 'madness would see itself, would be seen by itself – pure spectacle and absolute subject'.[31] And even though Freud introduced a linguistic moment into his psychoanalytic practice, he never abandoned entirely the specular bias of the psychiatric tradition. 'It would be fairer to say,' Foucault contended, 'that psychoanalysis doubled the absolute observation of the watcher with the endless monologue of the person watched – thus preserving the old asylum structure of non-reciprocal observation but balancing it, in a non-symmetrical reprocity, by the new structure of language without response.'[32] In fact, only in the non-psychiatric discourse of artists like Goya and de Sade were the marginalized claims of darkness and the night allowed to reassert themselves in the modern world, thus providing a prototype for the recovery of 'unreason' in art, the reverse side of madness.[33]

The Birth of the Clinic has been called an 'extended postscript'[34] to *Madness and Civilization*, which is an especially apt description if its concentration on the complicity of visual domination with the rise of modern medicine is acknowledged. In this work, Foucault more explicitly underlines the disciplinary power of *le regard* (the gaze or the look), a word with powerfully negative connotations in French thought since the celebrated chapter devoted to it in Sartre's *Being and Nothingness*.[35] Here as elsewhere, a subterranean affinity between two thinkers normally understood as opposed can be discerned, insofar as both express variations of the anti-visual paradigm of recent French thought.[36]

Sartre, to be sure, is never mentioned in the work, but it is difficult to avoid hearing echoes of his chilling description of the alienating and objectifying power of the Other's gaze in Foucault's historical account of the rise of a specific medical practice in the classical age. Less conjectural is the role of another student of the power of sight in Western theory and practice, the distinguished historian of science Georges Canguilhem, who commissioned *The Birth of the Clinic* for a series of studies he edited in the history and philosophy of biology and medicine. Canguilhem, who had also been the official supervisor of *Madness and Civilization* for Foucault's *doctorat d'état*, had given a course at the Sorbonne in 1957 on the role of vision as the model of cognition in Western thought.[37] Although Foucault, who was still teaching in Uppsala, Sweden at the time, could not have attended the lectures, it is highly probable that he learned something of their content when he returned to Paris. Later, he would acknowledge Canguilhem's influence as a methodological model, but it is no less likely that Foucault also became sensitized to the importance of sight in constituting medical 'knowledge' in the eighteenth century through the example of his mentor.

The Birth of the Clinic, in fact, describes the medical innovation of the classical age in terms of an intensified faith in visual evidence. 'The breadth of the experiment,' he argues, 'seems to be identified with the domain of the careful gaze, and of an empirical vigilance receptive only to the evidence of visible contents. The eye becomes the depository and source of clarity.'[38] The new medical gaze differs, however, from the Cartesian privileging of internal vision at the cost of the actual senses. Instead, it emphasizes 'the sovereign power of the empirical gaze',[39] which plays over the solid and opaque surfaces of the body. 'No light could now dissolve them in ideal truths; but the gaze directed upon them would, in turn, awaken them and make them stand out against a background of objectivity. The gaze is no longer reductive, it is, rather, that which establishes the individual in his irreducible quality.'[40] But what is in fact 'seen' is not a given, objective reality open to an innocent eye. Rather, it is an epistemic field, constructed as much linguistically as visually, which is no more or less close to the 'truth' than what it replaced. 'In its sovereign exercise, the gaze took up once again the structures of visibility that it had itself deposited in its field of perception.'[41]

Although the initial focus on visible surfaces and symptoms gave way in 'the age of Bichat' to a more penetrating gaze into the internal organic landscape, the search was still for an 'invisible visibility'.[42] The unexpected result of the ever more curious visual penetration of the body, Foucault suggests, is a focus not on the vitality of the patient, but rather his morality:

> That which hides and envelops, the curtain of night over truth, is, paradoxically, life; and death, on the contrary, opens up to the light of day the black coffer of the body: obscure life, limpid death, the oldest imaginary values of the Western world are crossed here in a strange misconstruction that is the very meaning of pathological anatomy . . . Nineteenth-century medicine was haunted by that absolute eye that cadaverizes life and rediscovers in the corpse the frail, broken nervure of life.[43]

What makes this development in the seemingly limited field of medicine so fateful for Foucault was its function as a model for future investigations in all of the 'sciences of man'. 'It will no doubt remain a decisive fact about our culture,' he concludes, 'that its first scientific discourse concerning the individual had to pass through this stage of death.'[44] And because the importance of perception, sight in particular, in this cadaverization of life was so great, it is impossible, Foucault suggests, to turn to it for an antidote to positivist reification, as the phenomenologists had hoped. In a passage covertly directed against Merleau-Ponty, he wrote,

> when one carries out a vertical investigation of this positivism, one sees the emergence of a whole series of figures – hidden by it, but also indispensable to its birth – that will be released later, and, paradoxically, used against it. In particular, that with which phenomenology was to oppose it so tenaciously was already present in its underlying structures: the original powers of the perceived and its correlation with language in the original form of experience . . .[45]

The surprising convergence of positivism and phenomenology on the level of their common privileging of ocular perception, with its penchant for death over life, did not, however, exhaust the importance of vision in the modern experience, as Foucault interpreted it. The complicated interlacing of language and vision was also apparent in the literary experiments of the writer to whom he devoted a very different kind of study at the same time as he was writing the history of the clinical gaze, Raymond Roussel.[46] Often neglected because of its seeming irrelevance to Foucault's more central concerns, the book demonstrates the complexity of his fascination with vision. That he thought it fundamental to Roussel's work is witnessed by his publishing a short piece specifically on saying and seeing in Roussel a year before its publication.[47] In the longer book, he expanded his analysis to cover the entire *oeuvre* of a writer whose experimental prose intrigued French intellectuals from the Surrealists to Robbe-Grillet.[48] Roussel is perhaps best known for his game of beginning a novel with a sentence which was phonetically repeated at its end, with only one element changed to make the meaning of the two sentences utterly different. Roussel's blithe disdain for the representative or referential function of language made him an obvious candidate for praise on the part of those who wanted to privilege the complete self-referentiality of language.

But significantly, in developing his unique style, Roussel revealed as well a preoccupation with vision, expressed even in the titles of certain of his works, such as *La Vue* and *La Poussière de Soleils*. According to Robbe-Grillett, 'sight, the privileged sense in Roussel, rapidly achieves an obsessive acuity, tending to infinity'.[49] Foucault, whose interest in the catachrestic dimensions of Roussel's language had been remarked,[50] was also very sensitive to the role of vision in his work. Like Robbe-Grillet, he emphasized its function as an impediment to meaningfulness in the novels. Contrary to the Surrealists, who were bent on seeking a hidden significance beneath the surface of Roussel's mysterious prose, Foucault insisted that his work 'systematically imposes an unformed, divergent, centrifugal uneasiness, oriented not towards the most reticent of secrets, but towards the redoubling and the transmutation of the most visible forms'.[51] Roussel's repetitive linguistic play was 'like the redoubling of the mask above the face; it would open on the same eclipse of being',[52] thus revealing in infinite reflection of mirrors without a privileged point of origin.

In places, Foucault seemed to appropriate Merleau-Ponty's terms in describing the 'interlacing' of the visible and the invisible in 'exactly the same tissue, the same indissoluble substance',[53] or in claiming *La Vue* presented a universe without perspective or, more precisely, 'combining the vertical point of view (which permits everything to be embraced as in a circle) and the horizontal point of view (which places the eye at ground level and gives to sight only the first dimension) so well that everything is seen in perspective and yet each thing is envisaged in its complete context'.[54] But rejecting Merleau-Ponty's optimism, Foucault emphasized the meaninglessness of Roussel's visual universe, where light was cast on a world which only reabsorbed it in the 'mutism of objects'.[55] Roussel's writing, he argued, invoked 'images visibly invisible, perceptible but not decipherable, given in a lightning flash and without possible reading, present in a radiance that repelled the gaze'.[56] Although Foucault noted a shift between the early and late Roussel – the works up to *La Vue* were illuminated by a dazzling, homogeneous light, the light of a sun too bright to permit any nuanced shadows, whereas everything written after, most notably the *Nouvelles Impressions de l'Afrique*, was cloaked in the darkness of a 'closed-in sun' (*soleil enfermé*) – the implication was the same: the visual in Roussel provided only 'an empty lens' (*lentille vide*) incapable of focusing on a clear and distinct world.[57] Genuine transparency, in the sense of a medium which completely dissolved to reveal an unequivocal truth or unambivalent meaning, was thus denied to both language and perception.

It was, in fact, Foucault's awareness of the visually opaque dimension within language itself, which he called its perpetually rebus-like character,[58] that makes it problematic to characterize him primarily as a structuralist, even of a heterodox kind.[59] There is no enigma to be decoded, no spatial coherence to be mapped out in two-dimensional terms. Roussel was not the only figure to whom Foucault was drawn because of his debunking of this hope; the Belgian Surrealist painter René Magritte, was another. In an essay written in 1968 and then expanded into a little book five years later, Foucault explored a more explicitly visual version of the phenomenon he had discerned in Roussel.[60] Describing Magritte's canvases as the opposite of *trompe l'oeil* because of their undermining of the mimetic conventions of realistic painting, he also referred to them as 'unraveled calligrams' because they refused to close the gap between image and word. In the terms he had introduced in *The Order of Things*, written between the Roussel and Magritte studies, the Surrealist had discarded art's claim to provide representative 'resemblances' of the external world in favour of repetitive 'similitudes', which circulate a series of visual and linguistic signs without an external referent.[61] Whereas resemblances always affirmatively assert the irreducible sameness of image and object, similitude, Foucault argued, 'multiplies different affirmations, which dance together, tilting and tumbling over one another'.[62]

Foucault's celebration of difference, heterogeneity and the dance of otherness in *This is Not a Pipe* clearly demonstrates his affinity with one of the most seductive voices in the anti-visual discourse of twentieth-century French thought, that of Georges Bataille. His contribution to *Critique*'s 1963 homage to Bataille shows how drawn Foucault was to Bataille's attempt to valorize a transgressive experience, 'where the subject who speaks has just vanished, where the spectacle topples over before an upturned eye'.[63] The upturned, unseeing eye referred to Bataille's celebrated pornographic novel *The Story of the Eye*, with its metaphoric exchange of ocular symbols – eggs, testicles, the sun, etc. – all pierced, bleeding, enucleated, overflowing and blind. Foucault recognized Bataille's fundamental challenge to the hierarchical privileging of vision in the Western tradition, its fateful linkage, as Freud pointed out,[64] with man's vertical posture, the repression of his sexual and anal erotic urges and the rise of 'civilization'. He also noted its challenge to the visually derived constitution of the reflective, Cartesian subject:

> Bataille reverses this entire direction: sight, crossing the globular limit of the eye, constitutes the eye in its instantaneous being, sight carries it away in this luminous stream (an outpouring fountain, streaming tears and, shortly, blood), hurls the eye outside of itself, conducts it to the limit where it bursts out in the immediately extinguished flash of its being. Only a small white ball, veined with blood, is left behind, only an exorbitated eye to which all sight is now denied . . . In the distance created by this violence and uprooting, the eye is seen absolutely, but denied the possibility of sight: the philosophizing subject has been dispossessed and pursued to its limit.[65]

As in Roussel, the ultimate blindness of sight, the opacity of the seemingly transparent, also suggested the limits of linguistic meaningfulness. For 'the upturned eye has no meaning in Bataille's language, can have no meaning since it marks its limit'.[66] Instead, it signals the point at which language explodes 'in laughter, tears, the overturned eyes of ecstasy, the mute and exorbitated horror of sacrifice'.[67] As such it shows the link between language, human finitude and the death of God, 'a sun that rotates and the great eyelid that closes upon the world'.[68]

The eclipse of the solar divinity was linked for Foucault with the decline of his secular analogue, the humanist concept of Man. Hostility to visual primacy and the critique of humanism were intricately linked in the work which most vividly established Foucault's credentials as an anti-humanist, *The Order of Things*.[69] Significantly, the work begins with a now celebrated description of a visual scene, Velázquez's *Las Meninas*, and ends with a no less frequently cited visual metaphor of Man's face etched in the sand being erased by the waves at the edge of the sea.

Rather than focusing on these now widely discussed framing moments in the text,[70] I want to explore instead the arguments in between insofar as they bear on the question of vision. Whether or not the spatial preoccupations of the book betokened an affinity for Apollonian structuralism, as Megill, following Derrida, has claimed, or merely reflected Foucault's subject matter, as he himself later argued,[71] *The Order of Things* does not seem quite as obsessively fixed on *le regard* as does his earlier work. Or rather it seems to be so only in Foucault's account of the classical age. As in *Madness and Civilization*, he describes the onset of that period in terms of the breakdown of an assumed unity of word and image before the end of the sixteenth century. In a culture based on semantic resemblances, images were understood to be decipherable hieroglyphs of meaning. The result was 'a non-distinction between what is seen and what is read, between observation and relation, which results in the constitution of a single, unbroken surface in which observation and language intersect to infinity'.[72]

For reasons that are not clear and which Foucault unfortunately never deemed worthy of explication, the classical age emerges when this unity is undone and images no longer resemble readable texts. Both Bacon and Descartes, if for different reasons, denounce thinking through resemblances or similitudes and warn against the illusions to which it is prone. One implication of the breakdown of this unity, first evident in Cervantes, is the growing awareness of the binary and representative nature of the sign, which frees it from the assumption that it bears an intrinsic figural resemblance to what it signifies. As an arbitrary human tool, language is understood as a neutral medium of communication. Inclined towards nominalism, language in the classical age also privileged the most neutral verb possible: the verb 'to be'.

Another implication of the breakdown is the compensatory unleashing of perception in general, and vision in particular, as the sole means of ascertaining reliable knowledge about the external world. According to Foucault, 'the manifestations and sign of truth are to be found in evident and distinct perception. It is the task of words to translate the truth if they can; but they no longer have the right to be considered a mark of it. Language has withdrawn from the midst of beings themselves and has entered a period of transparency and neutrality.'[73] The classical age is thus dominated by a new faith in the power of direct and technologically improved observation and by a concomitant taxonomic ordering of its findings in the visible space of the table. Although such tables are necessarily linguistic, the names they arrange in spatial relations are assumed to be utterly without density of their own. The triumph of natural history is thus the triumph of the visual:

> One has the impression that with Tournefort, with Linnaeus or Buffon, someone has at last taken on the task of stating something that had been visible from the beginning of time, but had remained mute before a sort of invincible distraction of men's eyes. In fact, it was not an age-old inattentiveness being suddenly dissipated, but a new field of visibility being constituted in all its density.[74]

Other senses like touch or hearing are denigrated, as scientific language struggles to turn itself as much as possible into a transparent record of the observing gaze.

Moreover, to the extent that visual knowledge is dominant in the classical age, there is assumed an observing eye capable of seeing the visible tables, but from a position outside of them. It is in this sense that *Las Meninas*, as Foucault interprets it, is itself a representation of classical representation. For it is the absent sovereigns, there only in their reflections in the small mirror on the back wall of the painter's studio, who 'see' the picture in front of us. We are thus not yet in a fully humanist age characterized by the positive appearance of Man:

> In Classical thought, the personage for whom the representation exists, and who represents himself within it, recognizing himself therein as an image or reflection, he who ties together all the interlacing threads of the 'representation in the form of a picture or a table' – he is never to be found in that table himself. Before the end of the eighteenth century, *man* does not exist . . . [75]

If then, it is only with the end of the visual primacy of the classical age that full-fledged humanism emerges, what is the connection between ocularcentrism and the rise of man? At first, there does not seem to be any, which would call into question the importance of the anti-visual discourse in Foucault's work, at least at this stage of it. For when he comes to describe the end of natural history and its replacement by biology at the time of Cuvier, he explicitly stresses the new emphasis on invisible, anatomic and organic structures which supplant the empirical classifications of the classical table. 'The visible order, with its permanent grid of distinctions,' he writes, 'is now only a superficial glitter above an abyss.'[76] With the concomitant emergence of historical consciousness, functional analogy and succession – temporal rather than spatial values – replace the static order of the classical age. Life, labour and language all break free from the domination of the taxonomic gaze. The putative transparency of language gives way to a growing opacity which culminates in the appearance of pure 'literature' in Mallarmé.

And yet, in a subtle way, the postclassical, humanist *episteme*, as Foucault describes it, is still hostage to the primacy of sight. We can become sensitive to this continuity across the seemingly abrupt rupture in discursive formations if we remember Foucault's argument about Bichat, Pinel and Freud in *Madness and Civilization* and his highly speculative claim about the link between the later sciences of man and the medical gaze in *The Birth of the Clinic.* In those works, he insisted that even as the surface of the body was penetrated to let the hitherto invisible become the object of inquiry, even as language was introduced to supplement the psychiatric gaze, vision did not falter as the dominant cognitive sense. It is for this reason that at the same time modern biology was positing 'life' as its object, it paradoxically discovered 'death' at its heart.[77]

But in an even more fundamental sense, the primacy of the visual was preserved in Foucault's account of the rise of the human sciences. For with the eclipse of the classical age,

> man appears in his ambiguous position as an object of knowledge and as subject that knows; enslaved sovereign, *observed spectator*, he appears in the place belonging to the king, which was assigned to him in advance by *Las Meninas*, but from which his real presence has for so long been excluded. As if, in that vacant space towards which Velázquez's whole painting was directed, but which it was nevertheless reflecting only in the chance presence of a mirror, and as though by stealth, all the figures whose alternation, reciprocal exclusion, interweaving, and fluttering one imagined (the model, the painter, the king, the spectator) suddenly stopped their imperceptible dance, immobilized into one substantial figure, and demanded that the entire space of the representation should at last be related to one corporeal gaze.[78]

In this extremely important paragraph, Foucault reveals the extent to which humanism is based in his view on the replacement of the absent spectator, the king, by the 'observed spectator', man in a still visually constituted epistemological field. Thus, the arrival of this 'strange empirico-transcendental doublet'[79] means that 'man' functions both as an allegedly neutral metasubject of knowledge and as its proper object, viewed from afar. Even phenomenology, Foucault insists once again, falls prey to this way of perceiving the world, showing its 'insidious kinship, its simultaneously promising and threatening proximity, to empirical analyses of man'.[80]

Only with the triumph of an opaque and self-referential concept of language does the visually determined humanist *episteme* begin to be effaced enough for Foucault to claim that 'man had been a figure occurring between two modes of language'.[81] Perhaps with writers like Roussel and Bataille – as well as others Foucault mentions, like Artaud and Blanchot – the crisis of the primacy of sight has reached a point at which an epistemic shift is on the horizon. Now those hitherto forbidden elements that had been consigned to the realm of darkness ever since the onset of the classical age, such as madness, difference and transgressive eroticism, can be rescued from the domination of light, transparency and the Same. For with the weakening of ocular primacy goes a concomitant questioning of the translucency of language, which had been its handmaiden ever since the breakdown of the preclassical unity of word and image. But rather than a return to that prelapsarian state in which latent meaning was available to be deciphered, the posthumanist condition will be characterized more by the mutual opacity we have seen Foucault celebrate in his study of Roussel.

The Order of Things marked the last great instance of what has become known as Foucault's archaeological period, which was brought to a close by his summary, if somewhat cryptic, methodological statement, *The Archaeology of Knowledge*. In a footnote in that work, he noted that 'the term *"regard medical"* used in my *Naissance de la clinique* was not a very happy one',[82] which may suggest a certain weakening of his earlier visual preoccupations; but in fact, all it implied was a more heightened awareness of the anthropocentric fallacies involved in positing a synthetic, unified subject doing the looking. For it was precisely this apparently transcendental subject that *The Order of Things* claimed was a function of ocularcentrism rather than a precondition for it. Vision, he now seemed to suggest, could help constitute an *episteme* without the implied presence of an absent sovereign or his humanist surrogate, whose gaze totalized the discursive field. Here, interestingly, he showed a continued filiation to Sartre, whose paranoid ontology of *le regard* in *Being and Nothingness* did not require an actual subject looking at an objectified other. According to Sartre, 'the look will be given just as well on occasion when there is a rustling of branches, or the sound of a footstep followed by silence, or the slight opening of a shutter, or a light movement of a curtain'.[83] This generalizable experience of being observed by an unknown and omnipresent 'eye' is, of course, precisely what Foucault described in his powerful investigation of panopticism in his next major work, *Discipline and Punish*.[84]

Foucault had been sensitive to the relations between social and political constraint and the objectifying power of the gaze as early as *The Birth of the Clinic*, where he linked the rise of modern medicine to the reforms of the French Revolution:

This medical field, restored to its pristine truth, pervaded wholly by the gaze, without obstacle and without alteration, is strangely similar, in

its implicit geometry, to the social space dreamt of by the Revolution
. . . The ideological theme that guides all structural reforms from 1789
to Thermidor Year II is that of the sovereign liberty of truth: the
majestic violence of light, which is in itself supreme, brings to an end
the bounded, dark kingdom of privileged knowledge and establishes
the unimpeded empire of the gaze.[85]

But it was only in *Discipline and Punish*, the first major fruit of his
so-called genealogical method, that he discovered the more subtle
social mechanism which allowed ocular domination to extend
beyond the boundaries of an all-seeing sovereign or a despotic
revolutionary state.

Foucault's analysis, to be sure, begins with an evocation of the
spectacle of sovereign power in the classical age. With characteristic
visual *éclat*, he describes the torture and execution of the failed
regicide Damiens in 1757 as a 'theatrical representation of pain'[86] in
which the power of the monarch was literally inscribed in the visible
flesh of the condemned man. As in his earlier accounts of the
constitution of madness, the medical gaze in the clinic and the
taxonomic system of natural history, the privileging of vision is
evident. Not only does it appear in the 'spectacle of the scaffold' of
the *ancien régime*, it continues as well through the 'great theatrical
ritual'[87] of the Revolutionary guillotine.

But as in his earlier analysis, Foucault notes the decay of the
classical mode in favour of a more complicated, but still visually
determined alternative in the nineteenth century. Although he
acknowledges its prototype in the military schools, military camps
and clinics of the eighteenth century – and he might have added the
court society at the end of Louis XIV's reign[88] – he chooses
Bentham's model prison as the most explicit version of the new ocular
technology of power. For it was here that the disciplining and
normalizing function of the gaze was at its most blatant. Reversing
the principle of the dungeon, the Panopticon, with its hidden
supervisor watching from a central tower like an omniscient but
invisible God, is an architectural embodiment of the most paranoid of
Sartrean fantasies about the 'absolute look'.[89] The object of power is
everywhere penetrated by the benevolently sadistic gaze of a diffuse
and anonymous power, whose actual existence soon becomes su-
perfluous to the process of discipline. The Panopticon is a 'machinery
that assures dissymmetry, disequilibrium, difference. Consequently, it
does not matter who exercises power. Any individual, taken almost at
random, can operate the machine.'[90]

Complementing the role of the gaze – or rather the sensation of always being its target – in the control and rehabilitation of criminals is the prophylactic power of surveillance, which is designed to prevent potential transgressions of the law. Here the external look becomes an internalized and self-regulating mechanism, which extends the old religious preoccupation with the smallest detail, whose importance 'in the sight of God'[91] was immense. The normalizing function of the institutions and practices of surveillance was successful enough, according to Foucault, to dispense with the more heavy-handed displays of sovereign power needed earlier to render the population docile. Napoleon was the transitional moment, as he 'combined in a single symbolic, ultimate figure the whole of the long process by which the pomp of sovereignty, the necessarily spectacular manifestations of power, were extinguished one by one on the daily exercise of surveillance, in a panopticism in which the vigilance of intersecting gazes was soon to render useless both the eagle and the sun.'[92] Thus, implicitly taking issue with Marxists like Guy Debord, who castigated the consumer-oriented 'society of the spectacle',[93] Foucault concluded that 'our society is one not of spectacle, but of surveillance . . . We are neither in the amphitheatre, nor on the stage, but in the panoptic machine'.[94]

That our imprisonment in this machine owed much to the well-intentioned goals of the enlightenment and the Revolution it helped spawn Foucault did not doubt. 'The "Enlightenment", which discovered the liberties,' he contended, 'also invented the disciplines.'[95] Unlike more sympathetic defenders of the *siècle des lumières*, like Jürgen Habermas,[96] who emphasized its contribution to a public sphere centred on talking and listening, Foucault tended to privilege its visual dimension instead. And although he protested near the end of his life against 'the intellectual blackmail of "being for or against the Enlightenment" ',[97] it is difficult to miss a certain hostility in such observations as the following remarks in an interview called 'The Eye of Power':

> I would say Bentham was the complement to Rousseau. What in fact was the Rousseauist dream that motivated many of the revolutionaries? It was the dream of a transparent society, visible and legible in each of its parts, the dream of there no longer existing any zones of darkness . . . Bentham is both that and the opposite. He poses the problem of visibility, but thinks of a visibility organized entirely around a dominating, overseeing gaze. He effects the project of a universal visibility which exists to serve a rigorous, meticulous power.

Thus Bentham's obsession, the technical idea of the exercise of an 'all-seeing' power, is grafted on to the great Rousseauist theme which is in some sense the lyrical note of the Revolution.[98]

Here, significantly, Foucault explicitly drew on the important analyses of Jean Starobinski, which were influential on other exemplars of the anti-visual discourse, such as Jacques Derrida and Sarah Kofman.[99] Rousseau's vain search for perfect transparency, both personal and political, could easily be turned into a target of reproach for those who detected in it a nostalgia for unmediated presence or a licence for coerced unanimity. Relying on a penetrating gaze which would pierce the surface of reality, it was no less illusory than the theatrical perusal of 'mere' appearances in the spectacles of the classical age.

Although Foucault took pain to avoid the implication that all modern technologies of power derived from the Rousseauist-Benthamite principle of perfect visibility.[100] He nonetheless acknowledged its importance in constituting and then controlling the next phenomenon he investigated, that of sexuality. 'With these themes of surveillance, and especially in the schools,' he claimed, 'it seems that control over sexuality becomes inscribed in architecture. In the Military Schools, the very walls speak the struggle against homosexuality and masturbation.'[101] The sciences of man, intended to help in the macro-logical control of populations as well as the micro-logical normalizing of individuals, drew on the mixture of the gaze and discourse which Foucault had identified with psychoanalysis as early as *The Birth of the Clinic*. Although he now stressed the power of discourse, such as that of the confession, in creating the very notion of sexuality, he insisted on the importance of spatial, visual controls in policing it. Nowhere was this function as evident as in the ostracism of the sexual 'pervert' whose very deviance was 'written immodestly on his face and body because it was a secret that always gave itself away'.[102]

In so arguing, Foucault demonstrated his implicit debt to yet another central text in the anti-visual discourse of twentieth-century French thought, Sartre's *Saint Genet*. For according to that work, not only was Genet compelled to label himself a 'thief' because he was observed by the 'other' in the act of stealing, he was also forced into assuming the character of the homosexual by the same gaze. As Sartre put it,

Sexually, Genet is first of all a raped child. This first rape was the gaze of the other, who took him by surprise, penetrated him, transformed him forever into an object . . . Undressed by the eyes of decent folk as women are by those of males, he carries his fault as they do their breasts and behind . . . Having been caught stealing *from behind*, his back opens when he steals; it is with his back that he awaits human gazes and catastrophe.[103]

Although Foucault never wrote about Genet and would have likely rejected Sartre's existentialist insistence on the victim heroically choosing to identify with his labels, his more general account of the ocular objectification of the deviant fits well with the analysis of *le regard* in *Saint Genet*.

To mention Genet is to reopen the question of possible resistance to the process of visual objectification. For certain of his works, such as the film he made with Jean Cocteau, *Un Chant d'Amour*, have been interpreted as visual challenges to the voyeuristic sadism of modern culture.[104] Can Foucault himself be said to have offered a visual antidote to the disciplinary power of the gaze? How strong a weapon was that 'optic of astonishment' noted by de Certeau in Foucault's struggle against the policing of space? Or perhaps did he implicitly draw on other senses in his evocation of 'bodies and pleasures' as a counterweight to the domination of sexuality and desire?

At times, Foucault did explicitly call on the disruptive power of images, especially against the claims of language to represent a perfectly self-contained and self-sufficient system. Thus, for example, in his introduction to Binswanger, he criticized psychoanalysis in general and Lacan in particular for failing to credit the visual dimension of dreams, which they reduced instead to merely linguistic phenomena.[105] And, as we have seen, his analyses of Roussel and Magritte emphasized the power of sight to subvert the homogenizing drive towards the 'same' implicit in naive linguistic versions of representation. What in *The Order of Things* he called 'hetero-topias'[106] were disturbingly inconsistent spatial configurations which undermined the alleged coherence of linguistic systems. Indeed, one might say that against both linguistic and visual *trompe l'oeil*, he preferred a kind of catachresis, which preserved ambiguity, otherness and chiasmic intersection.

And yet, in all of these cases, the role of vision remained essentially negative. Like Jean-François Lyotard in *Discours, figure*,[107] he pitted vision against language, especially in its structuralist incarnations, but did so only in order to emphasize its viewing a world of opaque meaninglessness. As we have seen in his frequent criticisms of Merleau-Ponty, Foucault never felt attracted towards an ontology of embodied vision in which a different kind of perception might provide answers to the unresolved problems raised in philosophies of consciousness. Unlike many non-French commentators on the implications of vision,[108] he resisted exploring its reciprocal, inter-subjective, communicative function, that of the mutual glance. *Le regard* never assumed its alternative meaning in English of caring or esteeming. As de Certeau has pointed out,[109] Foucault focused so insistently on the dangers of panopticism that he remained blind to other micro-practices of everyday life that subvert its power. In short, despite his obvious delight in visual phenomena, he remained very much in thrall to the anti-visual discourse so pervasive in French thought in this century. For Foucault, the upturned eye was always preferable to the empire of the gaze.

Nor is it likely that he held out much hope for another sense as the antidote to ocularcentrism, as is the case with other critics of visual primacy such as Luce Irigaray.[110] Feminists may choose to turn to touch or smell as more consonant with female than male sexuality, but Foucault was always too sceptical of any search for essentializing immediacy – and also, too unconcerned with female sexual experi-ence – to feel that this choice provided an answer. Indeed, as he emphasized in one of his last interviews, 'I am not looking for an alternative . . . What I want to do is not the history of solutions, and that's the reason why I don't accept the word *alternative*. I would like to do the genealogy of problems, of *problématiques*. My point is not that everything is bad, but that everything is dangerous.'[111]

Which dangers one chooses to stress are, of course, more than an arbitrary decision. It has been the purpose of this paper to demonstrate that Foucault was particularly sensitive to the putative dangers of ocularcentrism because of his embeddedness in a larger discourse, which he never himself problematized. It is only by understanding his debt to that discourse, I would argue in conclusion, that we can make sense of one of the most perplexing dimensions of his work: the source of its undefended but deeply felt critical impulse. Foucault's failure or unwillingness to probe the normative basis for his 'history of the present' has frequently troubled commentators eager to uncover the roots of his outrage.[112] When pressed, as he often was, to defend himself, Foucault would fall back at times on a weak separation of facts and values that echoed Weber at his most neo-Kantian. But his practice was very different from Weber's because of the current of ethical commitment that ran throughout virtually all of his writings. Although in his last years Foucault began to reflect on the ethical impulse of his work,[113] he never developed a fully satisfactory account of it. Perhaps the explanation can be found in his unavoidable inability to 'see' beyond the horizon of his own *episteme* and question the premises and implications of the anti-visual discourse itself.

The generative power of that discourse in revealing hitherto unproblematized dimensions of our culture cannot be denied; Foucault's own work shows how fecund its influence can be. And yet for those not completely caught in its gravitational field, it may be time to begin probing the costs as well as benefits of the anti-ocular counter-enlightenment. Its own genealogy needs to be demystified, not in order to restore a naive faith in the nobility of sight, but rather to cast a little light on the manifold implications of its new ignobility.

Notes

1 Charles C. Lemert and Garth Gillan, *Michel Foucault: Social Theory and Transgression* (New York: Columbia University Press, 1982), p. 2.
2 Michel Foucault, *The Archaeology of Knowledge and the Discourse on Language*, trans. A. M. Sheridan Smith (New York: Pantheon, 1972), p. 54.
3 I have attempted to apply similar analysis to another figure who defies simple categorization in *Adorno* (London: Fontana, 1984).
4 Some attention to the visual implications of Foucault's work has recently been paid by Allan Megill in his *Prophets of Extremity: Nietzsche, Heidegger, Foucault and Derrida* (Berkeley: University of California Press, 1985) and Scott Lash, 'Postmodernity and desire', *Theory and Society*, vol. 14 (January 1985), pp. 1–33. Although the title is promising, 'Der böse Blick des Michel Foucault', *Neue Rundschau*, vol. 82 (1972) by Martin Puder does not really investigate the problematic of vision in his work.
5 Hans Jonas, 'The Nobility of Sight' in *The Phenomenon of Life: Toward a Philosophical Biology* (University of Chicago Press, 1966); for an argument that restricts its period of ascendency to the bourgeois era, see Donald M. Lowe, *History of Bourgeois Perception* (University of Chicago Press, 1982).
6 The gender choice here is not accidental, as many feminists now claim ocularcentrism and phallocentrism go together. For a somewhat critical analysis of this claim, see Evelyn Fox Keller and Christine R. Grontowski, 'The Mind's Eye', in Sandra Harding and Merrill B. Hintikka (eds), *Discovering Reality: Feminist Perspectives on Epistemology, Metaphysics, Methodology, and Philosophy of Science* (Boston: D. Reidel, 1983).
7 Richard Rorty, *Philosophy and the Mirror of Nature* (Princeton University Press, 1979).

8   See, for example, Gustav Mensching, 'Die Lichtsymbolik in der Religionsgeschichte' and Hans Blumenberg, 'Licht als Metapher der Wahrheit: In Vorfeld der philosophischen Begriffsbildung', both in *Studium Generale*, vol. 10 (1957).

9   Quoted in M. H. Abrams, *Natural Supernaturalism: Tradition and Revolution in Romantic Literature* (New York: Norton, 1973), p. 377. Abrams cites many other examples of the romantic visionary tradition.

10 For a discussion of the evil eye, see Tobin Siebers, *The Mirror of Medusa* (Berkeley: University of California Press, 1983).

11 The classic account of Rousseau's visual preoccupations is Jean Starobinski, *Jean-Jacques Rousseau: La transparence et l'obstacle* (Paris: Gallimard, 1971); see also his *L'Oeil vivant* (Paris: Gallimard, 1961). For a general discussion of psychoanalysis and vision, see David W. Allen, *The Fear of Looking or Scopophilic–exhibitionistic Conflicts* (Charlottesville, Va.: University Press of Virginia, 1974).

12 Augustine discusses ocular desire in chapter 35 of his *Confessions*, which ties it to the temptations of unchecked curiosity. Other psychological implications of vision have been explored by later thinkers, like Freud, who linked fears of blindness with castration anxiety and emphasized the relations between voyeurism and sadism.

13 For two accounts that stress the link between the privileging of vision and the rise of the modern age, see Lucien Febvre, *The Problem of Unbelief in the Sixteenth Century: The Religion of Rabelais*, trans. Beatrice Gottlieb (Cambridge, Mass.: Harvard University Press, 1982) and Robert Mandrou, *Introduction to Modern France, 1500–1640: An Essay in Historical Psychology*, trans. R. B. Hallmark (New York: Holmes and Meier, 1976).

14 René Descartes, *Discourse on Method, Optics, Geometry, and Meteorology*, trans. Paul J. Olscamp (Indianapolis: Bobbs-Merrill, 1965); Charles Baudelaire, 'The Modern Public and Photography', in *Art in Paris, 1845–1862*, trans. and ed. Jonathan Mayne (London: Phaidon, 1965); Roland Barthes, *Camera Lucida: Reflections on Photography*, trans. Richard Howard (New York: Hill and Wang, 1981); Gilles Deleuze, *L'Image-mouvement* (Paris: Minuit, 1983).

15 A representative sample of their work on painting would include the following texts: Maurice Merleau-Ponty, 'Cézanne's Doubt', in *Sense and Non-sense*, trans. Hubert L. Dreyfus and Patricia A. Dreyfus (Evanston: Northwestern University Press, 1964); Jean-Paul Sartre, 'Tintoretto: St George and the Dragon' in *Between Existentialism and Marxism*, trans. John Matthews (New York: William Morrow, 1974); Jacques Derrida, *La vérité en peinture* (Paris: Flammarion, 1978); Jean-François Lyotard, 'La peinture comme dispositif libidinal', in *Des dispositifs pulsionnels* (Paris: Christian Bourgois, 1973); Sarah Kofman, 'Balthus ou la pause', in *Mélancholie de l'art* (Paris: Galilée, 1985); Claude Lefort, 'Bitran ou la question de l'oeil', in *Sur une colonne absente: Ecrits autour de Merleau-Ponty* (Paris: Gallimard,

1978); Louis Marin, *Détruire la peinture* (Paris: Galilée, 1977); Gilles Deleuze, *Francis Bacon: Logique de la sensation*, 2 vols (Paris: Editions de la Différance, 1981); Jean Starobinski, *1789: The Emblems of Reason*, trans. Barbara Bray (Charlottesville, Va.: University Press of Virginia, 1982); and Michel Foucault, *This is Not a Pipe*, trans. and ed. James Harkness (Berkeley: University of California Press, 1982).

Although I have not done a systematic comparison, it is likely that German thought during this same period would show a far less central preoccupation with visual phenomena. From the time of Schopenhauer and Nietzsche up to that of Adorno, music rather than painting has been the primary aesthetic model for many German philosophers. And the hermeneutic tradition dating back to the Reformation, with its stress on the word of God, has always privileged hearing and speech over sight, a bias still evident in contemporary thinkers like Gadamer and Habermas. Perhaps the only visually oriented text that immediately leaps to mind as a counterexample is Heidegger's famous discussion of Van Gogh's peasant shoes in 'The origin of the work of art', which Derrida discussed in *La vérité en peinture*.

16   Adelaide M. Russo, 'From visual to verbal in Jean Tardieu's *Les Portes de Toile*', *Substance*, vol. 14 (1985), p. 76.

17   According to Hannah Arendt, *The Life of the Mind* (New York: Harcourt Brace, Jovanovich, 1978), p. 122, 'Since Bergson, the use of the sight metaphor in philosophy has kept dwindling, not un-surprisingly, as emphasis and interest have shifted entirely from contemplation to speech, from *nous* to *logos*.' Anticipations of the shift, however, can be found somewhat earlier in, for example, the Decadents' interest in synaesthesia. Huysman's *Against the Grain* is an excellent instance of the search for other sensual experience beyond the visual.

18   Any explanation would have to include discussions of technological changes in the capacity to see in the nineteenth and early twentieth centuries, the impact of World War I, and the general crisis of representation that appeared at that time in many areas. For a useful commentary on some of these changes, see Stephen Kern, *The Culture of Time and Space, 1880–1918* (Cambridge, Mass.: Harvard University Press, 1983).

19   Megill, *Prophets*, p. 218. The inspiration for Megill's characterization comes from Derrida's critique of Foucault in *Writing and Difference*, trans. Alan Bass (University of Chicago Press, 1978).

20   Michel de Certeau, 'Le rire de Michel Foucault', *Revue de la Bibliothèque Nationale*, vol. 14 (Winter 1984), p. 15. Elsewhere, de Certeau invokes Foucault's narrative rhetoric as his antidote to panopticism. See his 'Micro-techniques and panoptic discourse: a quid pro quo', *Humanities in Review*, vol. 5 (Summer and Fall 1982), p. 264.

21   Martin Heidegger, 'The Age of the World View', in *The Question*

Concerning Technology and Other Essays, trans. William Lovitt (New York: Harper and Row, 1977). A more literal translation of *Weltbild* would be 'world picture'.

22 For an argument claiming Foucault misread Merleau-Ponty and overemphasized their differences, see Richard A. Cohen, 'Merleau-Ponty, the Flesh and Foucault', *Philosophy Today*, vol. 28 (Winter 1984). For another consideration of the Merleau-Ponty–Foucault relationship, see Hubert L. Dreyfus and Paul Rabinow, *Michel Foucault: Beyond Structuralism and Hermeneutics* (University of Chicago Press, 1982).

23 Foucault, *The Archaeology of Knowledge*, p. 203. In *The Visible and the Invisible*, ed. Claude Lefort, trans. Alphonso Lingis (Evanston: Northwestern University Press, 1968), p. 139, Merleau-Ponty did, in fact, claim that 'there is a fundamental narcissism of all vision'.

24 For a discussion of Nietzsche on vision, see Sarah Kofman, *Nietzsche et la métaphore* (Paris: Galilée, 1983), pp. 149f.

25 Foucault, *Madness and Civilization: A History of Insanity in the Age of Reason*, trans. Richard Howard (New York: Random House, 1965); *The Birth of the Clinic: An Archaeology of Medical Perception*, trans. A. M. Sheridan (London: Tavistock, 1973); *Raymond Roussel* (Paris: Gallimard, 1963); 'A Preface to Transgression', in *Language, Counter-Memory, Practice: Selected Essays and Interviews*, ed. Donald F. Bouchard, trans. Donald F. Bouchard and Sherry Simon (Ithaca, N.Y.: Cornell University Press, 1977).

26 Foucault, *Madness and Civilization*, p. 70.

27 Ibid., p. 106.

28 Ibid., p. 108.

29 Ibid., pp. 108–9.

30 Ibid., p. 250.

31 Ibid., p. 262.

32 Ibid., pp. 250–1.

33 Goya was also the figure Starobinski chose to represent the move away from the Enlightenment in *1789: The Emblems of Reason*. De Sade, of course, was heroized by a wide variety of twentieth-century thinkers, including Bataille and others important in the anti-visual discourse we are discussing in this paper.

34 Alan Sheridan, *Michel Foucault: The Will to Truth* (London: Tavistock, 1980), p. 37.

35 Jean-Paul Sartre, *Being and Nothingness: An Essay on Phenomenological Ontology*, trans. Hazel E. Barnes (New York: Washington Square Press, 1966), pp. 310f. On Sartre's critique of *le regard*, see François George, *Sur Sartre* (Paris: Christian Bourgois, 1976), pp. 303f; and Deena Weinstein and Michael Weinstein, 'On the visual constitution of society: the contributions of Georg Simmel and Jean-Paul Sartre to a sociology of the senses', *History of European Ideas*, vol. 5 (1984), pp. 349–62.

36 For other links between Sartre and Foucault, see Mark Poster, *Foucault, Marxism and History* (London: Blackwell, 1984).

37 Sarah Kofman mentions this course in *Camera obscura: De l'id-éologie* (Paris: Galilée, 1937), p. 17. Foucault's general debt to the heterodox philosophy of science tradition in France, which would include Bachelard as well as Canguilhem, is a topic still to be explored fully. For a useful introduction, see Lemert and Gillan, *Foucault: Social Theory and Transgression*. They emphasize the importance of discontinuity and rupture in their respective epistemologies. Equally important is their common hostility to phenomenalism, which may have turned Foucault away from perception. I am indebted to Robert d'Amico for this suggestion.

38 Foucault, *The Birth of the Clinic*, p. xiii.

39 Ibid.

40 Ibid., p. xiv.

41 Ibid., p. 117.

42 Ibid., p. 165.

43 Ibid., p. 166.

44 Ibid., p. 197.

45 Ibid., p. 199.

46 Foucault, *Raymond Roussel*.

47 Foucault, 'Dire et voir chez Raymond Roussel', *Lettre ouverte*, no. 4 (Summer 1962), pp. 38–51.

48 For Robbe-Grillet's appreciation, see his 'Enigmas and Transparency in Raymond Roussel', in *For a New Novel: Essays on Fiction*, trans. Richard Howard (New York: Grove Press, 1965). Although this essay was actually a review of Foucault's book, which first appeared in *Critique*, vol. 199 (December 1963), Robbe-Grillet oddly never mentions Foucault's book.

49 Ibid., p. 86.

50 See for example Hayden White, 'Michel Foucault', in John Sturrock (ed.), *Structuralism and Since: From Lévi-Strauss to Derrida* (Oxford University Press, 1979), pp. 87f.

51 Foucault, *Raymond Roussel*, pp. 19–20.

52 Ibid., p. 28.

53 Ibid., p. 132.

54 Ibid., p. 138.

55 Ibid., p. 134.

56 Ibid., p. 75.

57 'Le soleil enfermé' is the title of chapter 8 of the book; 'La lentille vide' is that of chapter 7.

58 Ibid., p. 154. For another discussion of the rebus as a model of language, which also turns it against a purely linguistic structuralism purged of all visual elements, see Jean-François Lyotard, *Discours, figure* (Paris: Klincksieck, 1971), pp. 295f.

59 Perhaps because he doesn't treat *Raymond Roussel*, Allan Megill is able to claim that the spatial preoccupations of the early Foucault, most obvious in *The Order of Things*, allow him to be justly called a structuralist *malgré lui* in the special sense of the term Megill derives

from Derrida. He cites, for example, Foucault's statement about 'the table upon which . . . language has intersected space' in the preface to the book (p. xviii), but he neglects to note that Foucault begins his sentence with a reference to Roussel and his catechrestic use of the 'table' as an imaginary place where Lautréamont's famous sewing machine and umbrella meet. It is not so much, in other words, a question of the homology between spatial form and linguistic structure as the tension between them. As Foucault says in *Raymond Roussel* (p. 148) 'This discourse forms a tissue where the texture of the verbal is already crossed with the chain of the visible.'

60 Foucault, *This is Not a Pipe*. For a useful discussion of the book, see Guido Almansi, 'Foucault and Magritte', *History of European Ideas*, vol. 3 (1982), pp. 305–9.
61 It should be noted that although the terms are the same in *The Order of Things* and *This is Not a Pipe*, the meaning has shifted somewhat. In the former, 'resemblances' and 'similitudes' are used as virtual synonyms, denoting the allegedly inherent relationship between a signifier and a signified. As such, they are contrasted with 'representation' in which the arbitrary nature of that link is stressed. In the book on Magritte, however, Foucault writes (p. 44), 'Resemblance serves representation, which rules over it; similitude serves repetition, which ranges across it. Resemblance predicates itself upon a model it must return to and reveal; similitude circulates the simulacrum as an indefinite and reversible relation of the similar to the similar.' Ironically, in a letter reprinted at the end of the work (p. 57), Magritte himself chastises Foucault for distinguishing between resemblances and similitudes.
62 Foucault, *This is Not a Pipe*, p. 46.
63 Foucault, 'A Preface to Transgression', p. 40. In addition to *The Story of the Eye*, Bataille revealed his ocular obsessions in many other works, several of which have recently been translated in *Visions of Excess: Selected Writings, 1927–1939*, ed. with intro. Allan Stoekl, trans. Allan Stoekl *et al.* (Minneapolis: University of Minnesota Press, 1985). In many cases, Bataille indicates a linkage between the anus and the eye, which Foucault did not explicitly discuss in his essay.
64 Sigmund Freud, *Civilization and its Discontents*, trans. James Strachey (New York: Norton, 1961), p. 46.
65 Foucault, 'A Preface to Transgression', pp. 45–6.
66 Ibid., p. 48.
67 Ibid., p. 48.
68 Ibid., pp. 48–9.
69 Foucault, *The Order of Things: An Archaeology of the Human Sciences* (New York: Random House, 1970).
70 Foucault's discussion of *Las Meninas* has stimulated an intense interest in the work. See for example John R. Searle, '*Las Meninas* and the paradoxes of pictorial representation', *Critical Inquiry*, vol. 6 (Spring

1980), pp. 477–88; Joel Snyder and Ted Cohen, 'Reflections on *Las Meninas*: Paradox Lost', *Critical Inquiry*, vol. 7 (1981), pp. 429–47; Svetlana Alpers, 'Interpretation without representation, or, the viewing of *Las Meninas*', *Representations*, no. 1 (February 1983), pp. 31–42. The famous parting image of *The Order of Things* is evoked whenever his anti-humanism is discussed. For a recent example, see Richard Wolin, 'Modernism vs. Postmodernism', *Telos*, vol. 62 (Winter 1984–5), p. 25.

71 Foucault, 'Space, Knowledge, Power', in Paul Rabinow (ed.), *The Foucault Reader* (New York: Pantheon, 1984), p. 254.

72 Foucault, *The Order of Things*, p. 39.

73 Ibid., p. 54. Foucault's analysis of the eclipse of language in the classical age has been disputed by implication in John W. Yolton, *Perceptual Acquaintance from Descartes to Reid* (Oxford University Press, 1984) which argues for the semantic dimension in the account of perception in Descartes and his followers.

74 Foucault, *The Order of Things*, p. 132.

75 Ibid., p. 308.

76 Ibid., p. 251.

77 Ibid., p. 232.

78 Ibid., p. 312 (italics added).

79 Ibid., p. 318.

80 Ibid., p. 326.

81 Ibid., p. 386. In French, of course, *figure* also means face, which suggests the final metaphor of the book.

82 Foucault, *The Archaeology of Knowledge*, p. 54.

83 Sartre, *Being and Nothingness*, p. 316.

84 Foucault, *Discipline and Punish: The Birth of the Prison*, trans. Alan Sheridan (New York: Vintage, 1979).

85 Foucault, *The Birth of the Clinic*, pp. 38–9.

86 Foucault, *Discipline and Punish*, p. 14. De Certeau, 'Micro-techniques and panoptic discourse: a quid pro quo', p. 264, notes that *Discipline and Punish* combines such representational tableaux with other optical figures, 'analytic tableaux (lists of ideological "rules" or "principles" relating to a single phenomenon) and figurative tableaux (seventeenth–nineteenth century engravings and photographs).'

87 Foucault, *Discipline and Punish*, p. 15. In an unpublished story entitled 'W.C'., Bataille included a drawing of the scaffold's eye, which he later described: 'solitary, solar' bristling with lashes, it gazed from the lunette of a guillotine' ('W.C.' Preface to *Story of the Eye*, trans. Joachim Neugroschel (New York: Berkley Books 1982), p. 120.

88 For an analysis of the shift from spectacle to surveillance at the court of Louis XIV, which places it around 1674, see Jean-Marie Apostolidès, *Le roi-machine: Spectacle et politique au temps de Louis XIV* (Paris: Minuit, 1981). Apostolidès argues that by the end of his reign, the Sun King had absented himself from the spectacle and become an empty place in the power structure of the monarchy, which gave the

impression of being able to see without being seen.

89 '*Le regard absolu*' is the title of François George's chapter on Sartre's critique of vision. See note 35.

90 Foucault, *Discipline and Punish*, p. 202.

91 Ibid., p. 140.

92 Ibid., p. 217.

93 Guy Debord, *Society of the Spectacle* (Detroit, Black and Red, 1983). This work provides another variant of the anti-visual discourse, Debord claiming that 'the spectacle is the heir of all the weaknesses of the Western philosophical project, which was to understand activity dominated by the categories of *seeing*' (p. 18, italics in original).

94 Foucault, *Discipline and Punish*, p. 217.

95 Ibid., p. 222.

96 Jürgen Habermas, *Strukturwandel der Öffentlichkeit. Untersuchungen au einer Kategorie der bürgerlichen Gesellschaft* (Berlin: Luchterhand, 1962). For Habermas's critique of Foucault's reduction of the human sciences to the disciplining gaze, see his *Der philosophische Diskurs der Moderne* (Frankfurt: Suhrkamp, 1985), p. 289. Another defender of the enlightenment, who emphasizes its aural rather than visual moment, is Agnes Heller. See her 'Enlightenment against fundamentalism: the example of Lessing', *New German Critique*, no. 23 (Spring/Summer 1981), pp. 13–26.

97 Foucault, 'What is Enlightenment?', *The Foucault Reader*, p. 45.

98 Foucault, 'The Eye of Power', in *Power/Knowledge: Selected Interviews and Other Writings, 1972–1977*, ed. Colin Gordon, trans. Colin Gordon *et al.* (New York: Pantheon, 1980), p. 152. There is, to be sure, a certain slippage here in Foucault's argument from the emphasis in *Discipline and Punish* on the theatrical spectacle of the revolutionary guillotine – a residue of the classical age's visual style – to the anti-theatrical surveillance of the nineteenth-century, anticipated by Rousseau.

99 See for example Jacques Derrida, 'Genesis and Structure of the *Essay on the Origin of Languages*', in *Of Grammatology*, trans. Gayatri Chakravorty Spivak (Baltimore: The Johns Hopkins University Press, 1976); and Sarah Kofman, *Camera obscura*, p. 58.

100 See his disclaimer in 'The Eye of Power', p. 148.

101 Ibid., p. 150.

102 Foucault, *The History of Sexuality*, vol. 1, *An Introduction*, trans. Robert Hurley (New York: Vintage, 1980), p. 43.

103 Sartre, *Saint Genet: Actor and Martyr*, trans. Bernard Frechtman (New York: G. Braziller, 1963), pp. 79–80.

104 See Laura Oswald, 'The Perversion of I/Eye in *Un Chant d'Amour*', *Enclitic*, vol. 7 (Fall 1983).

105 Foucault, 'Introduction' to Ludwig Binswanger, *Le Rêve et l'existence*, trans. Jacqueline Verdeaux (Paris: Desclée de Brouwer, 1954), p. 19.

106 Foucault, *The Order of Things*, p. xviii.

107 Lyotard, *Discours, figure*, p. 13.
108 See for example the stress on the mutual glance in the work of Simmel, discussed in the essay by Weinstein and Weinstein cited in note 35. See also the essay by Keller and Fox cited in note 6; John Berger, *Ways of Seeing* (London: Penguin, 1983), p. 9; and Hartmut Böhme, 'Sinne und Blick. Variationen zur mythopoetischen Geschichte des Subjects', in *Konkursbuch*, no. 13 (1984).
109 de Certeau, 'Micro-techniques and panoptic discourse: a quid pro quo', p. 259.
110 Luce Irigaray, *Speculum de l'autre femme* (Paris: Minuit, 1974).
111 Foucault, 'On the Genealogy of Ethics: An Overview of Work in Progress', in Rabinow (ed.), *The Foucault Reader*, p. 343.
112 See for example Nancy Fraser, 'Foucault on modern power: empirical insights and normative confusions', *Praxis International*, vol. 1 (October 1981).
113 Foucault, 'Politics and Ethics: An Interview', in Rabinow (ed.), *The Foucault Reader*.

I would like to thank the following readers for their helpful critiques of earlier drafts of this paper: Alan Megill, Robert D'Amico and Catherine Gallagher.

Foucault and the Tyranny of Greece

MARK POSTER

In *Foucault, Marxism and History*,[1] I argue that Foucault's writings, especially those of the 1970s, offer the most advanced positions available for the reconstitution of critical theory and history. In *Discipline and Punish* and *The History of Sexuality*, volume 1, he presents an effective critique of totalizing positions and traditional epistemological strategies. In addition he proposes a new kind of history based on the key concepts of discourse-practice and technologies of power which go a long way in overcoming the limitations of critical theory and historical writing. His texts treat the question of language in a manner that bypasses the theoretical obstacles inherent in dualist assumptions about idealism and materialism, thought and action, reason and nature, effectively opening new paths for analysis and critique. These texts also develop a position that reorients Critical Theory to the particular social context of what I call 'the mode of information'. More than anyone else, Foucault aligns his discursive strategy to the new constraints and systems of domination that are unique to the late twentieth century. In the present conjuncture a new social formation is emerging in which science is implicated in power, in which the process of production is dependent as never before on discourse and knowledge, in which organized systems of power (bureaucracies) rely upon information gathering, storing and retrieval, in which communication patterns increasingly consist of electronically mediated interactions. These new features of the social landscape, taken together, are what I call 'the mode of information'. And Foucault's later works, with all of their innovations, enable Critical Theory to analyse its important characteristics and explore the new multiple mechanisms of domination emerging within it. The question I address in this essay is whether and how volumes 2 and 3 of *The History of Sexuality* further the advances contained in the texts of the 1970s.

Sex is among the most difficult topics in the human sciences. Sex appears to be primordial, natural, a biological given that resists historical analysis and a critical theoretical perspective. Even diet, which is similar to sex in having a strong biological ground, is more amenable to analysis in terms of class differences, cultural patterning and elaborate social rituals. But sex seems either always to be the same thing or subject to variations that are of limited hermeneutic interest. Demographic studies treat variations in sex activity but do so in an objectified analysis that reduces sexual practice to reproduction.[2] Intellectual historians deal only with attitudes toward sex, suggestively relating them to other conceptual patterns but failing to embody the analysis in the important context of social practice.[3] Sex remains for historians of ideas a curious and marginal sector of the mansions of the mind. Freudians do a little better. They interpret sex in relation to personality formation and its vicissitudes in the adult psyche. Yet they are saddled with a notion of a fixed core of desire, an unchanging sediment of unconscious libido, an ontology of sex as a residue of nature in an evolving process of civilization.[4] To appreciate the significance of Foucault's recent and sadly final volumes in his project on the history of sexuality it is necessary to remind oneself of the limited success this topic has had in the field of the human sciences.

Many readers will be disappointed by the recently published volumes. They might argue that the new books do not sustain the powerful problematic developed in *Discipline and Punish* and *The History of Sexuality*, volume 1, a problematic that seemed to be the culmination of Foucault's work since *Madness and Civilization*. The analytics of discourse-practice and technologies of power that were the theoretical centrepieces of the previous two works are almost completely gone. His splendid manoeuvre that bypassed the theory of repression in *The History of Sexuality*, volume 1, in favour of an analysis of discourses on sex is now abandoned. So too is the delicate, complex hermeneutic that displaced standard forms of intellectual history in favour of an analysis that successfully revealed the imbrication of discourse in power. Volumes 2–4 of *The History of Sexuality*, on the contrary, might appear to some to be an exercise in paraphraxis, a string of banal summaries of well-known texts, a succession of unimaginative readings of the classics by someone who is hardly versed in the field. Moreover the magnificent writing of the earlier books, it might be argued, writing that continually surprised and delighted the reader with rhetorical devices and conceptual twists, becomes in the new books flat, straightforward, even unimaginative.

Shortly before he died Foucault gave an interview, subsequently published in the journal *Les Nouvelles*,[5] in which he responded to some of these objections. On the question of style, for example, he retorted that he self-consciously adopted a new voice back in the mid-1970s as a result of adding a new dimension to his problematic of truth and power, that of the individual. Not every critic will be convinced by this response. Indeed many will attribute what they regard as a decline in the new books to an exhaustion of his creative powers. Alternatively they may complain that the books appeared prematurely and Foucault unwisely rushed to publication only because he knew he had little time left. Other even less kind critics will attribute the failings of the books to Foucault's inability to maintain a distance from a topic that was close to his own homosexuality. These criticisms, while partially valid, fail to address the main issue in *L'Usage des plaisirs*, *Le Souci de soi* and *Les Aveux de la chair*, which is the constitution of the self through discourses on sex, a problematic that would have yielded its full potential, I am convinced, only with the completion of the project in volumes devoted to the modern period.

In the later volumes of *The History of Sexuality* there are only fleeting references to Foucault's interpretive strategy of genealogy.[6] This does not mean that these books reject the older method. On the contrary, Foucault introduces *L'Usage des plaisirs* with a methodological discussion that adheres to the tenets of genealogical analysis. He dismisses attempts to write a history of sex as a history of regulative codes or a history of ideas. To the surprise of the reader, he shows that at the level of codes things have not changed all that much. The Greeks and Romans were often like the Christians and the moderns in preferring monogamous, heterosexual, procreative sex. To obtain an adequate grasp of sexual phenomena it is necessary, Foucault contends, to leave the terrain of desire and its repressions and move to a problematic in which sex is understood in relation to the moral level of self-constitution. The important question for him — and it is a brilliant manoeuvre — is to reverse the normal expectation and ask why and in what ways is sex a problem for the individual in his or her effort to lead a moral life. 'In brief, in this genealogy the idea was to investigate how individuals have been led to exercise on themselves, and on others, a hermeneutic of desire in which their sexual behavior has no doubt been the focus but certainly not the exclusive one.'[7] Today we assume that sex is central to our identity; Foucault asks why is it, why has it been and how have its forms of being so changed.

The History of Sexuality is genealogical in that it opens up for questioning in an historical manner that which we assume to have always been the case. It is also genealogical in the sense that this opening displaces earlier methods of analysing the problem and attempts to sustain the method of discourse-practice employed in earlier studies. Instead of placing the analysis of texts in sex on the couplet science–ideology, he attempts to look at the way discourses and practices generate an experience of sex. In this regard, Foucault is unable to sustain the level of analysis of his earlier works. There is simply too much discourse and not enough practice. His chapters read too much like intellectual histories of different writings on sex, with few references to social practice. In this sense these volumes are uncharacteristic of Foucault, a shortcoming that might be due to the paucity of evidence from Greek, Hellenistic, Roman and early Christian periods. That question will be decided by those more expert than I in the fields. The result is that the fine balance so evident in previous works between the analysis of discourse and the play of practices is too often lost in the later volumes. In the *History of Sexuality* discourse is the only practice.

There is another aspect of genealogical analysis on which Foucault's later books are more successful but which is easily overlooked. The question may be raised, Why go back to the Greeks? In his earlier works Foucault never crossed the line that divides the modern world from its antecedents and in the 1970s his custom was to begin with the eighteenth century. Besides he is surely taking a risk by going back so far in time to a period with which he cannot be very familiar. Although he does make reference to many important primary and secondary works on the ancient periods, it is unlikely that he had the mastery of the materials of these epochs that he displayed in works on modernity. There is every reason to look carefully at the cause for his departure from his habitual terrain. The answer lies in the requirements of the method of genealogy.

One of the salient features of Foucault's work has been that he begins at a point of difference. In *Madness and Civilization* it was the ship of fools; in *The Order of Things* it was the *episteme* of correspondences; in *Discipline and Punish* it was the torture system of punishment. In each case a phenomenon was addressed and analysed which appears strange, discomforting, unfamiliar, vaguely threatening to the modern sensibility. The same procedure is followed in *The History of Sexuality*. The Greeks are the starting point for Foucault because in their sexual practice the love between free, adult males and boys was the central question. What is more, love for boys is not merely a point of difference with regard to sexual desire. It is also different in that sexual desire was not the problem for the Greeks, rather it was that of individual freedom or ethics.

Foucault begins his *History of Sexuality* with the Greeks because only by going back that far in time does he locate a point where the question of sex is posed in terms of a different relationship (adult males to boys) than that of the present and where sex is placed in a different register from that of the present (freedom rather than desire). The result of this genealogical strategy is to let us see with fresh eyes our own sexuality in comparison with the point of difference. What must be avoided at all costs is reversing poles of the values at stake. Thus Foucault does all he can to undermine a nostalgic presentation of Greek sexuality, a problem he finds in the work of others, who have trodden a similar path to pre-Christian sexual codes.[8] The critical intention of genealogical analysis is to reveal a difference in a phenomenon in such a way that it undermines the self-certainty of the present without presenting the past as an alternative. An underlying drama in the text of *L'Usage des plaisirs* is that Foucault wants to present the Greek practice of the love of boys as a point of difference without adding any positive valuation to it, even though he was himself a homosexual, and was associated with the gay rights movement (although he expressed reservations about various tendencies within that movement, especially those concerning the ideology of 'rights' and 'liberation'). To be sure contemporary homosexuality bears little resemblance to Greek practices – a point underscored by Foucault. Nonetheless there are enough superficial similarities to cause concern. Perhaps Foucault overcompensates for the likeness by denying all similarities.

The great achievement of the genealogical analysis of sex rests with its ability to present a critical history, history that undermines the unquestioned legitimacy of the present by offering a re-creation of a different past. The rupture between the past and the present generates the space for critique. This history avoids both teleology or progressivism and nostalgia. Foucault's history is a form of rationalist asceticism, rigorously denying to the historian all utopian impulses.

In *The History of Sexuality* there are no Golden Ages and no inevitable evolutions toward perfection in the future. Nonetheless by undermining the implicit universality of the pattern of sexuality in the present, Foucault's genealogy opens up the question of the limitations of sex in the present, implicitly inviting those disadvantaged by it to develop strategies to change it. In this sense Foucault is a historical materialist in the best Marxist sense of the term.

Even more than to Marx, Foucault demonstrates his debt to Nietzsche, especially in *The History of Sexuality*, in this case on terrain that is close to the anchorite of the nineteenth century. In *The Genealogy of Morals*,[9] Nietzsche contrasted the good–bad morality of the master class with the good–evil morality of the slaves. The Greek ruling class was one of the chief examples of the master morality for Nietzsche, who was trained in the classics and in methods of philology. The social position of the master led directly, acccording to him, to a spontaneous valuation of what was considered good along with a corresponding distaste for or negative valuation of what was considered bad. Like Nietzsche, Foucault attributes to this master class a morality of freedom, a sense of unrestrictedness, so foreign to the present morality with its compulsions and its guilt. Even when the Greek masters introduced themes of austerity into their morality, these must be understood, Foucault insists, as an 'elaboration and stylization of an activity in the exercise of power and the practice of freedom'.[10] In the context of a luxurious, open life situation, the Greek masters, in Foucault's text, determine their individual constraints or, in his terms, constitute their own selves. Neither Nietzsche nor Foucault idealize the master morality: Nietzsche saw in the masters uninteresting stupidity; Foucault finds the Greek rulers mired in 'a profound error'.[11]

Nietzsche and Foucault differ in the accents they give to the Greek master morality. Nietzsche emphasizes the great healthiness (*die grosse Gesundheit*) of the Greeks, the exuberance and power of their morality; Foucault stresses the constraints that, although self-imposed, they wrestled with. The love of boys was the central, nagging moral issue for the Greeks because that practice, Foucault argues, brought into question their style of life. For most writers in the fourth to the second centuries BC, there were no constraints on sexual passion. Anyone could become a love object for a Greek master: wife, mistress, slave, boy. To lead a moral life a Greek master need only actively decide on a course of action. This ruling class valued the active posture because it alone was commensurate with their freedom, and their freedom alone insured the health of the polis. With regard to sexual practice, they associated activity with penetration. The moral issue for them concerned the question of placing boys from the ruling class in a passive position during sexual relations with free adult males.[12] An elaborate etiquette and numerous discourses were developed by the masters of this period because they feared that the practice of the love of boys might inure the boys to patterns of passivity, hence undermining their freedom and the freedom of the polis. In this way sex became a moral problem in a culture where desire itself was not a moral issue. The love of boys was the leading preoccupation in the elaboration of techniques of the self by which the masters constituted themselves in their freedom.

Foucault outlines several features of these techniques of the self which underscore the difference between Greek and modern forms of sexuality. The codes and restrictions that governed sex were minimal, a sharp contrast with the Christian period where regulations over sex were detailed and comprehensive. Then too, for the Greeks sex was good, for the Christians it was bad or evil. Also the Greeks did not place sexual practice in a universalist context; individuals had to determine the pattern of their own sexual objects and practices. Again the opposite of the Christians. Marriage for the Greeks was more a social and political arrangement than a joining of two souls in a sacred relationship as it would later become. Thus for the Greeks there was no preoccupation with the self as a desiring subject, no careful scrutiny over the validity of one's sexual impulses. It followed that the Greeks did not characterize individuals by their sexual practices or desires and the distinction between heterosexual and homosexual did not exist. Since desire was not a moral object, the liberation of desire, a salient theme in the West since the 1920s, was not a political issue. The Greeks were different because the question of sexuality was placed in the register of the free activity of the individual to constitute himself. In short, sex was an aesthetic question, a matter of life-style.

If Foucault's depiction of Greek sexuality is convincing, one can see how sharp is the break between it and modern sexuality. His personal and political interest in gay liberation, even granting his reservations about the movement, is strongly supported by his argument, even though he places no special value on the Greek love of boys, or better, precisely because he does not do so. The power of his analysis derives from its ability to constitute the past as different, not as an alternative to the present, an option for current political strategy. That could only be accomplished by presenting the past in its specificity, ascetically reducing its ideological function to the minimum of difference itself. To raise Greek sexuality to the status of a standard for the present, to advocate the Greeks' love of boys as a political focus today, would destroy the critical value of the work. That is precisely what Marxist historians do when they glorify the heroic struggles of the proletariat of previous times, or present the trials of the working class in tones of unrelenting horror. The value of Foucault's *History of Sexuality* for critical theory lies precisely in its ascetic denial of teleology, its sharp constraint on rationalist universalism and its genealogical presentation of difference.

The precise object constituted by Foucault as his historical field is '. . . the forms and modalities of the relation to self by which the individual is constituted and recognizes himself as subject.'[13] Characteristically Foucault does not spend much time defining his categories of analysis, in this case those of 'self' and 'subject'. It appears from the text that 'self' is a neutral, ahistorical term, almost a synonym for 'individual'. 'Subject' is an active, historical term that refers to a process of interiorization. Foucault, of course, continues to reject philosophies of consciousness by which the individual ontologically constitutes himself or herself through mental activities.[14] Still, there is some ambiguity in Foucault's use of the term 'subject'. It is not always clear that he consistently avoids a 'subjectivist' use of the term. This is especially so in *The History of Sexuality*, volumes 2 and 3, where the text often reads like a traditional intellectual history. The paraphrase of one Greek thinker's ideas follows that of another. The verification of this complaint may safely be left to the reader, since it is a judgement based on the characterization of long sections of the texts and cannot be demonstrated by a selection of quotations or citations.

Foucault's intention, if I may use that term, apparently is to define the subject experientially and historically. The key to understanding this use of the term subject is his Nietzschean concept of truth. Since Foucault rejects the notion of absolute truth he also rejects the concept of the subject as source or foundation of truth. His notion of the subject is both de-centred and relativist. The subject takes shape through historically experienced discourses-practices. In this way the role of sex in the constitution of the self as subject becomes clear. It appears that the overall project of *The History of Sexuality* is to trace the path, by no means a straight one, through which individuals become, in the modern period, subjects whose truth is their sexuality.

If that is the case the place of the Greeks in the historical trajectory takes on new meaning.

From the perspective of the history of the subject the Greeks are not so much a point of difference as a point of origin. The rudiments of the modern subject can be traced to the Greek problematization of the self in the practice of the love of boys. Sex becomes a moral problem for the Greeks of the fourth to the second centuries BC because the passive positioning of free males contradicts the ethics of freedom. The Greek masters caught themselves in a conundrum which was creative. In wrestling with their dilemma of the love of boys, they gave birth to the subject. Only in this sense does sex play a role in Foucault's history of the Greeks.

It must be admitted that Foucault is not entirely convincing on this issue. Everything seems to hinge on the identification of sexual penetration with 'activity' and activity with freedom; also on the identification of being sexually penetrated with passivity and passivity with slavery.[15] Foucault writes that the young man's honour 'depends in part on the use he makes of his body . . . which will also to some extent determine his reputation and his future role'.[16] As a free citizen he will be judged by his ability to lead a dignified and beautiful life. If the boy allows himself to be the passive object of another's pleasure he will not be able to command the respect that it is necessary for a master to have. And yet it is not at all clear that in the sexual relation the boy is any more an object of another's pleasure than is the adult. Foucault relies on the work of historians of Greece to determine that such was indeed the case for the ancients.[17] But the determination of the fact of the passivity of Greek boys in sexual relations with adult males does not resolve the interpretive question of why that was so. It appears that Foucault assumes that a sexual relation in which one partner is required *exclusively* to play an active role and the other partner *exclusively* to play a passive role is possible, as if the fact of 'activity' and 'passivity' were not ambiguous from the start, as if the Greek *interpretation* of the sexual relation of man and boy as one of 'activity' and 'passivity' can be noted as an observation by the historian and left at that.

Foucault never asks, although it seems necessary to do so, why the Greeks attributed a passive role to the boys in the sexual relation but never doubted the active role of the adult males. In the absence of such an interrogation, the locus of the problematization of sex in the love of boys is thrown into doubt. From Foucault's description of the detailed elaboration of the practice of the love of boys there is little reason to question his argument that the relation was indeed a problematic one for the Greeks. What is in question, however, is why that was so. It is possible that the man–boy sexual relationship was problematic to the man not simply because the boys' 'passive' role contradicted their later position of dominance (an issue that Foucault notes), but also because in that relationship a reversal of roles was always possible. The man might at some moment be in a 'passive' position physically or emotionally and the boy might be in the 'active' position. Sexual relations are certainly volatile and ambiguous, especially if their emotional side is taken into account. That indeed might be the great lacuna of Foucault's history of sexuality: a relative and remarkable absence of discussion about the affective nuances of sexual relations.

Foucault's reticence about the emotional side of sex is difficult to comprehend. Certainly he is interested in the constitution of the self, not in sex *per se*. Even if that is granted, one can still question his repression of the question of the complex emotionality inherent in the issue of the constitution of the self. Perhaps the reason for the omission lies in Foucault's aversion to Freudian discourse, laden as it is with the question of conscious and unconscious feelings. Indeed one could imagine a Freudian interpretation of the Greek love of boys that would differ considerably from Foucault's, throwing into question the larger framework of his work. A Freudian might see in the Greek love of boys an ambiguous sexual identity on the part of the adult males, an interpretation that presupposes a fixed libido and therefore precludes the kind of historical interpretation of sex that Foucault is after. Foucault, of course, rejects a Freudian interpretation of the history of sexuality; that much is clear from volume 1. So it is perhaps unfair to raise this objection. In any case this unresolved difficulty casts a shadow of doubt over volume 2 of *The History of Sexuality*.

During the first two centuries AD important changes occur in the place of sex in the constitution of the self. In *Le Souci de soi* Foucault discusses these changes by analysing certain texts of the period, especially those of the stoic Epictetus. Volume 3 is much drier than volume 2, with much more paraphrase and less analysis than the latter. Also the significance of the changes that occurred during the period is presented somewhat ambiguously. Some of the texts reveal little change, others more. Foucault seems to pick his way carefully – some would say, arbitrarily – through them, cautiously outlining the new configuration. The result is that the outlines of the new shape of sex are drawn lightly, easily receding into a shapeless chaos.[18] Yet in Foucault's opinion the most important single change in the entire history of sex in the West occurred during this period: an emerging prohibition against the love of boys along with a rising valuation of heterosexual love.[19]

In the passage from Ancient Greece to Hellenistic Rome the major change concerning sexuality was a shift of emphasis from the love of boys to the marriage tie. In order to comprehend this change properly Foucault describes a more general transformation that affected the masters. In the Greek period the free individual was preoccupied with controlling or managing his desires. He sought an idea of moderation, an ideal that was thought to enhance his freedom. In the first two centuries AD the emphasis was rather on what Foucault calls 'the culture of self', and intensification of concern with 'the relation to self'. Foucault speaks of the change as the attaining of the 'apex of a curve' rather than a rupture.[20] He relates the new preoccupation with self to the altered political circumstances. No longer directly in command of society, the elite under the Roman Empire was rather an administrative class. In the new political system, Foucault surmises, the rules of the game made it more difficult for the individual to attain a stable identity or to define the relations through which the subject was constituted. Political activity was more problematic, and this threw the individual into a certain doubt about himself. One's position depended on signs that were more difficult to grasp than under the smaller city states of earlier times. Hence the individual needed to scrutinize his actions much more carefully.

The emphasis on marriage developed in the Imperial context. As the political institution became more 'public', more complex, marriage became more 'private' and in turn more 'important, intense, difficult and problematic'.[21] Men sought a new kind of relationship with their wives, one that was more equal and more personal than in the Greek period. Marriage became a 'symmetrical bond', rendering problematic and intense the sexual relations of husband and wife. 'The woman-wife was valorized as the other par excellence; but the husband had also to recognize her as forming a unity with self. In comparison to traditional forms of matrimonial relations, the change was considerable'.[22]

In place of the elaborate subculture surrounding the love of boys, the wife became the centre of the man's sexuality and accordingly the locus in which he constituted his subjectivity.

In the new situation an effort was made for the first time to develop a universal ideal of the subject. Nature and reason became standards by which to judge and evaluate the individual's realization of the culture of self. Implicit in the universalization of the sexual subject was an intensification of the forms of prohibition. Foucault emphasizes that we are still not at the level of constraint that obtained in the Christian period with its elaborate codes and punishments. Still, a kind of threshold had been crossed during the early Empire. Sex, while not intrinsically evil or even bad, was seen as the source of many serious dangers for the self. The focus on the marital tie implied that intercourse with boys or servants was increasingly avoided. While extramarital relations were not strictly speaking prohibited, they became an area of question for the culture of the self. In sum, the Hellenistic period witnessed a shift in sexual objects, an intensification of prohibitions concerning sexuality and a deepening subjectification of the self.

Le Souci de soi manifests a loosening of the grip Foucault has on his theoretical strategy. His presentation of the constitution of the self in the Hellenistic period fails to display convincingly the level of analysis that characterized his earlier work. The problem can clearly be seen if the text is evaluated as an example of archaeology.[23] Foucault mentions the term 'archaeology' only once in volumes 2 and 3 of *The History of Sexuality*. He explains the purpose of the volumes in terms of archaeology and genealogy and in relation to the corpus of his work:

> The archaeological dimension of the analysis permits the analysis of the forms themselves of problematization; its genealogical dimension permits the analysis of their formation starting from practices and their modifications. The problematization of madness and illness starting from social and medical practices defines a certain profile of 'normalization'. The problematization of life, language and work in discursive practices follows certain 'epistemic' rules. The problematization of crime and criminal behaviour starting from certain punitive practices follows a 'disciplinary' model. And now I would like to show how in Antiquity sexual activity and pleasures were problematized through practices of self, setting into play criteria of an 'aesthetic of existence'.[24]

In *Madness and Civilization*, *The Birth of the Clinic*, *The Order of Things* and *Discipline and Punish* – the works referred to above, all but one of which were written before the elaboration of the methods of archaeology and genealogy – Foucault achieved considerable success in accomplishing his goals. Can the same be said of *The History of Sexuality*?

In *The Archaeology* Foucault outlines a method of analysing texts which set aside the intentions of the authorial subject. He asks how the 'statements' in a given discourse are possible. His theoretical strategy is, by working within the texts themselves, to develop an analysis of the text as discourse, as an objective field of positions or statements. This analysis proceeds a level beneath that of the consciousness of the author, hence the term 'archaeology'. *Discipline and Punish* locates the disciplinary statements in discourses on punishment even though the writers, like Bentham, were motivated to establish methods for the rehabilitation of criminals, not the institution of systems of discipline. In this method, everything hinges on the ability of the critic to go beyond the intentional level of the discourse to locate a system of problematics that are at once outside the text and within it, and once elaborated reveal a new level of significance in the text.

Foucault's method works pretty well in *L'Usage des plaisirs*; the problematization of sex, specifically the love of boys, in relation to the constitution of the self captures the texts of the ancients at a new level and displaces their intentional meaning. But in *Le Souci de soi* things do not turn out as well for Foucault. The difference is a subtle one, perhaps remaining an ambiguous question of interpretation. At issue is not the changes outlined by Foucault in the history of sex and in the shape of the constitution of the self. The question is whether these changes are presented through archaeological and genealogical analyses. I think not, and I think not because *Le Souci de soi* reads like a traditional study in the history of ideas, relying too heavily on the intentional level of meaning, direct arguments and explicit phrases of the author. *Le souci de soi* does not seem to get beyond a standard Aristotelian reading; it simply rearranges these sorts of readings to construct the analysis that Foucault desires to make. And if that is so, Foucault leaves himself open to traditional methods of critique: does he force the text to yield the meaning he wants?; does he select texts only because they display positions that conform to his 'bias' and interpretation?; and so forth. These are questions for empiricist historians to ask. From the perspective I am pursuing – the adequacy of Foucault's position for a reconstituted critical theory – the problem is different. For me, the inadequacy of the archaeological level of interpretation explains, I think, the failure of the text to further the development of critical theory.

One example will suffice to make my case. Foucault argues, as we have seen, that there is a shift in the locus of problematization of sex from the love of boys to the marriage tie. He finds traces of the change in the writings of Musonius. 'It is in Musonius that one finds articulated in the greatest detail the principle of symmetrical, conjugal fidelity.'[25] And further on, 'This integral conjugalization of sexual practice that one finds in Musonius, and the principle of a strict monopoly of *aphrodisia* reserved for marriage, are no doubt exceptional . . .'[26] The reader finds a detailed description of Musonius's position, presented at the level of what he says in the text; the meaning of the text conforms to the change argued for by Foucault; the unrepresentative status of the text is announced by Foucault. The genealogical level of 'practices and their modifications' is not a problem. Foucault does little with the level of practices in this text, yet what he writes about the emergence of a 'culture of self' appears to be sound. The archaeological level, on the contrary, never seems to be reached. The objectivist level of reading statements in texts is forgotten in favour of a recitation of what the author says.

Nonetheless the change outlined by Foucault from the Greek constitution of the self through discourses on the sexual practice of the love of boys to the Christian constitution of the self through elaborate restrictive codes against the pleasures of the flesh is a dramatic and fascinating story.[27] Foucault again has presented a fresh and vigorous interpretation of an obscure topic. The completion of his project with volumes carrying the history forward to modern times would certainly have resulted in a most important statement and remains a task for others. Based on what has been done in volumes 1 through 4, it is possible to draw the main lines of such a history, or at least suggest one direction the story might take.

Like Nietzsche, Foucault sees the main historic rupture occurring with Christianity. For Nietzsche all morality since the Christian epoch has been a set of variations on that slave morality. For Foucault the basic technique of the self of the last 1,800 years was developed by the Christians. They instituted an elaborate code, universally applicable, to regulate sexual conduct and thoughts. They based the code on a principle of the sinful nature of the flesh. They established a practice of confession through which their discourse on sex governed social action and thought. And above all they established sex as the truth about the self. The coupling of truth and sex was an innovation that would endure through all the profound changes that discourse would undergo in the modern period. Starting in the eighteenth century, when discourses on sex began to appear in a rationalist and then scientific register, the same coupling of truth and sex would persist. As Foucault argued in *La Volonté de savoir*, the past two centuries have witnessed an increasing proliferation of discourses on sex – the writings of medical men in the eighteenth and nineteenth centuries, the formation of psychoanalysis in the late nineteenth century, the multiplication of sex therapies and research in the late twentieth century – all sharing the premise that some deep truth about individuals was bound up with their sexuality.

If that serves as an admittedly crude outline of how the history of sex might proceed along lines traced by Foucault, certain limitations of the project need briefly to be mentioned. These concern two areas especially in which contemporary sex is implicated but which do not appear neatly to fit into Foucault's scheme. The first is the increasing diminution of social networks in the context of postindustrial society, or what I prefer to call the mode of information. As electronic systems are substituted, at all points of the social field, for face-to-face communication situations, individuals experience and are subject to new linguistic experiences. The relation of discourse to practice is profoundly changed. One example of this phenomenon is TV advertising, which in many cases attempts to co-ordinate the consumption of commodities with sexual fantasies. It is not clear that Foucault's theoretical strategy is adequate for an analysis of this phenomenon. Some type of semiological theory appears to be more appropriate, a theory that can unpack the linguistic mechanisms at play in the linguistic communication of TV advertising.

The other area in which Foucault's method seems inappropriate but which is crucial to the constitution of the self in sex is the family. When Foucault treats the family he does so through systems of discourse which are external to it but act upon it, most notably that of the medical profession. However, the family is also constituted internally through the constellation of interactions, especially at the emotional level, between its members. Only a psychological theory can adequately grasp these phenomena, a level of theory that Foucault ignores or is critical of. In sum, *The History of Sexuality* opens up a new level of understanding but it is unclear if its completion would have fully satisfied the requirements of a critical theory of sex.

Notes

1 (Oxford: Blackwell, 1984).
2 See for example E. Shorter's piece on illegitimacy and the debate surrounding it, 'Illegitimacy, Sexual Revolution, and Social Change in Modern Europe', in T. Rabb and R. Rotberg (eds), *The Family in*

History (New York: Harper & Row, 1971), pp. 48–84.

3 See for example Paul Robinson, *The Modernization of Sex* (New York: Harper & Row, 1976).

4 See for example Herbert Marcuse, *Eros and Civilization* (Boston: Beacon, 1955).

5 (28 June–5 July 1984), pp. 37–41.

6 To be exact in Foucault, *The History of Sexuality*, vol. 3, *Le Souci de Soi*, p. 11.

7 Ibid., p. 11.

8 See his discussion of this problem in *Les Nouvelles* (28 June–5 July 1984), pp. 39–40.

9 Trans. W. Kaufman (New York: Random House, 1967).

10 Foucault, *Histoire de la sexualité*, vol. 2, *L'Usage des plaisirs* (Paris: Gallimard, 1984), p. 30.

11 *Les Nouvelles*, p. 38.

12 Foucault, *L'Usage des plaisirs*, p. 277.

13 Ibid., p. 12.

14 Foucault discusses this question briefly in the interview in *Les Nouvelles*, p. 41.

15 Foucault does not mention penetration as a factor until volume 3, p. 43, which is most peculiar since it is implied throughout volume 2.

16 Foucault, *L'Usage des plaisirs*, p. 235.

17 Foucault, in a review of the French translation of *Greek Homosexuality* by J. Dover, notes with praise the author's discussion of the question of activity and passivity in Greek social and sexual relations. This review appeared in *Liberation* (1 June 1982), p. 27.

18 For two eloquent statements of opposing views see Michael Ignatieff's review of the two recent books in *TLS* (28 September 1984), pp. 1071–2 and David Hoy's review of recent Foucault literature in *London Review of Books* (1–14 November 1984), pp. 7–9.

19 Foucault does not stress this point in the text. However he told it to me in a conversation we had in July 1981.

20 Foucault, *Histoire de la sexualité*, vol. 3, *Le Souci de soi* (Paris: Gallimard, 1984), p. 59.

21 Ibid., p. 96.

22 Ibid., p. 192.

23 It has been argued that Foucault gave up the strategy of archaeology in the early 1970s. This is the position of Dreyfus and Rabinow in *Michel Foucault* (University of Chicago Press, 1984). But I do not think that is the case in light of his use of the term as cited below.

24 Foucault, *L'Usage des plaisirs*, p. 18.

25 Foucault, *Le Souci de soi*, p. 201.

26 Ibid., p. 202.

27 The promised volume 4 of Foucault's *History of Sexuality, Les Aveux de la chair*, which deals with the early Christian era, has not appeared on schedule and may be delayed for some time.

Archaeology, Genealogy, Ethics

ARNOLD I. DAVIDSON

Three main domains of analysis can be found in Michel Foucault's work as a whole: an analysis of systems of knowledge, of modalities of power, and of the self's relationship to itself. In each of these domains Foucault employed very specific forms of analysis, which he called, respectively, archaeology, genealogy, and ethics. Archaeology and genealogy are the two best-known key words of Foucault's so-called methodology. To get an initial approximation to how he understood these two terms one can do no better than to recall a pair of suggestions he advanced at the end of 'Truth and Power', an interview given in the late seventies: ' "Truth" is to be understood as a system of ordered procedures for the production, regulation, distribution, circulation and operation of statements. . . . "Truth" is linked in a circular relation with systems of power which produce and sustain it, and to effects of power which it induces and which extend it. A "regime" of truth.'[1] Since Foucault is usually his own best interpreter, I like to think of the first suggestion here as his own succinct retrospective interpretation of his archaeological method, while the second suggestion is his equally succinct interpretation of his genealogical method. Let me turn first to the method of archaeology.

If the working hypothesis of archaeology was that truth is to be understood as a system of ordered procedures for the production, regulation, distribution, circulation, and operation of statements, then it should not be surprising that Foucault undertook to write a history of statements that claim the status of truth, a history of these ordered procedures. To attempt to write such a history one must isolate certain kinds of discursive practices – practices for the production of statements – which will be 'characterized by the

222					Arnold I. Davidson

delimitation of a field of objects, the definition of a legitimate perspective for the agent of knowledge, and the fixing of norms for the elaboration of concepts and theories. Thus, each discursive practice implies a play of prescriptions that designates its exclusions and choices.'[2]

Foucault's project, announced in the foreword to the English edition of *The Order of Things*, was to write the history of what Ian Hacking has called the *immature sciences* – those sciences that, in Foucault's words, are 'considered too tinged with empirical thought, too exposed to the vagaries of chance or imagery, to age-old traditions and external events, for it to be supposed that their history could be anything other than irregular'[3] – from the standpoint of an archaeology of discursive practices.[4] Foucault made the assumption, perhaps commonplace now, but bold and even radical when he first wrote, that this kind of empirical knowledge possesses a well-defined regularity, that the history of this knowledge exhibits systems of rules, and their transformations, which make different kinds of statements possible. These rules are, however, never formulated by the participants in the discursive practices; they are not available to their consciousness, but constitute what Foucault once called the 'positive unconscious of knowledge'.[5] If these rules are both relatively autonomous and anonymous, if they are rules which make it possible for individuals to make the claims they do when they do, then a history of such rules and such knowledge will not look like the kind of history with which one is most familiar. It will not, for example, group sets of regularities around individual works or authors; nor will it rest content with the ordinary boundaries of what we think of as a science or a discipline. It will rather force regroupings of statements and practices into 'a new and occasionally unexpected unity'.[6] Thus in *The Order of Things*, Foucault wanted to show that there were rules of formation common to the apparently unrelated sciences of natural history, economics, and grammar, as well as that these rules of formation, sometimes called the *episteme* of the classical period, were totally unlike what preceded and came after them.

With this conception of archaeology, the object of historical analysis could no longer remain theoretically unproblematic. Foucault's work placed itself in tension with the kind of history that was concerned with the already given, commonly recognized 'facts' or dated events, and whose task was to define the relations, of causality, antagonism, or expression, between these facts or events. The series of events to be explained or understood could no longer be taken as given, and so Foucault's aim could no longer be simply to understand where each given element of the series fitted *vis-à-vis* the other elements. As he wrote in *The Archaeology of Knowledge*, 'the problem now is to constitute series'[7] – to define the elements that belong to a series, to show where a series begins and ends, to formulate the laws of a series, and to describe the relations between different series. Foucault's work shares this aim with the *Annales* historians, but his perspective on the constitution of the series, in terms of the rules of formation and production of statements, gives his kind of analysis its own distinctive features.

Foucault's aim, in those of his books that worked out his archaeological method, was a thoroughly descriptive one. His task was not to provide explanations of the changes he described, nor to offer any kind of general theory of epistemic change, but to allow one to see the history of the immature sciences from a point of view that shifted what would count as a plausible or relevant explanation. Foucault's descriptive enterprise is a precondition of the explanatory task, since what needs to be explained will decisively depend on the details of one's descriptions. Someone who accepts Foucault's descriptions of the different *epistemes* in *The Order of Things* will look for explanations of a very different kind from those required by other descriptions of the very 'objects' that stand in need of explanation. The often repeated objection that Foucault's books are of no help, or even an obstacle, in understanding what causes specific changes in the sciences is so completely beside the point that it is no wonder Foucault gave it only a cursory response.

It is because Foucault wanted to describe discursive practices from the standpoint of archaeology that the theme of discontinuity was prominent in some of his major books. The unearthing of discontinuities between systems of knowledge is not an assumption of his method, but a consequence of it. If one sets out to describe the historical trajectories of the sciences in terms of anonymous rules for the formation and production of statements, then what looked continuous from some other perspective may very well appear radically discontinuous from this perspective. Problems of periodization and of the unity of a domain will be almost entirely transformed by the archaeological method. One will find, for example, that new kinds of statements which seem to be mere incremental additions to scientific knowledge are in fact only made possible because underlying rules for the production of discourse have significantly altered. However, the method of archaeology also makes possible the discovery of new continuities, overlooked because of a surface appearance of discontinuity. Archaeology makes no presumption about the predominance of discontinuity over continuity in the history of knowledge; but it does make it extremely likely that what one took to be natural groupings actually turn out, from this new level of analysis, to be quite unnatural indeed.

Genealogy, that aspect of Foucault's methodology most clearly employed in his later works, has a wider scope than archaeology. Its central area of focus is the mutual relations between systems of truth and modalities of power, the way in which there is a 'political regime' of the production of truth. Following Nietzsche, Foucault's pursuit of genealogy led him to be concerned with the origin of specific claims to truth, especially the claims, concepts, and truths of the human sciences. Yet what is distinctive about genealogy is not its interest in origins, but the form its interest takes, and the kind of origins it isolates for analysis. Genealogy does not look to origins to capture the essence of things, or to search for some 'immobile form' that has developed throughout history; the secret disclosed by genealogy is that there is no essence or original unity to be discovered. When genealogy looks to beginnings, it looks for accidents, chance, passion, petty malice, surprises, feverish agitation, unsteady victories, and power. As Foucault says in his essay on Nietzsche, a crucial essay in understanding his own thought, 'historical beginnings are lowly: not in the sense of modest or discreet like the steps of a dove, but derisive and ironic, capable of undoing every infatuation.'[8] One thinks immediately of a passage in *Discipline and Punish*, extraordinary in its implications, that appears in the midst of Foucault's discussion of the new means of 'correct training' that produce docile and disciplined bodies:

> . . . small techniques of notation, of registration, of constituting files, of arranging facts in columns and tables that are so familiar to us now, were of decisive importance in the epistemological 'thaw' of the sciences of the individual. One is no doubt right to pose the Aristotelian problem: is a science of the individual possible and legitimate? A great problem needs great solutions perhaps. But there is the small historical problem of the emergence, towards the end of the eighteenth century, of what might generally be termed the 'clinical' sciences, the problem of the entry of the individual (and no longer the species) into the field of knowledge; the problem of the entry of the individual description, of the cross-examination, of anamnesis, of the 'file' into the general functioning of scientific discourse. To this simple question of fact, one must no doubt give an answer lacking in

'nobility': one should look into these procedures of writing and registration, one should look into the mechanisms of examination, into the formation of the mechanisms of discipline, and of a new type of power over bodies. Is this the birth of the sciences of man? It is probably to be found in these 'ignoble' archives, where the modern play of coercion over bodies, gestures and behavior has its beginnings.[9]

This passage is a fine example of Foucault's astonishing ability to take a standard philosophical problem – how is a science of the individual possible? – to look to its lowly, genealogical beginnings – procedures of writing and registration, mechanisms of examination, techniques of discipline applied to gestures and behaviour – and, as a result, totally to transfigure how one might approach the problem in the first place. It is the kind of ignobility Nietzsche would have loved. Genealogy does not try to erect shining epistemological foundations. As any reader of Foucault learns, it shows rather that the origin of what we take to be rational, the bearer of truth, is rooted in domination, subjugation, the relationship of forces – in a word, power.

Genealogy converges with archaeology in placing 'everything considered immortal in man' within a process of development.[10] It disturbs what is considered immobile, fragments what is thought to be unified, and shows the heterogeneity of what is taken to be homogeneous: 'We believe that feelings are immutable, but every sentiment, particularly the noblest and most disinterested, has a history ... "Effective" history differs from traditional history in being without constants. Nothing in man – not even his body – is sufficiently stable to serve as the basis of self-recognition or for understanding other men.'[11] New configurations of power linked to new rules of formation exclude a quest for the 'rediscovery of ourselves'.[12] It is procedures such as these that helped to produce the special kind of history of madness, life, the body, and sexuality that Foucault practised. One only has to compare other attempts to write a history of the body with Foucault's histories of the body in order to see how particularly profitable his methodological background turned out to be.

Perhaps the most important effect of Foucault's preoccupation with genealogy was to force him to articulate some general rules for the study of power, providing not so much a new theory of power as a new approach to the problems of power in modern societies. Some of the most significant of these rules, elaborated in *Discipline and Punish* and in two lectures given in 1976, are the following: first, do not study power merely as a form of repression or prohibition, but look at its positive effects, at what it produces; analyse power and its techniques in terms of their own specificity, and do not reduce it to a consequence of legislation and social structure; along with this second suggestion, Foucault advocates that one conduct an ascending analysis of power, 'starting, that is, from its infinitesimal mechanisms, which each have their own history, their own trajectory, their own techniques and tactics, and then see how these mechanisms of power have been – and continue to be – invested, colonised, utilised, involuted, transformed, displaced, extended, etc., by ever more general mechanisms . . .'[13] – that is, write a micro-physics of power; this will lead one to view power not as the homogeneous domination of one group or class over another, but as a net-like, circulating organization; finally, one should not analyse power at the level of 'conscious intention or decision', should not ask what certain people want and why they want to dominate others, but should ask, instead, 'how things work at the level of on-going subjugation, at the level of those continuous and uninterrupted processes, which subject our bodies, govern our gestures, dictate our behaviours, etc.',[14] those processes which constitute us as subjects. These kinds of rules for directing the study of power are Foucault's implicit critique of both juridical and Marxist conceptions of power. Neither the juridical model of the sovereign and his subjects, the model of the individual who by exercising his rights imposes limitations on sovereign power, nor the Marxist model of base and superstructure and its resulting primacy of the economic, are adequate conceptualizations, according to Foucault, of how power operates in modern societies. Both of these models embed directives for studying power that miss or mask the operation of power at the level of on-going subjection. Genealogy not only links systems of truth and modalities of power, but also shows how to conceptualize the very notion of a modality of power in a way that adds a new dimension to the investigation of social relations.

In undertaking an analysis of 'sexuality', for example, archaeology would attempt to show how, in the mid-nineteenth century, a mutation in the rules for the production of discourse first made it possible to speak about sexuality, and not merely about sex. These same rules permitted new talk about diseases of sexuality, allowing doctors to isolate these diseases as distinct morbid entities and bringing about an unprecedented discourse on perversion. Genealogy would follow Foucault's lead that '"sexuality" was far more a positive product of power than power was ever repression of sexuality'.[15] It would insist, for instance, that infantile sexuality was not a natural phenomenon waiting to be repressed, but was rather incited by techniques of surveillance and examination, such as the helpful hints in medical manuals for parents on how they might examine their children's bedsheets for evidence of their solitary nocturnal activity.[16]

Archaeology attempts to isolate the level of discursive practices and formulate the rules of production and transformation for these practices. Genealogy, on the other hand, concentrates on the forces and relations of power connected to discursive practices; it does not insist on a separation of rules for production of discourse and relations of power. But genealogy does not so much displace archaeology as widen the kind of analysis to be pursued. It is a question, as Foucault put it in his last writings, of different axes whose 'relative importance . . . is not always the same for all forms of experience.'[17] These axes of analysis are complementary rather than contradictory. No analysis of modalities of power, however detailed, will be able to account, for instance, for the rules of production of discourse in eighteenth- or nineteenth-century medicine. Many of these rules, as well as their transformations, will only be intelligible when one takes a standpoint internal to the development of medical knowledge. The level of discursive practices must maintain its theoretical independence, even though it must also be shown to enter into convoluted relations with the techniques and forces of power. Foucault never denied, to quote a remark from the preface to the second volume of *The History of Sexuality*, that scientific knowledge is 'endowed with its own rules for which external determinations could not account – its own structure as discursive practice'.[18] Archaeology does not suffer from some intrinsic methodological failure, as some commentators have argued, but rather gets placed in a wider framework in which, naturally enough, its significance seems somewhat transformed. However, it would be a mistake to think that Foucault ever abandoned his archaeological method; and from an epistemological point of view, it is a good thing indeed that he did not surrender it, for the archaeological level is an indispensable and distinct level of analysis whose abandonment would inevitably result in distortion.

Foucault called the third axis of his analyses 'ethics' (developed in the second and third volumes of *The History of Sexuality*, the fourth volume, left unpublished at his death, and in 'On the Genealogy of Ethics', published in *The Foucault Reader*). In Foucault's writings, ethics is a study of the self's relationship to itself, *rapport á soi*, an understanding of ethics that many Anglo-American philosophers will find extremely idiosyncratic. But Foucault was, I believe, aware of how different his conceptualization of ethics was from that of other philosophers, and his purpose, already attempted in his previous works, was to isolate a distinctive stratum of analysis, typically overlooked by others. Foucault took ethics to be one part of the study of morals. In addition to ethics, morals consists of people's actual behaviour, that is, their morally relevant actions, and of the moral code which is imposed on them. By the moral code Foucault understood, for example, the rules that determine which actions are forbidden, permitted, or required, as well as that aspect of the code that assigns different positive and negative values to different possible behaviours. The study of people's actual moral behaviour is the usual domain of a sociology of morals, while moral philosophers stand-ardly concern themselves with elaborating a justifiable moral code and defending its structure. Foucault wanted to shift the emphasis to 'how the individual is supposed to constitute himself as a moral subject of his own actions',[19] without, however, denying the importance of either the moral code or the actual behaviour of people.

The relationship to oneself which Foucault called ethics has four major aspects. The first aspect, the ethical substance, is that part of ourselves or our behaviour which is taken to be the relevant domain for ethical judgement. Are ethical judgements to be applied to feelings, intentions, or desire? What part of ourselves is to be the substance or matter of ethics? Foucault believed that the ethical substance of Graeco-Roman ethics was quite different from both the Christian and modern categories of ethical substance, and these differences were one major theme of the second volume of *The History of Sexuality*. Our ethical substance will determine what part of ourselves needs to be taken into account in the formulation of the moral code.

The mode of subjection is the second major aspect of ethics. This aspect concerns 'the way in which people are invited or incited to recognize their moral obligations'.[20] We might recognize moral obligations as being revealed by divine law; or as imposed by the demands of reason; or as resting on convention; or, to use one of Foucault's most interesting examples, as deriving from 'the attempt to give your existence the most beautiful form possible'.[21] Foucault wanted to show that different people and distinct historical periods may be subjected to the same rules in different ways. So, for example, faithfulness to one's spouse may be imposed as a requirement of reason or as a consequence of a certain aesthetics of existence. The mode of subjection provides the linkage between the moral code and the self, determining how this code is to get a hold on our selves.

The third aspect of ethics concerns the means by which we change or elaborate ourselves in order to become ethical subjects, our self-forming activity (*practique de soi*) or 'asceticism' in a broad sense. In Christianity, for instance, self-examination has the form of a self-deciphering, and gives rise to a set of techniques that help to change us into the kind of being who can behave ethically. Ascetic manuals are one excellent source of self-forming activity, but so too are many nineteenth- and twentieth-century self-help books. And what Foucault calls the Californian cult of the self is almost defined by its elaboration of techniques that permit one to liberate the true self, a necessary step, at least in California, in allowing one to behave ethically.

The final aspect of ethics, called the *telos*, is the kind of being to which we aspire when we behave morally. Should we become 'pure, or immortal, or free, or masters of ourselves . . .?'[22] What is the goal to which our self-forming activity should be directed? So Foucault's schema for understanding morals looks like this:

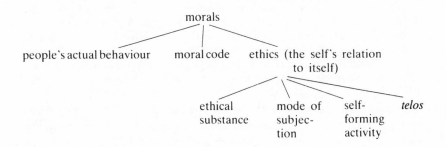

Although Foucault believed that there were relationships among the four aspects of ethics, he also thought that there was 'a certain kind of independence between them'.[23] When the *telos* of ethics changed with the emergence and consolidation of Christianity, when the goal became purity and immortality, the other aspects of ethics also underwent transformation. But it was possible, for example in Greek culture, for the ethical substance to remain the same, even while the mode of subjection gradually altered. The second and third volumes of Foucault's history of sexuality can be read as a study of the relations, the kinds of dependence and independence, among these four aspects of ethics in Greek and Roman society.

Foucault's originally announced project was a six-volume study on the history of sexuality, concentrating on the eighteenth and nineteenth centuries, and including volumes on women, children, and perverts. His published volumes, and the forthcoming fourth volume, markedly diverge from that announced project, the most obvious divergence being the immense chronological displacement to the ancient world. One reason for this displacement on Foucault's part was that the experience of sexuality in the eighteenth and nineteenth centuries was decisively informed by systems of knowledge arising from biology, medicine, and psychiatry, and by the imposition on sexual behaviour of normative systems of power coming from education and the law, among other places. This conjunction of circumstances

> made it hard to distinguish the form and effects of the relation to the self as particular elements in the constitution of this experience . . . I found myself spanning eras in a way that took me farther and farther from the chronological outline I had first decided on, both in order to address myself to periods when the effect of scientific knowledge and the complexity of normative systems were less, and in order eventually to make out forms of relation to the self different from those characterizing the experience of sexuality. And that is how, little by little, I ended up placing the work's emphasis on what was to have been simply the point of departure or historical background . . .[24]

This is another example of the gradually widening focus of Foucault's work. Ethics neither displaces genealogy and archaeology nor makes them irrelevant, but it does alter the final methodological implications of both. In order to show how the study of ethics could be carried out, in order to distinguish it as sharply as possible from the genealogical study of power and the archaeological study of knowledge, Foucault shifted his attention backwards about two thousand years. An attempt to study modern sexuality would have to combine all three axes of analysis, the self, power, and knowledge, and would take many more volumes than even Foucault's originally projected six.

An exceptionally important lesson to draw from Foucault's last work is that the study of ethics can be fruitful even when there is little or no change in the moral codes examined. Foucault believed, and many other more traditional historians have defended the same view, that there was no great moral rupture between the Greek and Christian moral codes. Many of the more significant prohibitions remain the same, and even where there are important changes, the themes remain quite similar. I remember a lecture by a prominent British professor of divinity who, having argued that the Christian moral code was not a great innovation from previous pagan codes, behaved as if there was nothing else to say about the history of early Christian ethics. Foucault's conceptualization of ethics shows us where to locate the transvaluations consequent upon the emergence of Christian ethics. And, moreover, by isolating the relation to oneself as a separate component of ethics, he opened up a domain of analysis that can be profitably investigated both when moral codes are relatively static and when they undergo great upheaval.

His focus allows him to make wonderful suggestions, worthy of entire books. Thus, taking the three poles of sexual behaviour to be acts, pleasure and desire, he proposes the following scheme. First we have the Greek 'formula' in which 'what is underscored is "acts", with pleasure and desire as subsidiary'; in the Chinese formula, 'acts are put aside because you have to restrain acts in order to get the maximum duration and intensity of pleasure'; the Christian formula 'puts an accent on desire and tries to eradicate it. Acts have to become something neutral; you have to act only to produce children, or to fulfil your conjugal duty. And pleasure is both practically and theoretically excluded . . . Desire is practically excluded – you have to eradicate your desire – but theoretically very important'; and as for the modern formula, Foucault thinks it is desire 'which is theoretically underlined and practically accepted, since you have to liberate your own desire. Acts are not very important and pleasure – nobody knows what it is!'[25] What we have here is nothing less than a prolegomena to any future study of the comparative history of ethical substance, whose articulation is made possible by conceiving of ethics in a decisively new way.

Most contemporary Anglo-American moral philosophy is exclusively focused on the level of the moral code. Virtually nothing about one's relation to oneself is thought to be relevant to ethics, and when one's relation to oneself does surface in these discussions, it is always with respect to the question of whether or not there are duties to oneself. Since ethics is conceived of as the elaboration and justification of a moral code, the only place one's relation to oneself can occupy is fixed by the wish to make the code complete, by the wish to know what specific duties, if any, one has to oneself. From Foucault's perspective, there is little philosophical difference between those writers who believe that there are duties to ourselves, the heirs to Kant, and those writers who believe there are no such duties, the successors to Schopenhauer. Both kinds of philosophers ignore the domain of ethics proper, the self's relation to itself conceived independently of the structure of the moral code. Furthermore, discussions by philosophers who do believe that we have some duties to ourselves typically take no more than a few pages in moral treatises, since it is agreed by all that our duties to others are far greater in number, complexity, and even interest than our duties to ourselves.

Alan Donagan's *The Theory of Morality*, an important contemporary work that does discuss duties to oneself, contains a very traditional list of prohibitions against suicide, self-mutilation, and impairment of one's health, as well as a duty to adopt a coherent plan of life by which one can develop one's mental and physical powers. Donagan tries to determine how rigorous these duties are, when exceptions are permissible, and what form these exceptions may take – that is, he tries to determine the structure of the moral code with respect to duties to oneself. But he begins his discussion with the following claim: 'As we shall see, the relations which human beings can have to one another are more complex than those they can have to themselves.'[26] After Foucault, this claim is quite unbelievable. Even if our *duties* to others are more complex than our duties to ourselves, our relations to ourselves have all the complexity one could ever hope for, or fear. By showing how to embed our relations to ourselves in a grid of ethical intelligibility, Foucault has helped to articulate the kind of complexity these relations actually embody. Unless moral philosophers supplement their discussions of moral codes with ethics *à la* Foucault, we will have no excuse against the charge that our treatises suffer from an unnecessary but debilitating poverty.

Notes

1 Paul Rabinow (ed.), *The Foucault Reader* (New York: Pantheon, 1984), p. 74.
2 M. Foucault, 'History of Systems of Thought' in *Language, Counter-Memory, Practice* (Ithaca: Cornell University Press, 1977), p. 199.

3 Foucault, *The Order of Things* (New York: Random House, 1970), p. ix.
4 'Michel Foucault's Immature Science', *Nous*, vol. 13 (1979). Also see Hacking's 'The Archaeology of Foucault' in this collection.
5 *The Order of Things*, p. xi.
6 'History of Systems of Thought,' p. 200.
7 Foucault, *The Archaeology of Knowledge* (New York: Pantheon, 1972), p. 7.
8 P. Rabinow (ed.), *The Foucault Reader*, p. 79.
9 Ibid., pp. 202–3.
10 Ibid., p. 87.
11 Ibid., pp. 87–8.
12 Ibid., p. 88.
13 Foucault, 'Two lectures' in *Power/Knowledge* (New York: Pantheon, 1980), p. 99.
14 Ibid., p. 97.
15 P. Rabinow (ed.), *The Foucault Reader*, p. 62.
16 I discuss some of the issues raised by the project of an archaeology of sexuality in 'Sex and the emergence of sexuality', forthcoming in *Raritan*.
17 P. Rabinow (ed.), *The Foucault Reader*, p. 337.
18 Ibid., p. 337.
19 Ibid., p. 352.
20 Ibid., p. 353.
21 Ibid., p. 353.
22 Ibid., p. 355.
23 Ibid., p. 355.
24 Ibid., p. 339.
25 Ibid., p. 359.
26 Alan Donagan, *The Theory of Morality* (University of Chicago Press, 1977), p. 76.

Self-Improvement

IAN HACKING

In an exhilarating 1983 interview, Michel Foucault described some of his work in progress. Foucault agreed to the interview title 'On the Genealogy of Ethics';[1] indeed, many of his new ideas were captured in an only slightly unusual sense of the word '*ethics*'. Perhaps Foucault had written enough about what we say and do to other people. He had now become preoccupied with what we say and do to ourselves. Official or prevalent or private moral codes would be part of that story, but there is

> another side to the moral prescriptions, which most of the time is not isolated as such but is, I think, very important: the kind of relationship you ought to have with yourself, *rapport à soi*, which I call ethics, and which determines how the individual is supposed to constitute himself as a moral subject of his own action.[2]

Where previous nominalists thought of the self as making up its own categories, Foucault did not imagine that there is any self, any ego, any I, waiting to do that. Each human subject – you, me – is an artifact. Because of Foucault's almost doctrinaire loathing of most forms of repression, and his radical shake-up of standard accounts of it, many readers would still think of him as believing that the human subject is created by forces of repression. That is too limited an outlook. In this interview, he says 'we constitute ourselves as subjects acting on others' – as agents, that is, not as victims.

One domain of his projected genealogy of ethics was certainly the 'power' we exercise. Another was an account 'of ourselves in relation to truth through which we constitute ourselves as subjects of knowledge'. Again, it is *we* who are doing it, not having it done to us. The knowledge/power story has been elaborately illustrated in Foucault's books, but those are outer-directed narratives – what we say about others, say to others, have said to ourselves by others, do to others, or have done to ourselves. They leave out the inner monologue, what I say to myself. They leave out self-discipline, what I do to myself. Thus they omit the permanent heartland of subjectivity. It is seldom force that keeps us on the straight and narrow; it is conscience. It is less knowledge produced in the human sciences that we use as our guide in life than self-knowledge. To say this is not to return to subjectivity. There is nothing private about this use of acquired words and practical techniques. The cunning of conscience and self-knowledge is to make it *feel* private.

We have long been barraged by manuals giving techniques for self-improvement. A genealogy of ethics would be a study of what these techniques really are and how we use them upon ourselves. In the most superficial respect such work would be radically different from Foucault's other endeavours, for it would not involve abrupt transformations. According to Foucault, knowledge commonly undergoes sharp breaks, as do the forms of power, and much of his writing is about discontinuities, which for Foucault usually coincide with the arrival of Descartes and the bourgeois economy or with the French Revolution and Kant.

But moral codes change very slowly. It is not just that we swear on, and often swear by, books written millennia ago. By 'codes', Foucault means quite specific general instructions. The Ten Commandments form a model code. They are brief and quite easy to obey. In America today some version of most of them is still inculcated into infants, and the rules are honoured about as well as they were in the time of Isaiah, say. Christ's injunctions are something else. To live by them is to aspire to sanctity. They do not form a code but one way of working upon ourselves, of setting impossible ideals or creating guilt. It is worth recalling that most techniques of the self – meditation, confession, exercise, diet, exemplary role models – are as old as the old codes, but the ways they are employed may differ from generation to generation.

Foucault had been writing a good deal about early Christian, patristic practices, and those of the Greeks. He claimed that classical Greek texts are first of all concerned with health, and then with food.

At a famous banquet described by Plato – an occasion of much eating and drinking – abstinence was commended as the healthiest regime in both food and sex. There is a specific problem in such texts having to do with boys. It is not the case, claimed Foucault, that Greeks were untroubled by love for boys. On the contrary, that they write about it so much betrays malaise. The difficulty was that the boy was supposed to be passive, pleasureless, and this was inconsistent with the fact that the same boy was supposed to grow up to be an active citizen. But Greek sex, at any rate, had to do with the active pleasures of adults, pleasures that supposedly interfered with health. The early Christian evolution, which often adapted pagan practices and conceptions, made pleasure passive. Foucault had a complex story to tell here: of dreams, retreats, confessions, penance, and disciplines to control both mind and its physical outlets in the body.

Foucault was gifted at imposing new organization on old material. What I've just been mentioning he called 'ethical substance', the sheer stuff that you worry about if you are a moral agent. It is the part of ourselves and of our behaviour that is relevant for ethical judgement. The definition of this can differ substantially. For us, said Foucault, it is feelings. For Kant it was intentions. Foucault's own example in the interview is a contrast between an Athenian philosopher and Saint Augustine. The Athenian in love with a boy worries whether he should touch him or not. Not touching is valued; the emphasis is on the act linking pleasure and desire. Augustine, recalling a relationship with a young friend when he was eighteen, is worried about the nature of the desire itself. 'So you see that the ethical substance has changed.'

A second element in ethics is the 'mode of subjection': whatever it is that you use to internalize these concerns, and what you take as being the relevant Truth about them – Holy Writ, the voice of a drug, the sanction of reason, political conviction, personal obsession, anything from outside that we take as authority.

A third element of ethics is how we get it to work. 'What are we to do, either to moderate our acts, or to decipher what we are, or to eradicate our desires, or to use our sexual desire in order to obtain certain aims like having children, and so on?' Foucault calls that '*asceticism* in a very broad sense'. He also calls it 'the self-forming activity': 'in order to be faithful to your wife you can do different things to the self'.[3] This is asceticism because it is cutting off some possible ways to be or to behave, in order to serve some immediate end. Behind such an end we may present to ourselves the fourth element of ethics, a teleology, 'the kind of being to which we aspire when we behave in a moral way. For instance, whether we shall become pure, or immortal, or free, or masters of ourselves, and so on.'

What we more commonly call ethics has, in its nobler forms, tended to address the questions, What shall we do? What is of value? Foucault was in the terrible predicament of being rich in values and able in action, yet at the same time asking what makes the ethical question possible at all. It is common for intellectuals, be they self-styled pragmatists or Critical Theorists or academic social democrats, to harass Foucault about this supposed predicament:

'And what, then, shall we do?'

'Well, if you want to do something, why don't you start trying to make San Quentin less horrendous?'

'No, that doesn't answer the question. If you're in the tradition of unmasking the origins of moral codes and our ethical practices, then where do you stand? How can you have any values at all? How can you have any grounds for action, even for joining a league for prison reform?'

Even his generous interviewers, Dreyfus and Rabinow, have a sense that Foucault 'owes us a criterion of what makes one kind of danger more dangerous than another'.[4]

I am a little reminded of the tale told of David Hume's death. It is said that the rabble of Edinburgh congregated around his house demanding to know when the atheist would recant. I suspect it won't be long before the solemn clamour of the intellectuals about Foucault sounds as quaint as the baying of the Edinburgh mob. That expectation does not, however, help remove the present tension. For that purpose, it may be more useful to think of Kant than of Hume.

Foucault was a remarkably able Kantian. It is seldom remembered that his longest and perhaps most important book, *The Order of Things*,[5] arose from an attempt to write an introduction to a book Foucault had translated into French, Kant's *Anthropologie*. Kant had been the first to ask, as a professorial question, What is Man? Foucault's book is a prehistory of that question, ending with a probably misguided prediction that the question in its present forms will soon be erased. His actual and projected work on ethics could also use some Kantian spectacles, for a moment. I don't know what weight to put on the interview title 'Genealogy of Ethics'. There are overtones of Nietzsche's *Toward a Genealogy of Morals*, of course. Should we take the morals/ethics contrast seriously? Nietzsche used the German word *Moral*. Kant's titles use the word *Sitte*, which we translate as 'ethics'. The contrast does fit Foucault's concerns. He was writing about *Sitten*, not *Moral*. The German word *Sitte* refers to customs and practices, not exclusively moral. They were precisely what preoccupied Foucault.

But let us go further. What did Kant do? One thing was to make something quite new out of ethics. In ancient Greece the topic of ethics had been the good life. Values were out there in the world, and the good life could be perceived and, with diligence, lived. After that, after divine ethics, after Humean naturalized ethics, and after much else, Kant made ethics utterly internal, the private duty of reason. In that respect Foucault explicitly reverses Kant. 'Couldn't everyone's life become a work of art?' This was not some vapid plea for aestheticism, but a suggestion for separating our ethics, our lives, from our science, our knowledge. At present rhetoric about the good life is almost always based on some claim to know the truth about desire, about vitamins, about humanity or society. But there are no such truths to know.

That takes me to the Kantian side of Foucault's ethics. Among the radical novelties of Kant was the notion that we *construct* our ethical position. Kant said we do this by recourse to reason, but the innovation is not reason but construction. Kant taught that the only way the moral law can be moral is if we make it. Foucault's historicism combined with that notion of constructing morality leads one away from the letter and the law of Kant, but curiously preserves Kant's spirit. Kant founded his metaphysics of ethics on the idea of freedom. That was another radical departure: what on earth do ethics and freedom have to do with each other? Foucault was always sceptical of liberation movements, be they political or sexual, except as means, for they always assumed a knowledge of how the liberation would create the true and objectively desirable natural state of people. Kant made freedom something that is necessarily outside the province of knowledge. Only in the inherently unknowable could there be a Kantian *Foundations for a Metaphysics of Ethics*. 'Unknowable' is meant literally; it pertains not just to the knowledge of the physicist or the gnosis of the hermit, the mysticism of the visionary or the high of the jogger. It means that there is nothing to be said about freedom, except that within its space we construct our ethics and our lives. Those who criticize Foucault for not giving us a place to stand might start their critique with Kant.

Notes

1 Hubert L. Dreyfus and Paul Rabinow, *Michel Foucault: Beyond Structuralism and Hermeneutics* (University of Chicago Press, second edition,
   1983), pp. 229–52.
2 Ibid., pp. 237–8.
3 Ibid., p. 239.
4 Ibid., p. 264.
5 Michel Foucault, *The Order of Things: An Archaeology of the Human
   Sciences* (New York: Pantheon, 1971).

Index